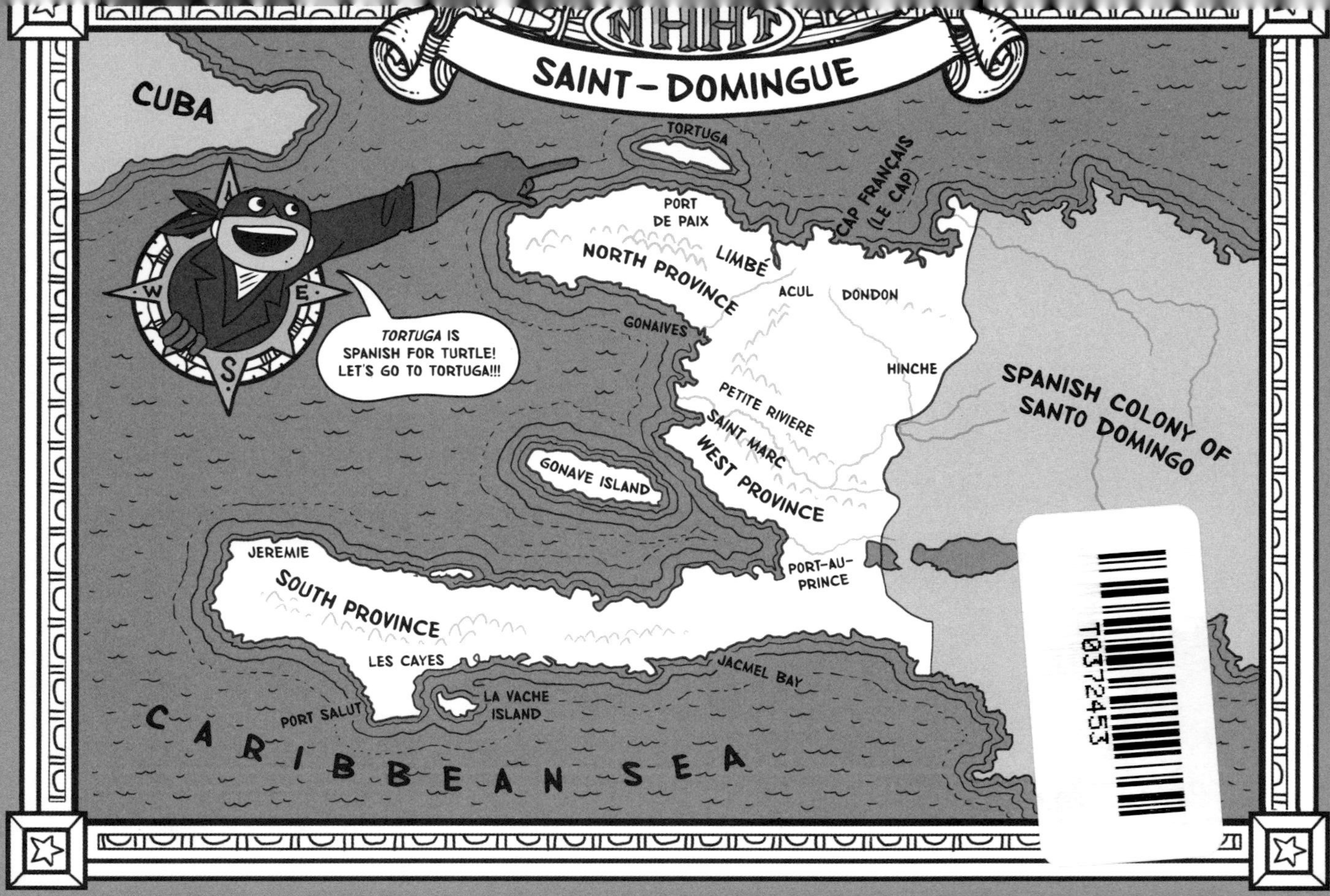
NHHT
SAINT-DOMINGUE
CUBA
TORTUGA
TORTUGA IS SPANISH FOR TURTLE! LET'S GO TO TORTUGA!!!
W
E
S
CAP FRANÇAIS (LE CAP)
PORT DE PAIX
LIMBÉ
NORTH PROVINCE
ACUL
DONDON
GONAIVES
HINCHE
SPANISH COLONY OF SANTO DOMINGO
PETITE RIVIERE
SAINT MARC
WEST PROVINCE
GONAVE ISLAND
JEREMIE
PORT-AU-PRINCE
SOUTH PROVINCE
LES CAYES
JACMEL BAY
LA VACHE ISLAND
PORT SALUT
CARIBBEAN SEA

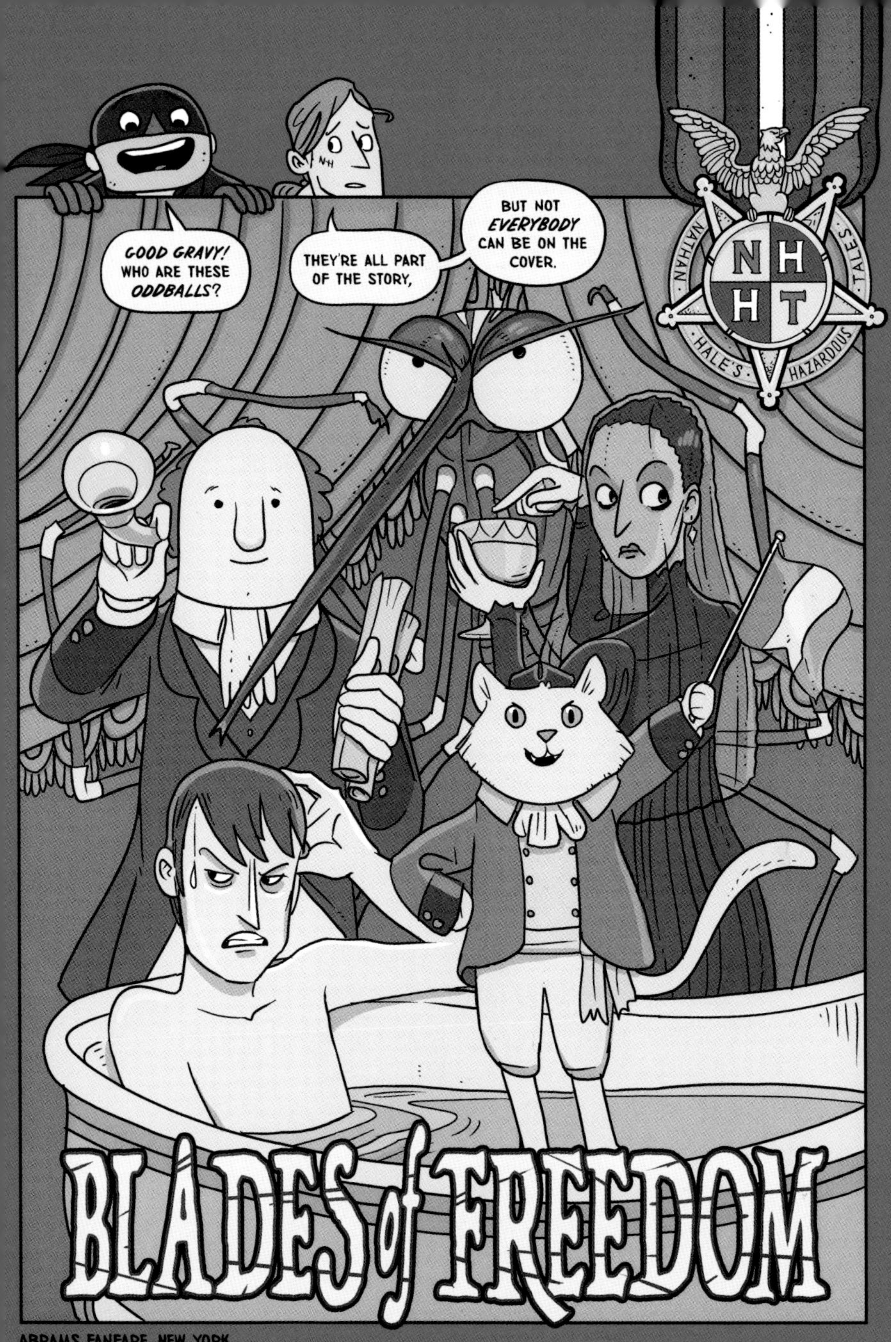
GOOD GRAVY! WHO ARE THESE ODDBALLS?
THEY'RE ALL PART OF THE STORY,
BUT NOT EVERYBODY CAN BE ON THE COVER.
NATHAN HALE'S HAZARDOUS TALES
NH HT
BLADES of FREEDOM

ABRAMS FANFARE, NEW YORK

CATALOGING-IN-PUBLICATION DATA HAS BEEN APPLIED FOR
AND MAY BE OBTAINED FROM THE LIBRARY OF CONGRESS.

ISBN 978-1-4197-4691-8

TEXT AND ILLUSTRATIONS COPYRIGHT © 2020 NATHAN HALE
BOOK DESIGN BY NATHAN HALE AND MEGAN KELCHNER
COLOR ASSISTANT LUCY HALE

PRINTED AND BOUND IN CHINA
14 13 12 11 10 9 8 7 6

ABRAMS FANFARE BOOKS ARE AVAILABLE AT SPECIAL
DISCOUNTS WHEN PURCHASED IN QUANTITY FOR
PREMIUMS AND PROMOTIONS AS WELL AS FUNDRAISING
OR EDUCATIONAL USE. SPECIAL EDITIONS CAN ALSO
BE CREATED TO SPECIFICATION. FOR DETAILS,
CONTACT SPECIALSALES@ABRAMSBOOKS.COM OR THE
ADDRESS BELOW.

ABRAMS FANFARE™ AND THE ABRAMS FANFARE LOGO ARE
TRADEMARKS OF HARRY N. ABRAMS, INC.

ABRAMS The Art of Books
195 Broadway, New York, NY 10007
abramsbooks.com

FOR THE GOOSE

NHHT

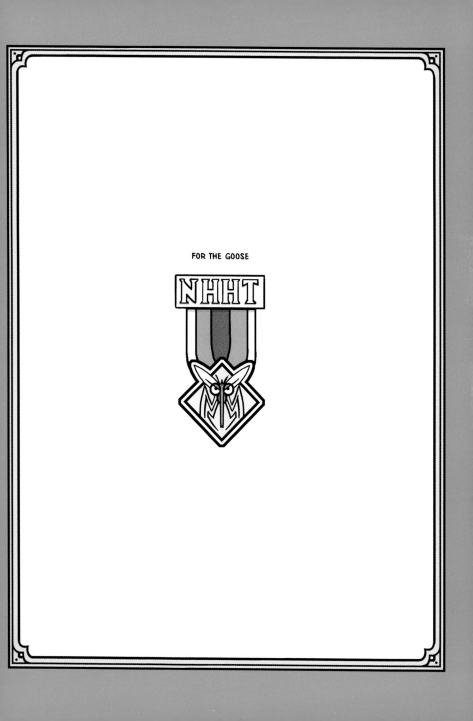

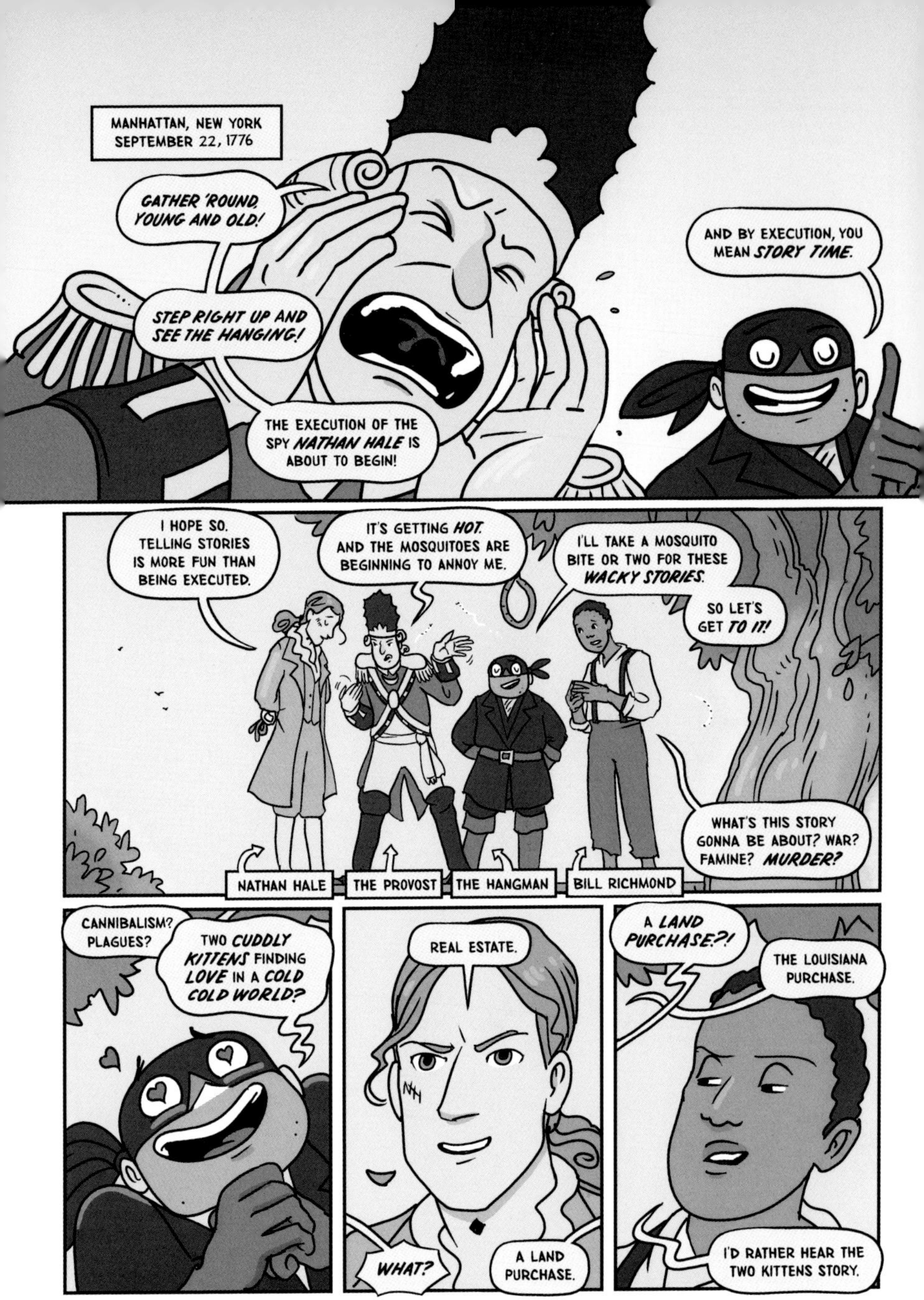

MANHATTAN, NEW YORK
SEPTEMBER 22, 1776
GATHER 'ROUND, YOUNG AND OLD!
STEP RIGHT UP AND SEE THE HANGING!
THE EXECUTION OF THE SPY NATHAN HALE IS ABOUT TO BEGIN!
AND BY EXECUTION, YOU MEAN STORY TIME.
I HOPE SO. TELLING STORIES IS MORE FUN THAN BEING EXECUTED.
IT'S GETTING HOT. AND THE MOSQUITOES ARE BEGINNING TO ANNOY ME.
I'LL TAKE A MOSQUITO BITE OR TWO FOR THESE WACKY STORIES.
SO LET'S GET TO IT!
WHAT'S THIS STORY GONNA BE ABOUT? WAR? FAMINE? MURDER?
NATHAN HALE
THE PROVOST
THE HANGMAN
BILL RICHMOND
CANNIBALISM? PLAGUES?
TWO CUDDLY KITTENS FINDING LOVE IN A COLD COLD WORLD?
REAL ESTATE.
WHAT?
A LAND PURCHASE.
A LAND PURCHASE?!
THE LOUISIANA PURCHASE.
I'D RATHER HEAR THE TWO KITTENS STORY.

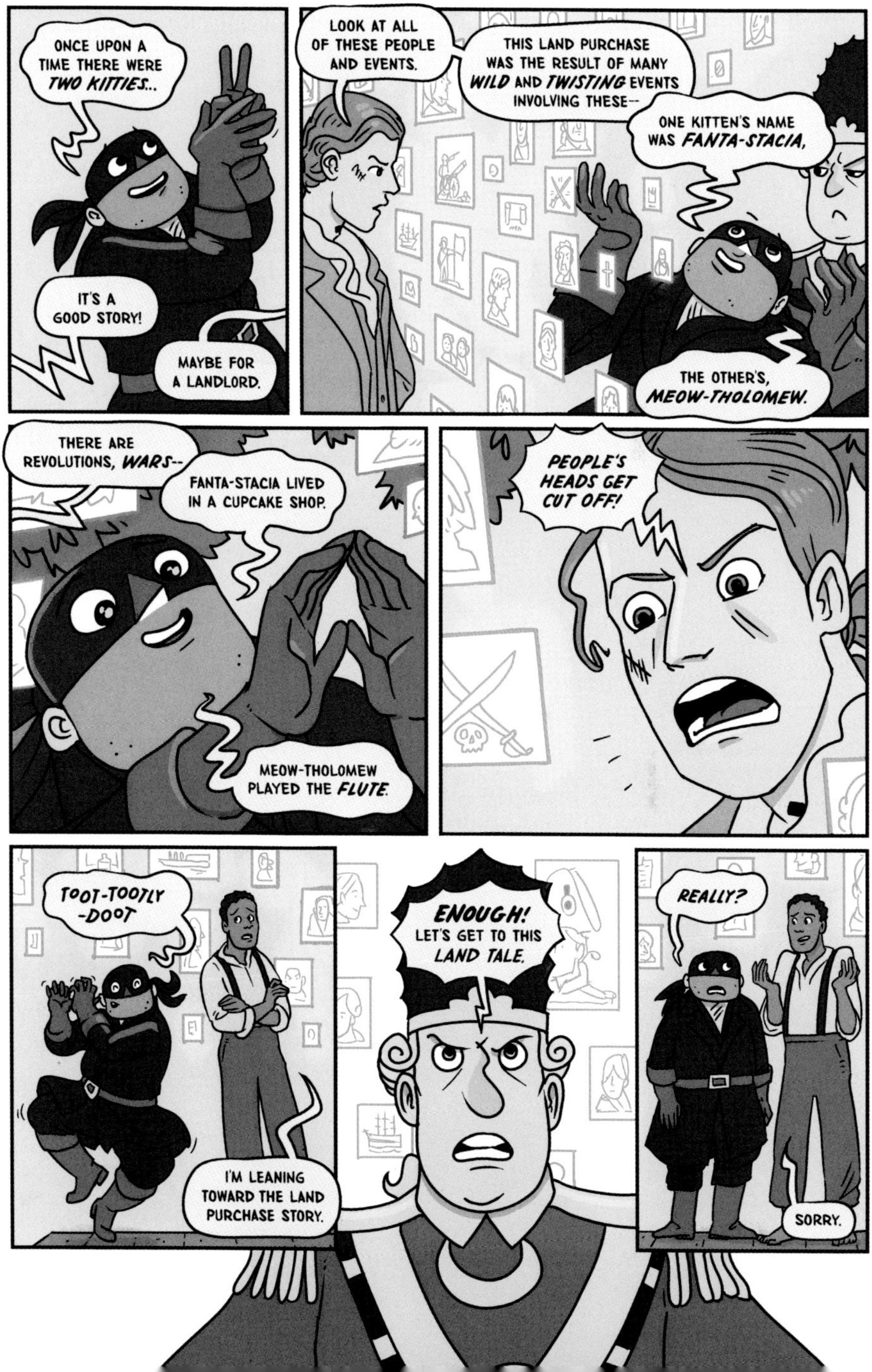
ONCE UPON A TIME THERE WERE *TWO KITTIES*...
IT'S A GOOD STORY!
MAYBE FOR A LANDLORD.
LOOK AT ALL OF THESE PEOPLE AND EVENTS.
THIS LAND PURCHASE WAS THE RESULT OF MANY *WILD* AND *TWISTING* EVENTS INVOLVING THESE--
ONE KITTEN'S NAME WAS *FANTA-STACIA*,
THE OTHER'S, *MEOW-THOLOMEW*.
THERE ARE REVOLUTIONS, *WARS*--
FANTA-STACIA LIVED IN A CUPCAKE SHOP.
MEOW-THOLOMEW PLAYED THE *FLUTE*.
PEOPLE'S HEADS GET CUT OFF!
TOOT-TOOTLY -DOOT
I'M LEANING TOWARD THE LAND PURCHASE STORY.
ENOUGH! LET'S GET TO THIS *LAND TALE*.
REALLY?
SORRY.

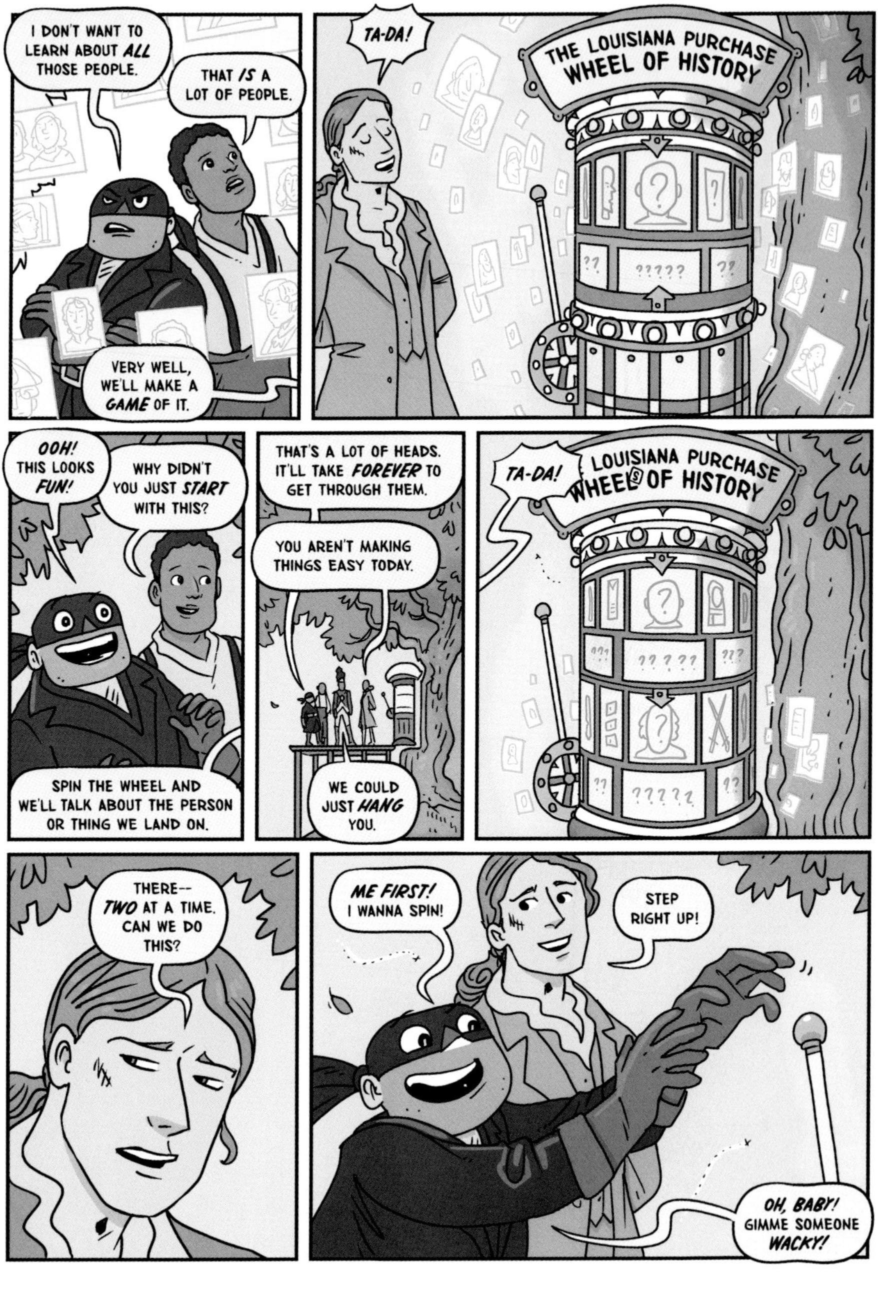
I DON'T WANT TO LEARN ABOUT ALL THOSE PEOPLE.
THAT IS A LOT OF PEOPLE.
VERY WELL, WE'LL MAKE A GAME OF IT.
TA-DA!
THE LOUISIANA PURCHASE WHEEL OF HISTORY
OOH! THIS LOOKS FUN!
WHY DIDN'T YOU JUST START WITH THIS?
SPIN THE WHEEL AND WE'LL TALK ABOUT THE PERSON OR THING WE LAND ON.
THAT'S A LOT OF HEADS. IT'LL TAKE FOREVER TO GET THROUGH THEM.
YOU AREN'T MAKING THINGS EASY TODAY.
WE COULD JUST HANG YOU.
TA-DA!
LOUISIANA PURCHASE WHEELS OF HISTORY
THERE-- TWO AT A TIME. CAN WE DO THIS?
ME FIRST! I WANNA SPIN!
STEP RIGHT UP!
OH, BABY! GIMME SOMEONE WACKY!

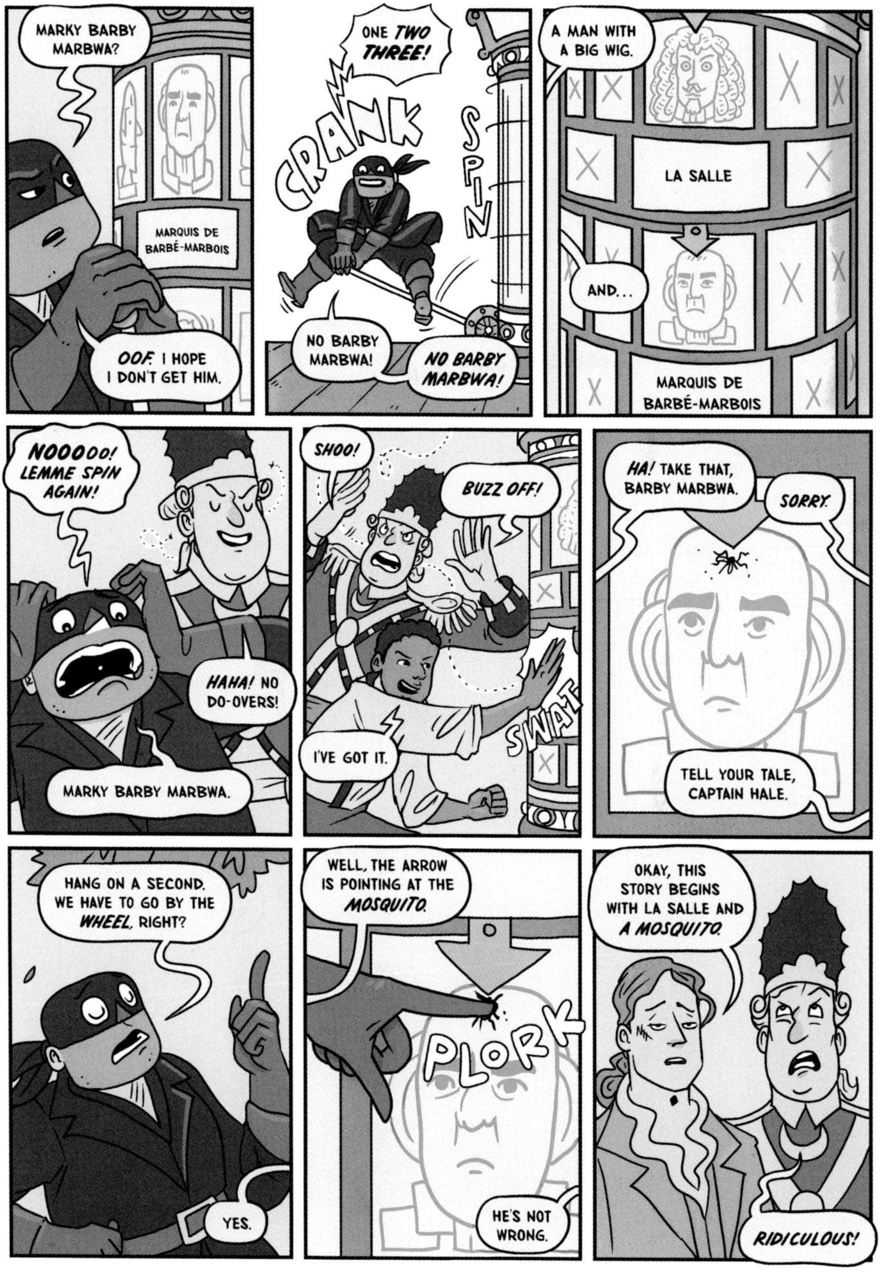
MARKY BARBY MARBWA?
MARQUIS DE BARBÉ-MARBOIS
OOF. I HOPE I DON'T GET HIM.
ONE TWO THREE!
CRANK
SPIN
NO BARBY MARBWA!
NO BARBY MARBWA!
A MAN WITH A BIG WIG.
LA SALLE
AND...
MARQUIS DE BARBÉ-MARBOIS
NOOOoo! LEMME SPIN AGAIN!
HAHA! NO DO-OVERS!
MARKY BARBY MARBWA.
SHOO!
BUZZ OFF!
SWAT
I'VE GOT IT.
HA! TAKE THAT, BARBY MARBWA.
SORRY.
TELL YOUR TALE, CAPTAIN HALE.
HANG ON A SECOND. WE HAVE TO GO BY THE WHEEL, RIGHT?
YES.
WELL, THE ARROW IS POINTING AT THE MOSQUITO.
PLORK
HE'S NOT WRONG.
OKAY, THIS STORY BEGINS WITH LA SALLE AND A MOSQUITO.
RIDICULOUS!

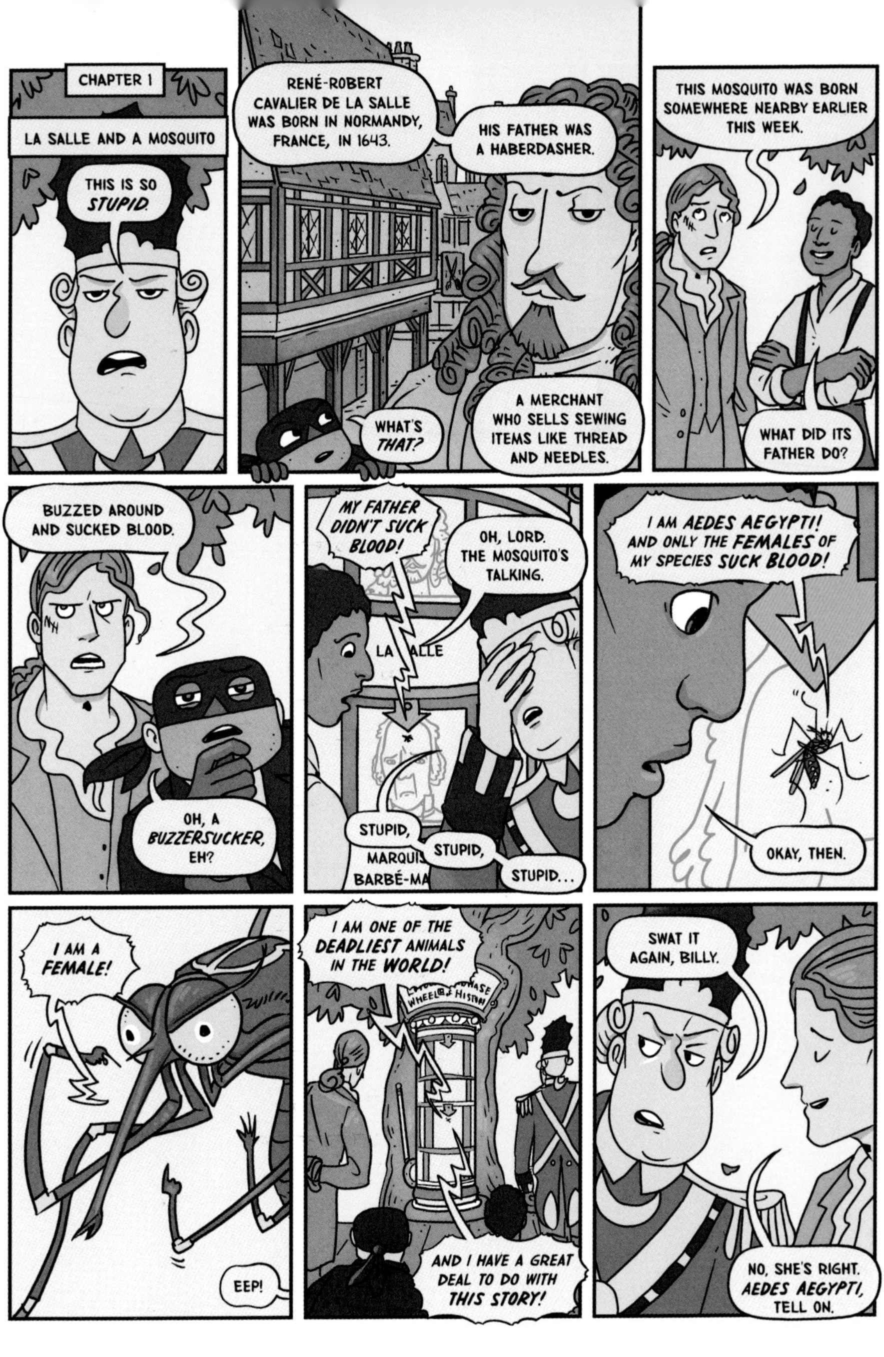

CHAPTER 1
LA SALLE AND A MOSQUITO
THIS IS SO *STUPID.*
RENÉ-ROBERT CAVALIER DE LA SALLE WAS BORN IN NORMANDY, FRANCE, IN 1643.
HIS FATHER WAS A HABERDASHER.
WHAT'S *THAT?*
A MERCHANT WHO SELLS SEWING ITEMS LIKE THREAD AND NEEDLES.
THIS MOSQUITO WAS BORN SOMEWHERE NEARBY EARLIER THIS WEEK.
WHAT DID ITS FATHER DO?
BUZZED AROUND AND SUCKED BLOOD.
OH, A *BUZZERSUCKER,* EH?
MY FATHER DIDN'T SUCK BLOOD!
OH, LORD. THE MOSQUITO'S TALKING.
LA ALLE
STUPID,
STUPID,
STUPID...
MARQUIS
BARBÉ-MA
*I AM **AEDES AEGYPTI!** AND ONLY THE **FEMALES** OF MY SPECIES **SUCK BLOOD!***
OKAY, THEN.
*I AM A **FEMALE!***
EEP!
*I AM ONE OF THE **DEADLIEST** ANIMALS IN THE **WORLD!***
WHEEL OF HISTO
*AND I HAVE A GREAT DEAL TO DO WITH **THIS STORY!***
SWAT IT AGAIN, BILLY.
NO, SHE'S RIGHT. *AEDES AEGYPTI,* TELL ON.

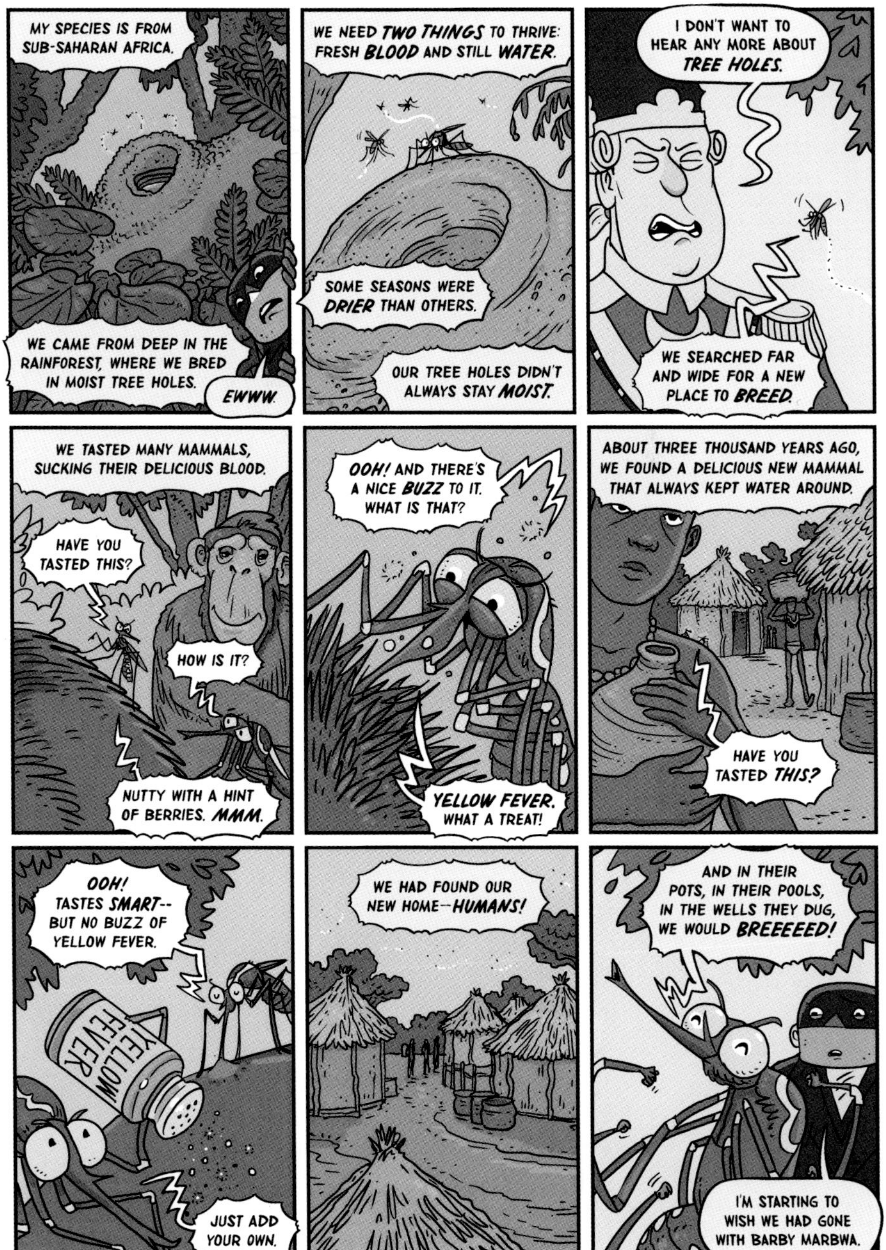
MY SPECIES IS FROM SUB-SAHARAN AFRICA.
WE CAME FROM DEEP IN THE RAINFOREST, WHERE WE BRED IN MOIST TREE HOLES.
EWWW.
WE NEED TWO THINGS TO THRIVE: FRESH BLOOD AND STILL WATER.
SOME SEASONS WERE DRIER THAN OTHERS.
OUR TREE HOLES DIDN'T ALWAYS STAY MOIST.
I DON'T WANT TO HEAR ANY MORE ABOUT TREE HOLES.
WE SEARCHED FAR AND WIDE FOR A NEW PLACE TO BREED.
WE TASTED MANY MAMMALS, SUCKING THEIR DELICIOUS BLOOD.
HAVE YOU TASTED THIS?
HOW IS IT?
NUTTY WITH A HINT OF BERRIES. MMM.
OOH! AND THERE'S A NICE BUZZ TO IT. WHAT IS THAT?
YELLOW FEVER. WHAT A TREAT!
ABOUT THREE THOUSAND YEARS AGO, WE FOUND A DELICIOUS NEW MAMMAL THAT ALWAYS KEPT WATER AROUND.
HAVE YOU TASTED THIS?
OOH! TASTES SMART-- BUT NO BUZZ OF YELLOW FEVER.
YELLOW FEVER
JUST ADD YOUR OWN.
WE HAD FOUND OUR NEW HOME--HUMANS!
AND IN THEIR POTS, IN THEIR POOLS, IN THE WELLS THEY DUG, WE WOULD BREEEEED!
I'M STARTING TO WISH WE HAD GONE WITH BARBY MARBWA.

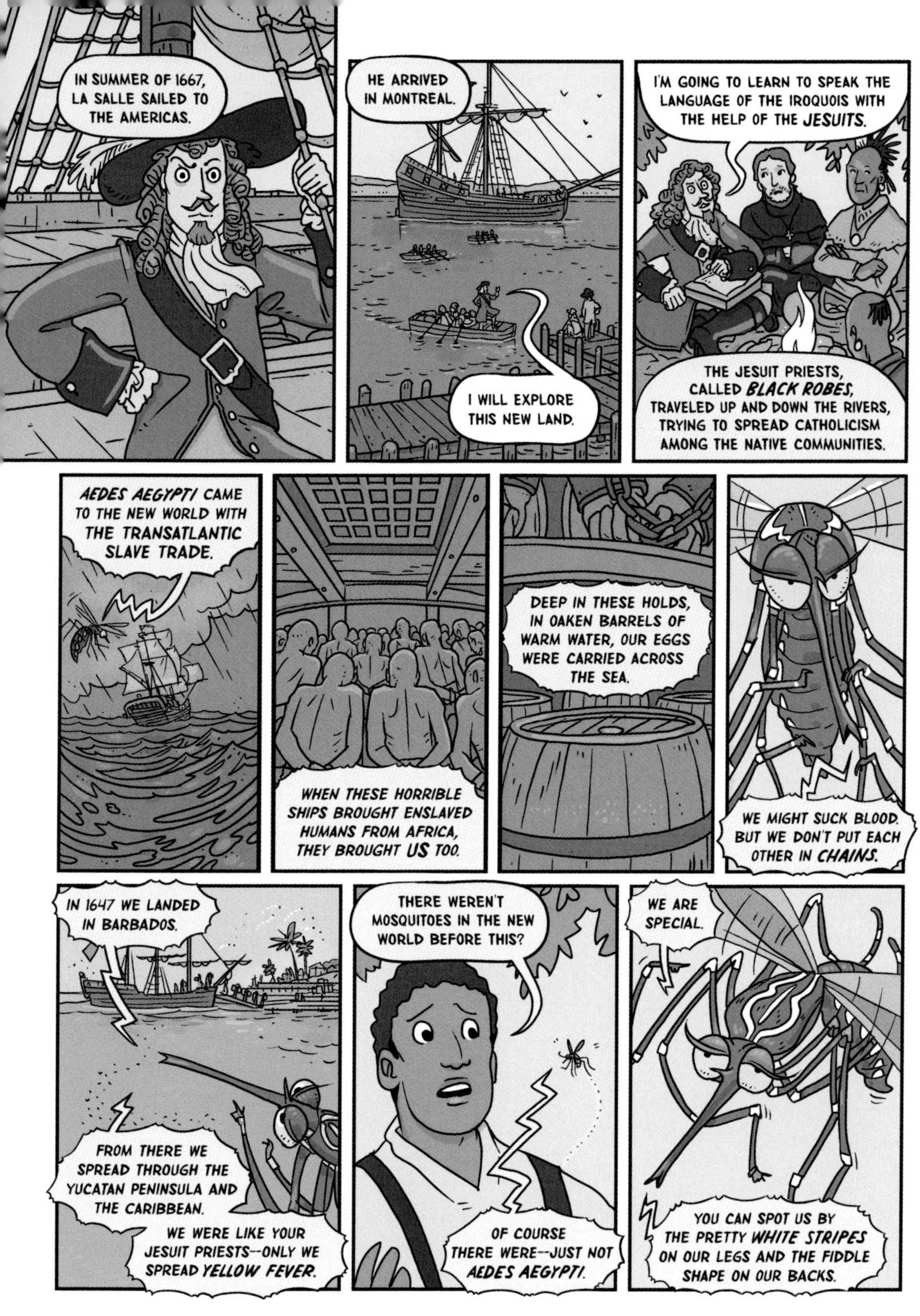

IN SUMMER OF 1667, LA SALLE SAILED TO THE AMERICAS.
HE ARRIVED IN MONTREAL.
I WILL EXPLORE THIS NEW LAND.
I'M GOING TO LEARN TO SPEAK THE LANGUAGE OF THE IROQUOIS WITH THE HELP OF THE JESUITS.
THE JESUIT PRIESTS, CALLED BLACK ROBES, TRAVELED UP AND DOWN THE RIVERS, TRYING TO SPREAD CATHOLICISM AMONG THE NATIVE COMMUNITIES.
AEDES AEGYPTI CAME TO THE NEW WORLD WITH THE TRANSATLANTIC SLAVE TRADE.
WHEN THESE HORRIBLE SHIPS BROUGHT ENSLAVED HUMANS FROM AFRICA, THEY BROUGHT US TOO.
DEEP IN THESE HOLDS, IN OAKEN BARRELS OF WARM WATER, OUR EGGS WERE CARRIED ACROSS THE SEA.
WE MIGHT SUCK BLOOD. BUT WE DON'T PUT EACH OTHER IN CHAINS.
IN 1647 WE LANDED IN BARBADOS.
FROM THERE WE SPREAD THROUGH THE YUCATAN PENINSULA AND THE CARIBBEAN.
WE WERE LIKE YOUR JESUIT PRIESTS--ONLY WE SPREAD YELLOW FEVER.
THERE WEREN'T MOSQUITOES IN THE NEW WORLD BEFORE THIS?
OF COURSE THERE WERE--JUST NOT AEDES AEGYPTI.
WE ARE SPECIAL.
YOU CAN SPOT US BY THE PRETTY WHITE STRIPES ON OUR LEGS AND THE FIDDLE SHAPE ON OUR BACKS.

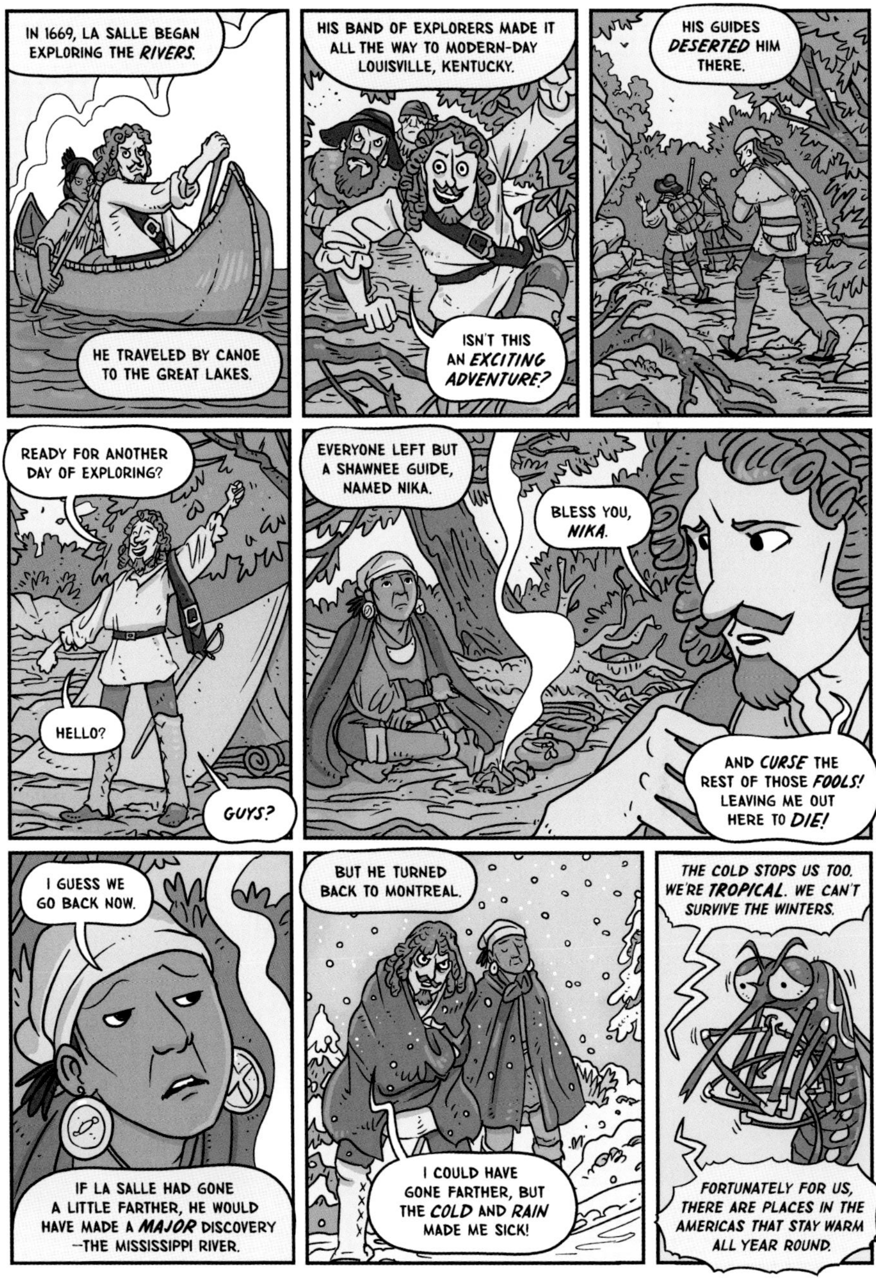
IN 1669, LA SALLE BEGAN EXPLORING THE *RIVERS*.
HE TRAVELED BY CANOE TO THE GREAT LAKES.
HIS BAND OF EXPLORERS MADE IT ALL THE WAY TO MODERN-DAY LOUISVILLE, KENTUCKY.
ISN'T THIS AN *EXCITING ADVENTURE?*
HIS GUIDES *DESERTED* HIM THERE.
READY FOR ANOTHER DAY OF EXPLORING?
HELLO?
GUYS?
EVERYONE LEFT BUT A SHAWNEE GUIDE, NAMED NIKA.
BLESS YOU, *NIKA*.
AND *CURSE* THE REST OF THOSE *FOOLS!* LEAVING ME OUT HERE TO *DIE!*
I GUESS WE GO BACK NOW.
IF LA SALLE HAD GONE A LITTLE FARTHER, HE WOULD HAVE MADE A *MAJOR* DISCOVERY —THE MISSISSIPPI RIVER.
BUT HE TURNED BACK TO MONTREAL.
I COULD HAVE GONE FARTHER, BUT THE *COLD* AND *RAIN* MADE ME SICK!
THE COLD STOPS US TOO. WE'RE ***TROPICAL***. *WE CAN'T SURVIVE THE WINTERS.*
FORTUNATELY FOR US, THERE ARE PLACES IN THE AMERICAS THAT STAY WARM ALL YEAR ROUND.

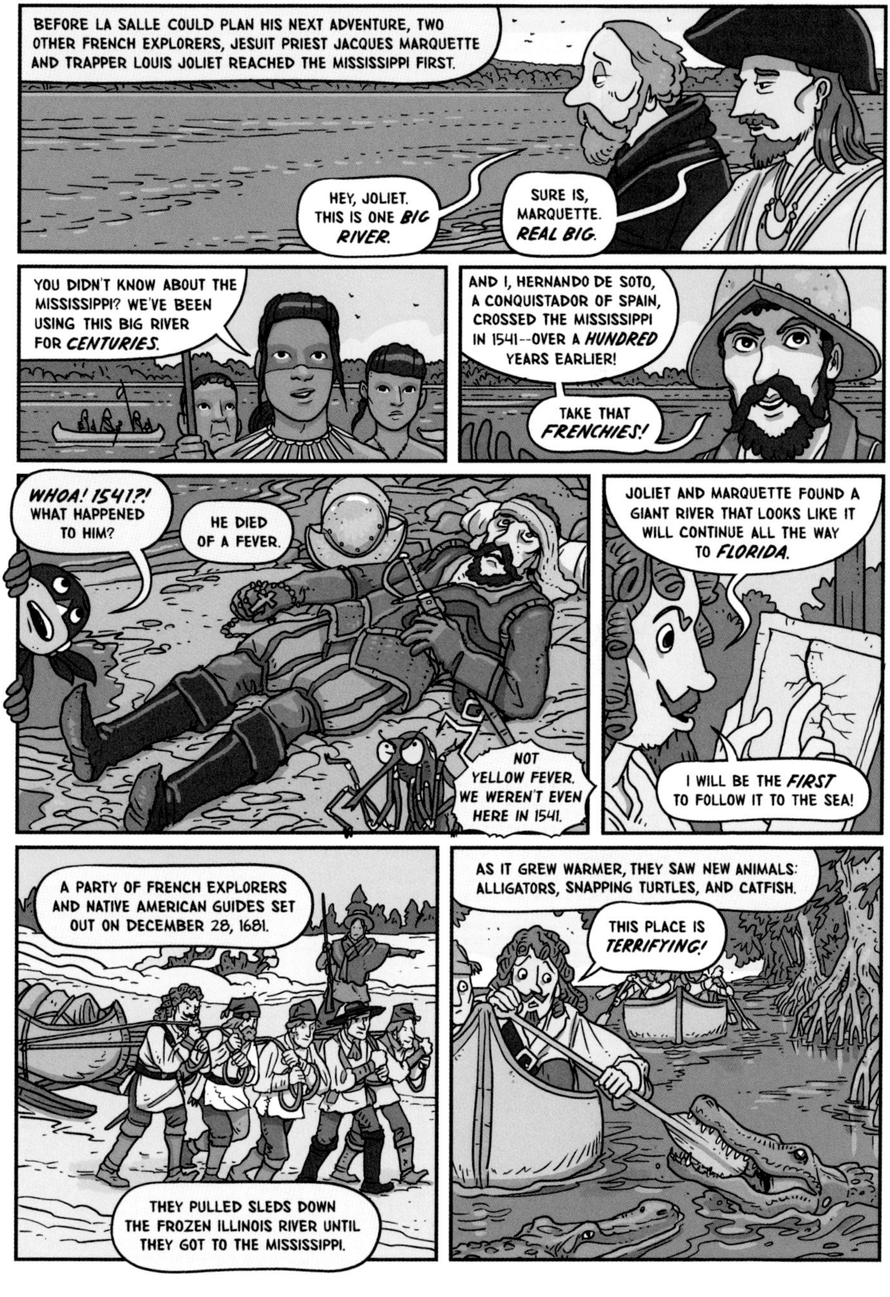

BEFORE LA SALLE COULD PLAN HIS NEXT ADVENTURE, TWO OTHER FRENCH EXPLORERS, JESUIT PRIEST JACQUES MARQUETTE AND TRAPPER LOUIS JOLIET REACHED THE MISSISSIPPI FIRST.
HEY, JOLIET. THIS IS ONE *BIG RIVER.*
SURE IS, MARQUETTE. *REAL BIG.*
YOU DIDN'T KNOW ABOUT THE MISSISSIPPI? WE'VE BEEN USING THIS BIG RIVER FOR *CENTURIES.*
AND I, HERNANDO DE SOTO, A CONQUISTADOR OF SPAIN, CROSSED THE MISSISSIPPI IN 1541--OVER A *HUNDRED* YEARS EARLIER!
TAKE THAT *FRENCHIES!*
WHOA! 1541?! WHAT HAPPENED TO HIM?
HE DIED OF A FEVER.
NOT YELLOW FEVER. WE WEREN'T EVEN HERE IN 1541.
JOLIET AND MARQUETTE FOUND A GIANT RIVER THAT LOOKS LIKE IT WILL CONTINUE ALL THE WAY TO *FLORIDA.*
I WILL BE THE *FIRST* TO FOLLOW IT TO THE SEA!
A PARTY OF FRENCH EXPLORERS AND NATIVE AMERICAN GUIDES SET OUT ON DECEMBER 28, 1681.
THEY PULLED SLEDS DOWN THE FROZEN ILLINOIS RIVER UNTIL THEY GOT TO THE MISSISSIPPI.
AS IT GREW WARMER, THEY SAW NEW ANIMALS: ALLIGATORS, SNAPPING TURTLES, AND CATFISH.
THIS PLACE IS *TERRIFYING!*

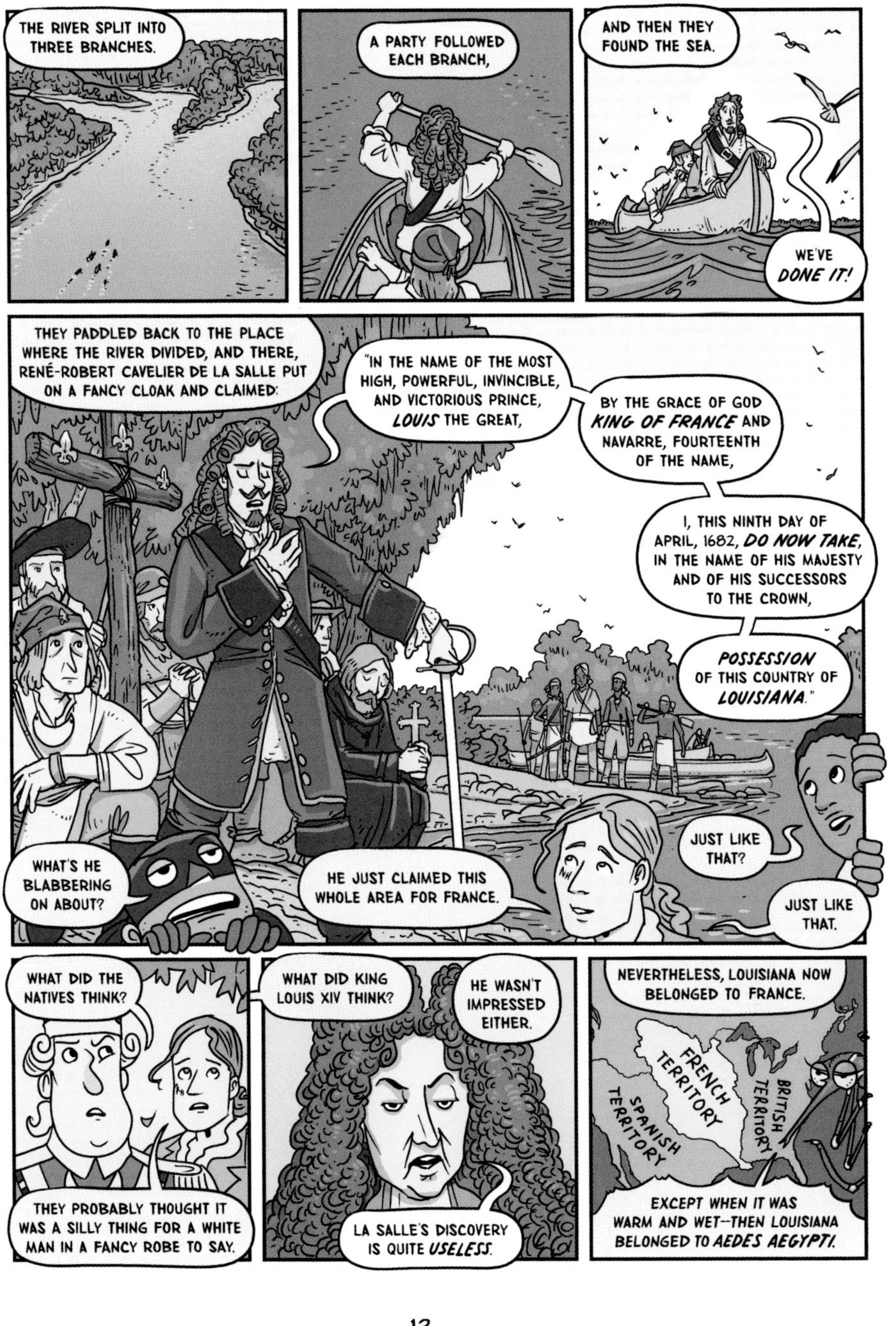
THE RIVER SPLIT INTO THREE BRANCHES.
A PARTY FOLLOWED EACH BRANCH,
AND THEN THEY FOUND THE SEA.
WE'VE *DONE IT!*
THEY PADDLED BACK TO THE PLACE WHERE THE RIVER DIVIDED, AND THERE, RENÉ-ROBERT CAVELIER DE LA SALLE PUT ON A FANCY CLOAK AND CLAIMED:
"IN THE NAME OF THE MOST HIGH, POWERFUL, INVINCIBLE, AND VICTORIOUS PRINCE, *LOUIS* THE GREAT,
BY THE GRACE OF GOD *KING OF FRANCE* AND NAVARRE, FOURTEENTH OF THE NAME,
I, THIS NINTH DAY OF APRIL, 1682, *DO NOW TAKE*, IN THE NAME OF HIS MAJESTY AND OF HIS SUCCESSORS TO THE CROWN,
POSSESSION OF THIS COUNTRY OF *LOUISIANA*."
WHAT'S HE BLABBERING ON ABOUT?
HE JUST CLAIMED THIS WHOLE AREA FOR FRANCE.
JUST LIKE THAT?
JUST LIKE THAT.
WHAT DID THE NATIVES THINK?
THEY PROBABLY THOUGHT IT WAS A SILLY THING FOR A WHITE MAN IN A FANCY ROBE TO SAY.
WHAT DID KING LOUIS XIV THINK?
HE WASN'T IMPRESSED EITHER.
LA SALLE'S DISCOVERY IS QUITE *USELESS*.
NEVERTHELESS, LOUISIANA NOW BELONGED TO FRANCE.
FRENCH TERRITORY
SPANISH TERRITORY
BRITISH TERRITORY
EXCEPT WHEN IT WAS WARM AND WET--THEN LOUISIANA BELONGED TO *AEDES AEGYPTI*.

CHAPTER 2

SEE HOW THIS WORKS?

I DO. IT'S A LITTLE WEIRD, BUT I LIKE IT.

BILL, IT'S YOUR TURN TO SPIN.

OH BOY!

SPIIINNNZZ

NAPOLEON BONAPARTE

FRANÇOIS MACKANDAL

NEVER HEARD OF HIM.

THIS IS AN INTERESTING COMBO. LET'S SEE IF THEY HAVE ANYTHING IN COMMON.

NAPOLEON BONAPARTE WAS BORN AUGUST 15, 1769, IN AJACCIO ON THE ISLAND OF CORSICA.

CORSICA

SARDINIA

MEDITERRANEAN SEA

THERE ARE MORE BOOKS WRITTEN ABOUT HIM THAN *ANYONE* IN MODERN HISTORY.

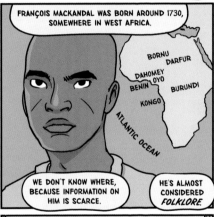

FRANÇOIS MACKANDAL WAS BORN AROUND 1730, SOMEWHERE IN WEST AFRICA.

BORNU

DARFUR

DAHOMEY

BENIN OYO

KONGO

BURUNDI

ATLANTIC OCEAN

WE DON'T KNOW WHERE, BECAUSE INFORMATION ON HIM IS SCARCE.

HE'S ALMOST CONSIDERED *FOLKLORE.*

IN 1769, THE YEAR NAPOLEON WAS BORN, CORSICA WAS TAKEN OVER BY FRANCE.

WE ARE FRENCH, BUT WE SPEAK ITALIAN.

MAMMA MIA!

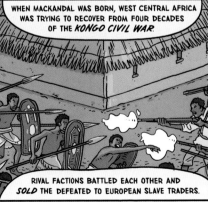

WHEN MACKANDAL WAS BORN, WEST CENTRAL AFRICA WAS TRYING TO RECOVER FROM FOUR DECADES OF THE *KONGO CIVIL WAR.*

RIVAL FACTIONS BATTLED EACH OTHER AND *SOLD* THE DEFEATED TO EUROPEAN SLAVE TRADERS.

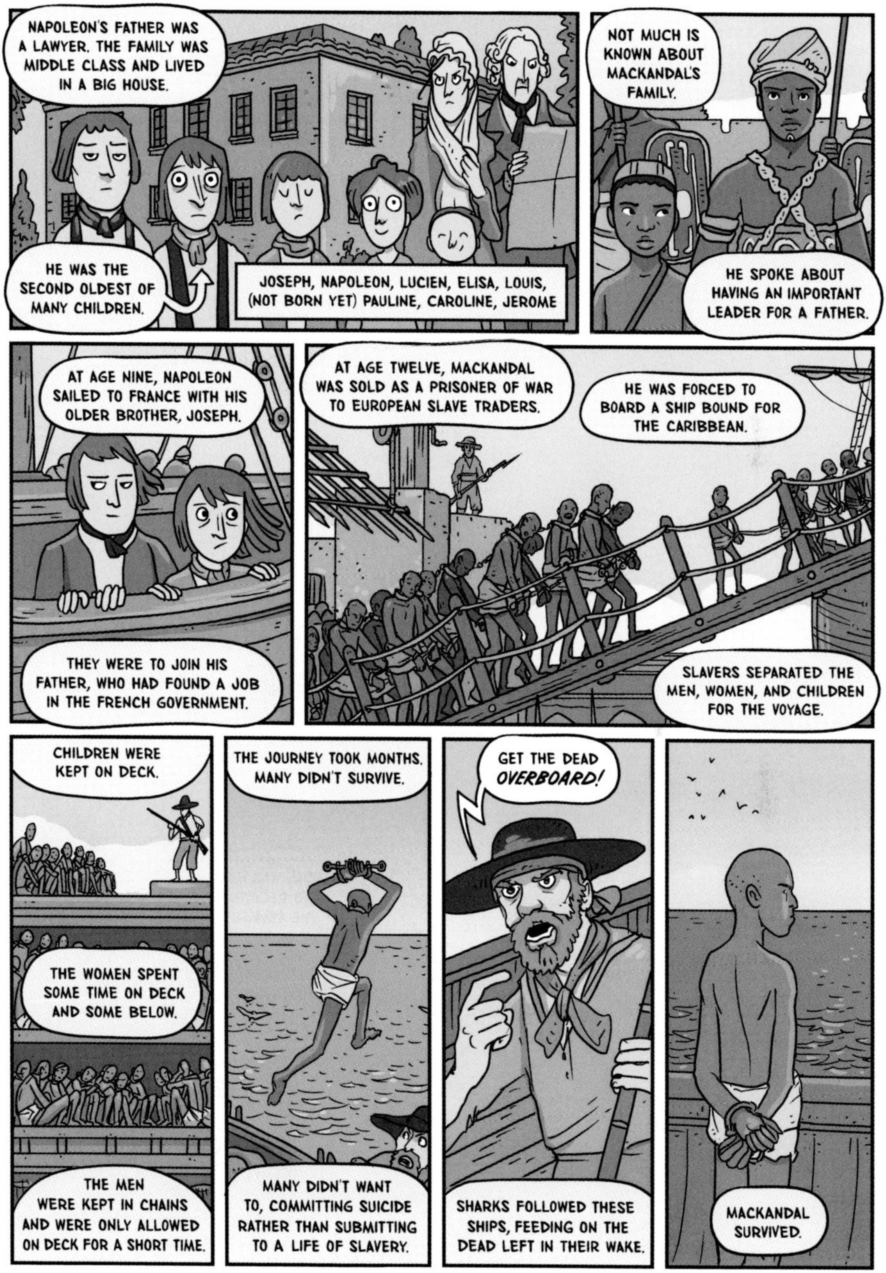
NAPOLEON'S FATHER WAS A LAWYER. THE FAMILY WAS MIDDLE CLASS AND LIVED IN A BIG HOUSE.
HE WAS THE SECOND OLDEST OF MANY CHILDREN.
JOSEPH, NAPOLEON, LUCIEN, ELISA, LOUIS, (NOT BORN YET) PAULINE, CAROLINE, JEROME
NOT MUCH IS KNOWN ABOUT MACKANDAL'S FAMILY.
HE SPOKE ABOUT HAVING AN IMPORTANT LEADER FOR A FATHER.
AT AGE NINE, NAPOLEON SAILED TO FRANCE WITH HIS OLDER BROTHER, JOSEPH.
THEY WERE TO JOIN HIS FATHER, WHO HAD FOUND A JOB IN THE FRENCH GOVERNMENT.
AT AGE TWELVE, MACKANDAL WAS SOLD AS A PRISONER OF WAR TO EUROPEAN SLAVE TRADERS.
HE WAS FORCED TO BOARD A SHIP BOUND FOR THE CARIBBEAN.
SLAVERS SEPARATED THE MEN, WOMEN, AND CHILDREN FOR THE VOYAGE.
CHILDREN WERE KEPT ON DECK.
THE WOMEN SPENT SOME TIME ON DECK AND SOME BELOW.
THE MEN WERE KEPT IN CHAINS AND WERE ONLY ALLOWED ON DECK FOR A SHORT TIME.
THE JOURNEY TOOK MONTHS. MANY DIDN'T SURVIVE.
MANY DIDN'T WANT TO, COMMITTING SUICIDE RATHER THAN SUBMITTING TO A LIFE OF SLAVERY.
GET THE DEAD *OVERBOARD!*
SHARKS FOLLOWED THESE SHIPS, FEEDING ON THE DEAD LEFT IN THEIR WAKE.
MACKANDAL SURVIVED.

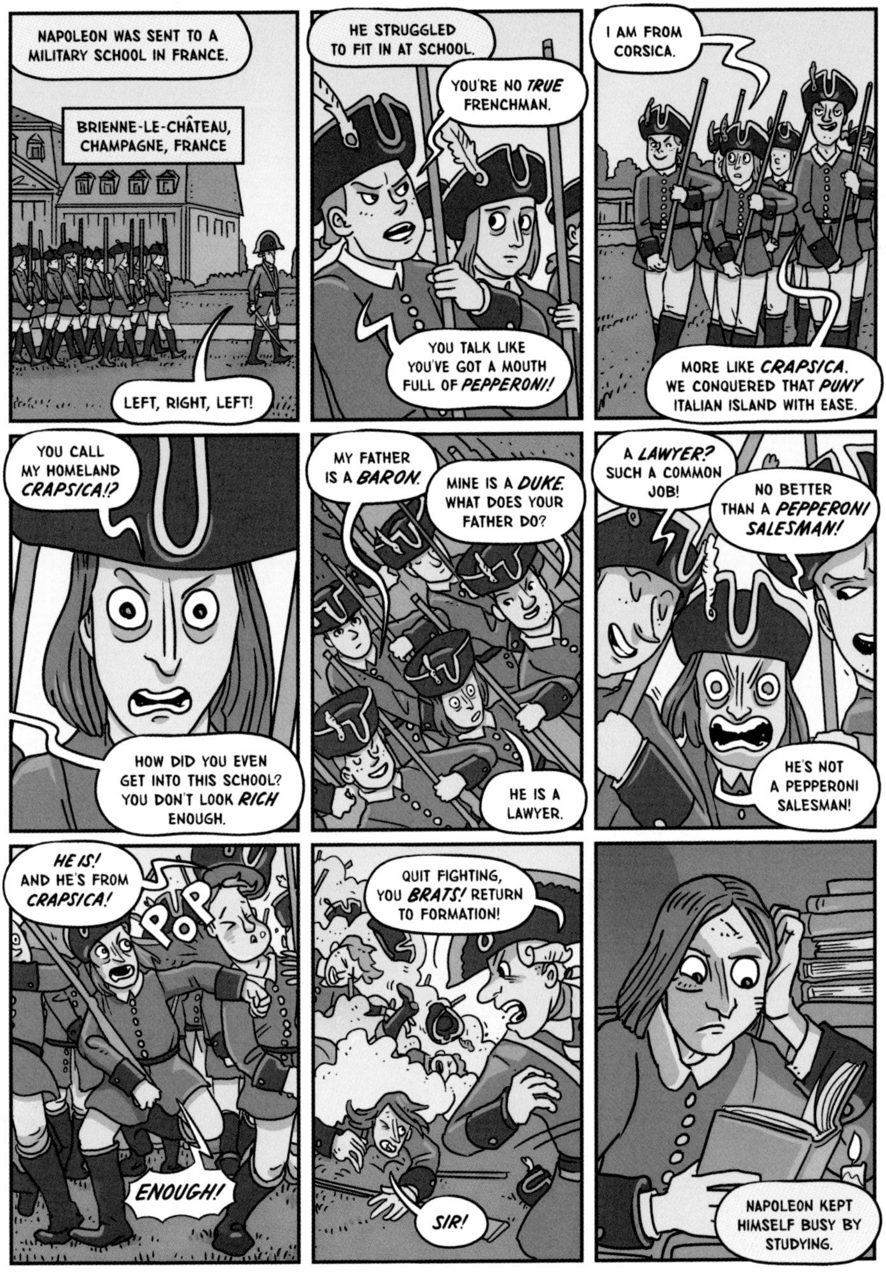
NAPOLEON WAS SENT TO A MILITARY SCHOOL IN FRANCE.
BRIENNE-LE-CHÂTEAU, CHAMPAGNE, FRANCE
LEFT, RIGHT, LEFT!
HE STRUGGLED TO FIT IN AT SCHOOL.
YOU'RE NO TRUE FRENCHMAN.
YOU TALK LIKE YOU'VE GOT A MOUTH FULL OF PEPPERONI!
I AM FROM CORSICA.
MORE LIKE CRAPSICA. WE CONQUERED THAT PUNY ITALIAN ISLAND WITH EASE.
YOU CALL MY HOMELAND CRAPSICA!?
HOW DID YOU EVEN GET INTO THIS SCHOOL? YOU DON'T LOOK RICH ENOUGH.
MY FATHER IS A BARON.
MINE IS A DUKE. WHAT DOES YOUR FATHER DO?
HE IS A LAWYER.
A LAWYER? SUCH A COMMON JOB!
NO BETTER THAN A PEPPERONI SALESMAN!
HE'S NOT A PEPPERONI SALESMAN!
HE IS! AND HE'S FROM CRAPSICA!
POP
ENOUGH!
QUIT FIGHTING, YOU BRATS! RETURN TO FORMATION!
SIR!
NAPOLEON KEPT HIMSELF BUSY BY STUDYING.

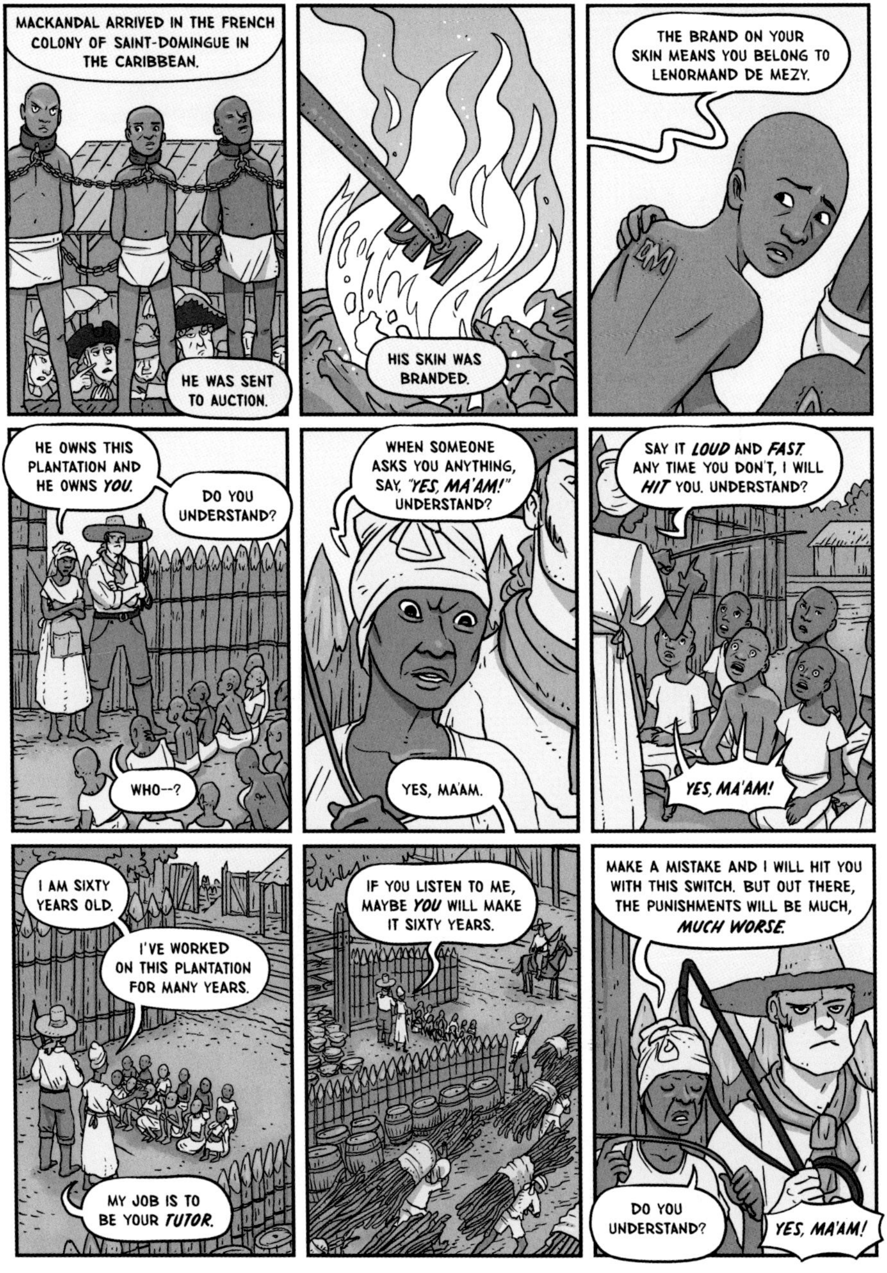
MACKANDAL ARRIVED IN THE FRENCH COLONY OF SAINT-DOMINGUE IN THE CARIBBEAN.
HE WAS SENT TO AUCTION.
HIS SKIN WAS BRANDED.
THE BRAND ON YOUR SKIN MEANS YOU BELONG TO LENORMAND DE MEZY.
HE OWNS THIS PLANTATION AND HE OWNS *YOU*.
DO YOU UNDERSTAND?
WHO--?
WHEN SOMEONE ASKS YOU ANYTHING, SAY, *"YES, MA'AM!"* UNDERSTAND?
YES, MA'AM.
SAY IT *LOUD* AND *FAST*. ANY TIME YOU DON'T, I WILL *HIT* YOU. UNDERSTAND?
YES, MA'AM!
I AM SIXTY YEARS OLD.
I'VE WORKED ON THIS PLANTATION FOR MANY YEARS.
MY JOB IS TO BE YOUR *TUTOR*.
IF YOU LISTEN TO ME, MAYBE *YOU* WILL MAKE IT SIXTY YEARS.
MAKE A MISTAKE AND I WILL HIT YOU WITH THIS SWITCH. BUT OUT THERE, THE PUNISHMENTS WILL BE MUCH, *MUCH WORSE*.
DO YOU UNDERSTAND?
YES, MA'AM!

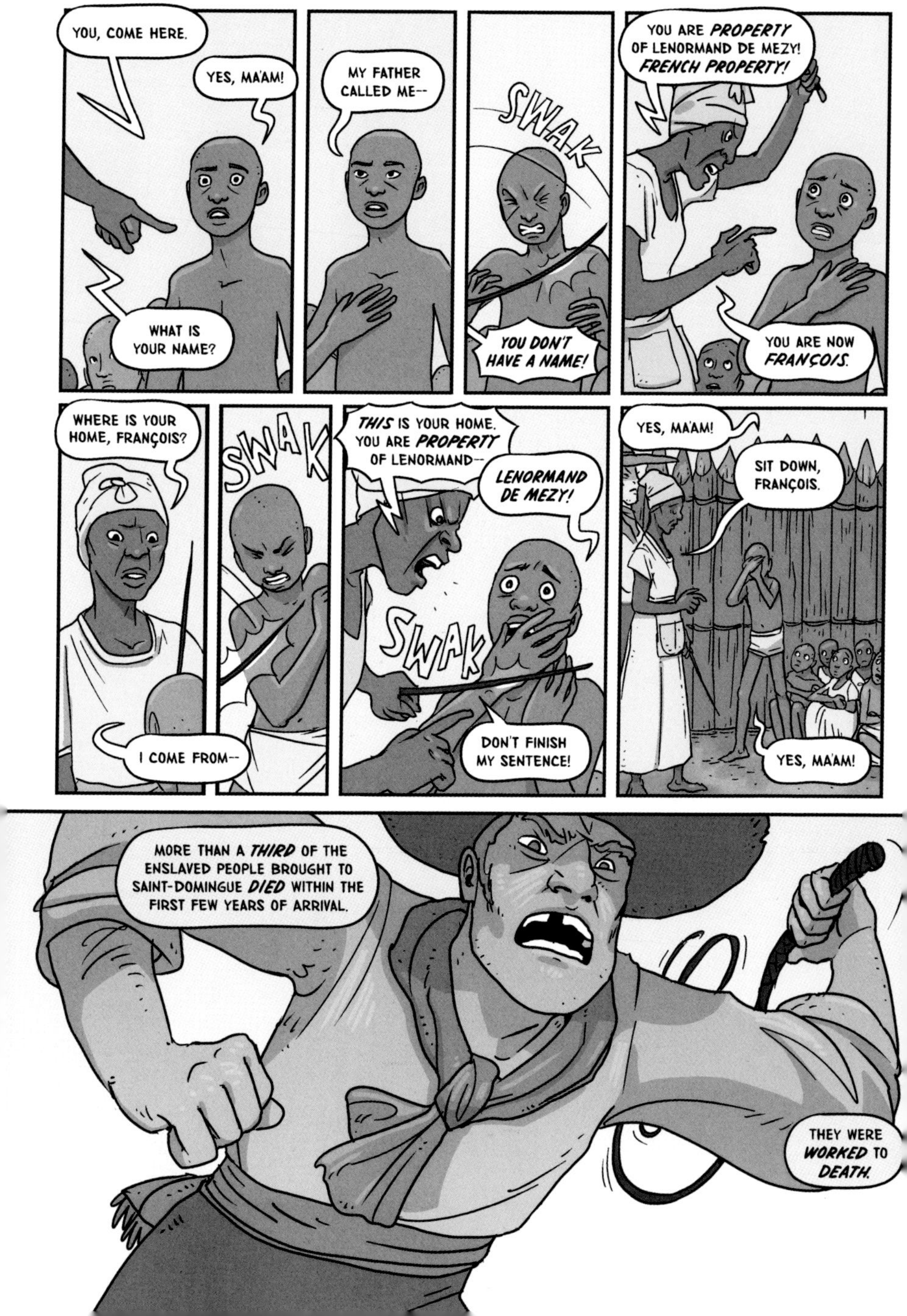
YOU, COME HERE.
YES, MA'AM!
WHAT IS YOUR NAME?
MY FATHER CALLED ME--
SWAK
YOU DON'T HAVE A NAME!
YOU ARE PROPERTY OF LENORMAND DE MEZY! FRENCH PROPERTY!
YOU ARE NOW FRANÇOIS.
WHERE IS YOUR HOME, FRANÇOIS?
I COME FROM--
SWAK
THIS IS YOUR HOME. YOU ARE PROPERTY OF LENORMAND--
LENORMAND DE MEZY!
SWAK
DON'T FINISH MY SENTENCE!
YES, MA'AM!
SIT DOWN, FRANÇOIS.
YES, MA'AM!
MORE THAN A THIRD OF THE ENSLAVED PEOPLE BROUGHT TO SAINT-DOMINGUE DIED WITHIN THE FIRST FEW YEARS OF ARRIVAL.
THEY WERE WORKED TO DEATH.

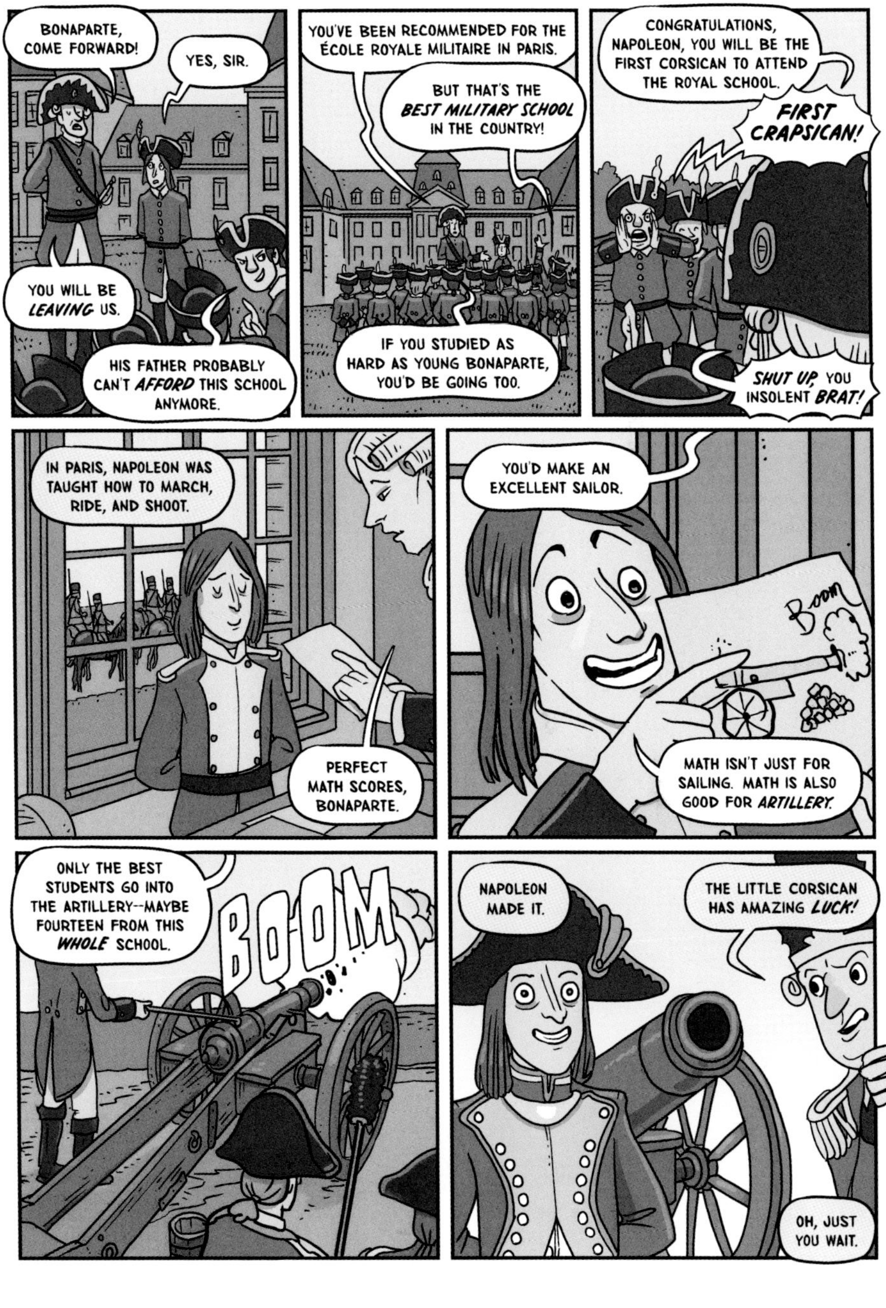
BONAPARTE, COME FORWARD!
YES, SIR.
YOU WILL BE *LEAVING* US.
HIS FATHER PROBABLY CAN'T *AFFORD* THIS SCHOOL ANYMORE.
YOU'VE BEEN RECOMMENDED FOR THE ÉCOLE ROYALE MILITAIRE IN PARIS.
BUT THAT'S THE *BEST MILITARY SCHOOL* IN THE COUNTRY!
IF YOU STUDIED AS HARD AS YOUNG BONAPARTE, YOU'D BE GOING TOO.
CONGRATULATIONS, NAPOLEON, YOU WILL BE THE FIRST CORSICAN TO ATTEND THE ROYAL SCHOOL.
FIRST CRAPSICAN!
SHUT UP, YOU INSOLENT *BRAT!*
IN PARIS, NAPOLEON WAS TAUGHT HOW TO MARCH, RIDE, AND SHOOT.
PERFECT MATH SCORES, BONAPARTE.
YOU'D MAKE AN EXCELLENT SAILOR.
BOOM
MATH ISN'T JUST FOR SAILING. MATH IS ALSO GOOD FOR *ARTILLERY.*
ONLY THE BEST STUDENTS GO INTO THE ARTILLERY--MAYBE FOURTEEN FROM THIS *WHOLE* SCHOOL.
BOOM
NAPOLEON MADE IT.
THE LITTLE CORSICAN HAS AMAZING *LUCK!*
OH, JUST YOU WAIT.

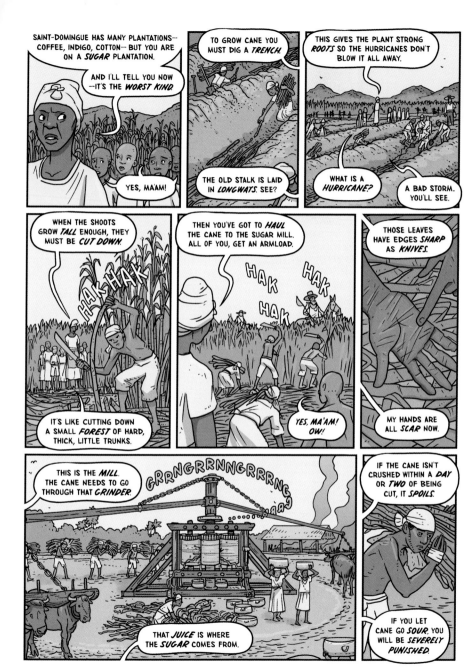

SAINT-DOMINGUE HAS MANY PLANTATIONS-- COFFEE, INDIGO, COTTON-- BUT YOU ARE ON A *SUGAR* PLANTATION.

AND I'LL TELL YOU NOW --IT'S THE *WORST KIND.*

YES, MA'AM!

TO GROW CANE YOU MUST DIG A *TRENCH.*

THE OLD STALK IS LAID IN *LONGWAYS.* SEE?

THIS GIVES THE PLANT STRONG *ROOTS* SO THE HURRICANES DON'T BLOW IT ALL AWAY.

WHAT IS A *HURRICANE?*

A BAD STORM. YOU'LL SEE.

WHEN THE SHOOTS GROW *TALL* ENOUGH, THEY MUST BE *CUT DOWN.*

HAK HAK

IT'S LIKE CUTTING DOWN A SMALL *FOREST* OF HARD, THICK, LITTLE TRUNKS.

THEN YOU'VE GOT TO *HAUL* THE CANE TO THE SUGAR MILL. ALL OF YOU, GET AN ARMLOAD.

HAK HAK HAK

YES, MA'AM! OW!

THOSE LEAVES HAVE EDGES *SHARP* AS *KNIVES.*

MY HANDS ARE ALL *SCAR* NOW.

THIS IS THE *MILL.* THE CANE NEEDS TO GO THROUGH THAT *GRINDER.*

GRRNGRRNNGRRRNG GRR

THAT *JUICE* IS WHERE THE *SUGAR* COMES FROM.

IF THE CANE ISN'T CRUSHED WITHIN A *DAY* OR *TWO* OF BEING CUT, IT *SPOILS.*

IF YOU LET CANE GO *SOUR,* YOU WILL BE *SEVERELY PUNISHED.*

20

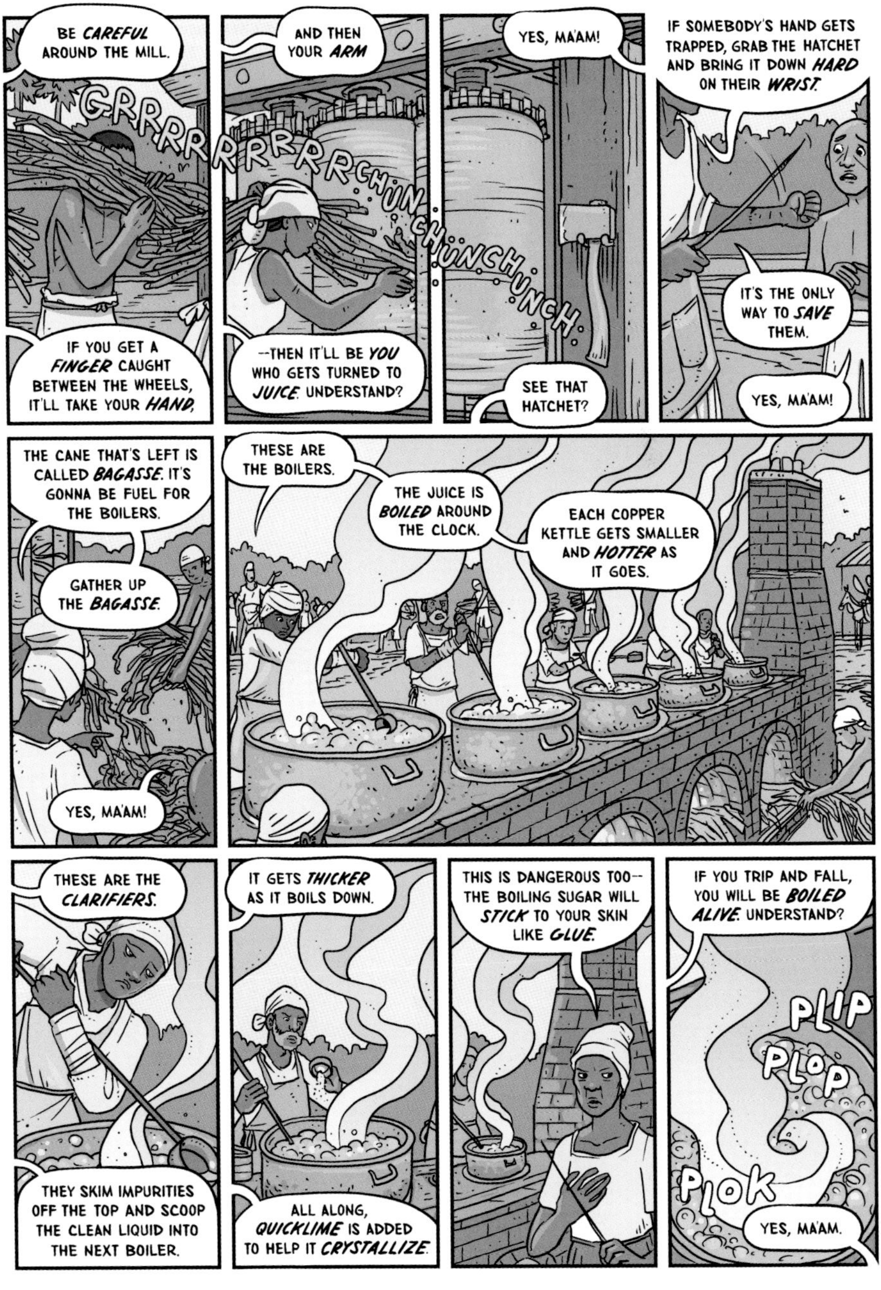
BE CAREFUL AROUND THE MILL.
GRRRRRRRRRRRCHUNCHUNCHUNCH
IF YOU GET A FINGER CAUGHT BETWEEN THE WHEELS, IT'LL TAKE YOUR HAND,
AND THEN YOUR ARM
--THEN IT'LL BE YOU WHO GETS TURNED TO JUICE. UNDERSTAND?
YES, MA'AM!
SEE THAT HATCHET?
IF SOMEBODY'S HAND GETS TRAPPED, GRAB THE HATCHET AND BRING IT DOWN HARD ON THEIR WRIST.
IT'S THE ONLY WAY TO SAVE THEM.
YES, MA'AM!
THE CANE THAT'S LEFT IS CALLED BAGASSE. IT'S GONNA BE FUEL FOR THE BOILERS.
GATHER UP THE BAGASSE.
YES, MA'AM!
THESE ARE THE BOILERS.
THE JUICE IS BOILED AROUND THE CLOCK.
EACH COPPER KETTLE GETS SMALLER AND HOTTER AS IT GOES.
THESE ARE THE CLARIFIERS.
THEY SKIM IMPURITIES OFF THE TOP AND SCOOP THE CLEAN LIQUID INTO THE NEXT BOILER.
IT GETS THICKER AS IT BOILS DOWN.
ALL ALONG, QUICKLIME IS ADDED TO HELP IT CRYSTALLIZE.
THIS IS DANGEROUS TOO-- THE BOILING SUGAR WILL STICK TO YOUR SKIN LIKE GLUE.
IF YOU TRIP AND FALL, YOU WILL BE BOILED ALIVE. UNDERSTAND?
PLIP
PLOP
PLOK
YES, MA'AM.

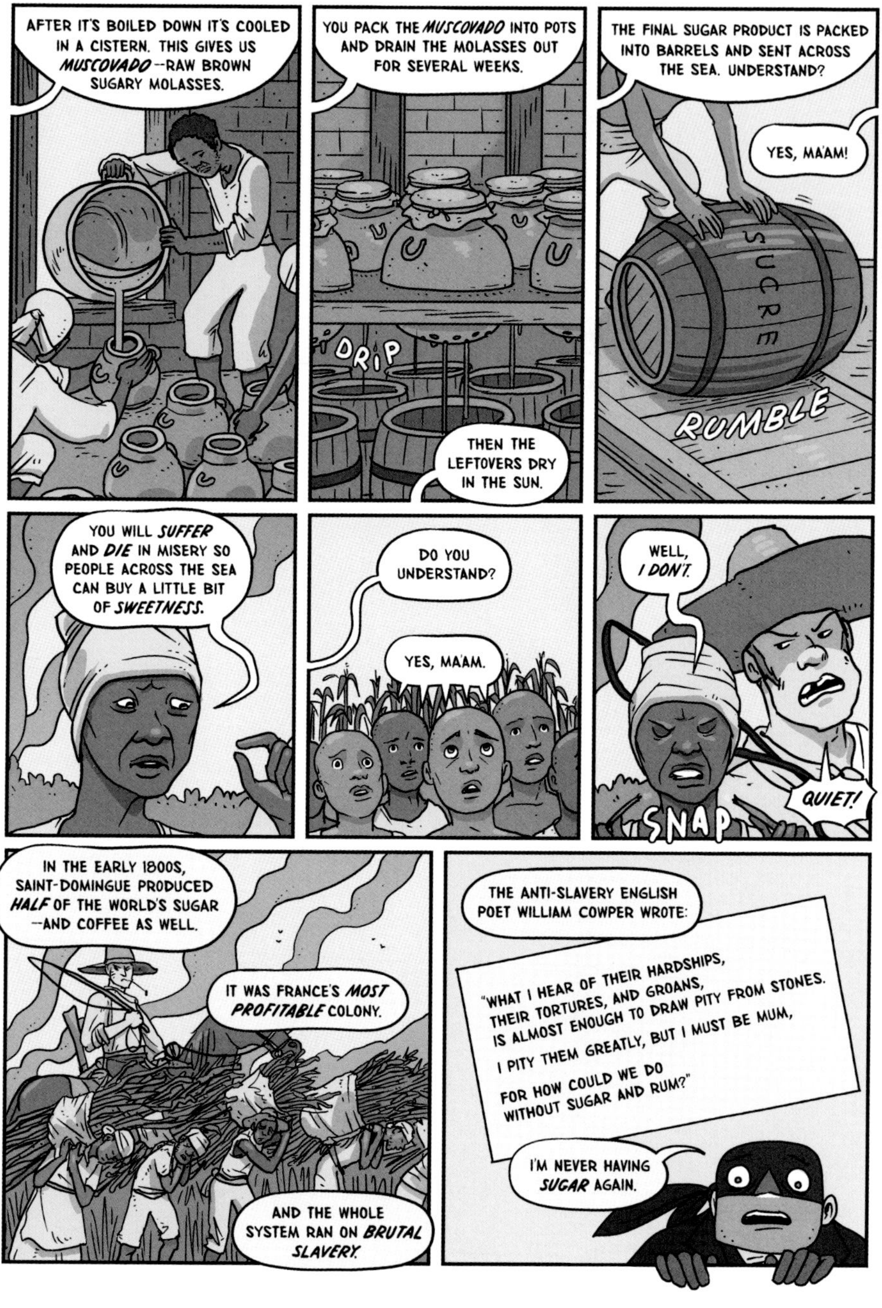
AFTER IT'S BOILED DOWN IT'S COOLED IN A CISTERN. THIS GIVES US *MUSCOVADO*--RAW BROWN SUGARY MOLASSES.
YOU PACK THE *MUSCOVADO* INTO POTS AND DRAIN THE MOLASSES OUT FOR SEVERAL WEEKS.
DRIP
THEN THE LEFTOVERS DRY IN THE SUN.
THE FINAL SUGAR PRODUCT IS PACKED INTO BARRELS AND SENT ACROSS THE SEA. UNDERSTAND?
YES, MA'AM!
SUCRE
RUMBLE
YOU WILL *SUFFER* AND *DIE* IN MISERY SO PEOPLE ACROSS THE SEA CAN BUY A LITTLE BIT OF *SWEETNESS*.
DO YOU UNDERSTAND?
YES, MA'AM.
WELL, *I DON'T*.
SNAP
QUIET!
IN THE EARLY 1800S, SAINT-DOMINGUE PRODUCED *HALF* OF THE WORLD'S SUGAR --AND COFFEE AS WELL.
IT WAS FRANCE'S *MOST PROFITABLE* COLONY.
AND THE WHOLE SYSTEM RAN ON *BRUTAL SLAVERY*.
THE ANTI-SLAVERY ENGLISH POET WILLIAM COWPER WROTE:
"WHAT I HEAR OF THEIR HARDSHIPS,
THEIR TORTURES, AND GROANS,
IS ALMOST ENOUGH TO DRAW PITY FROM STONES.
I PITY THEM GREATLY, BUT I MUST BE MUM,
FOR HOW COULD WE DO
WITHOUT SUGAR AND RUM?"
I'M NEVER HAVING *SUGAR* AGAIN.

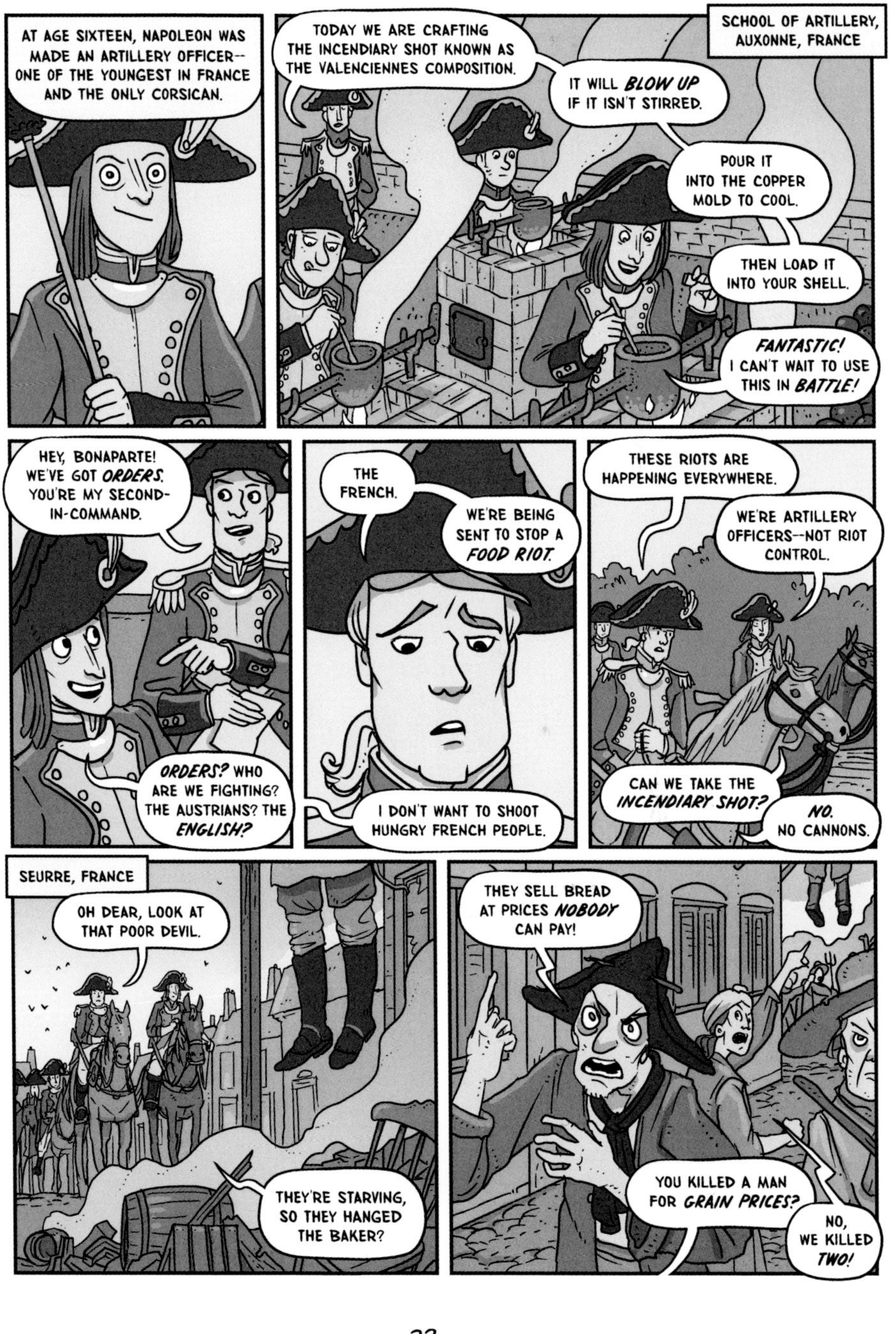

AT AGE SIXTEEN, NAPOLEON WAS MADE AN ARTILLERY OFFICER--ONE OF THE YOUNGEST IN FRANCE AND THE ONLY CORSICAN.
SCHOOL OF ARTILLERY, AUXONNE, FRANCE
TODAY WE ARE CRAFTING THE INCENDIARY SHOT KNOWN AS THE VALENCIENNES COMPOSITION.
IT WILL BLOW UP IF IT ISN'T STIRRED.
POUR IT INTO THE COPPER MOLD TO COOL.
THEN LOAD IT INTO YOUR SHELL.
FANTASTIC! I CAN'T WAIT TO USE THIS IN BATTLE!
HEY, BONAPARTE! WE'VE GOT ORDERS. YOU'RE MY SECOND-IN-COMMAND.
ORDERS? WHO ARE WE FIGHTING? THE AUSTRIANS? THE ENGLISH?
THE FRENCH.
WE'RE BEING SENT TO STOP A FOOD RIOT.
I DON'T WANT TO SHOOT HUNGRY FRENCH PEOPLE.
THESE RIOTS ARE HAPPENING EVERYWHERE.
WE'RE ARTILLERY OFFICERS--NOT RIOT CONTROL.
CAN WE TAKE THE INCENDIARY SHOT?
NO. NO CANNONS.
SEURRE, FRANCE
OH DEAR, LOOK AT THAT POOR DEVIL.
THEY'RE STARVING, SO THEY HANGED THE BAKER?
THEY SELL BREAD AT PRICES NOBODY CAN PAY!
YOU KILLED A MAN FOR GRAIN PRICES?
NO, WE KILLED TWO!

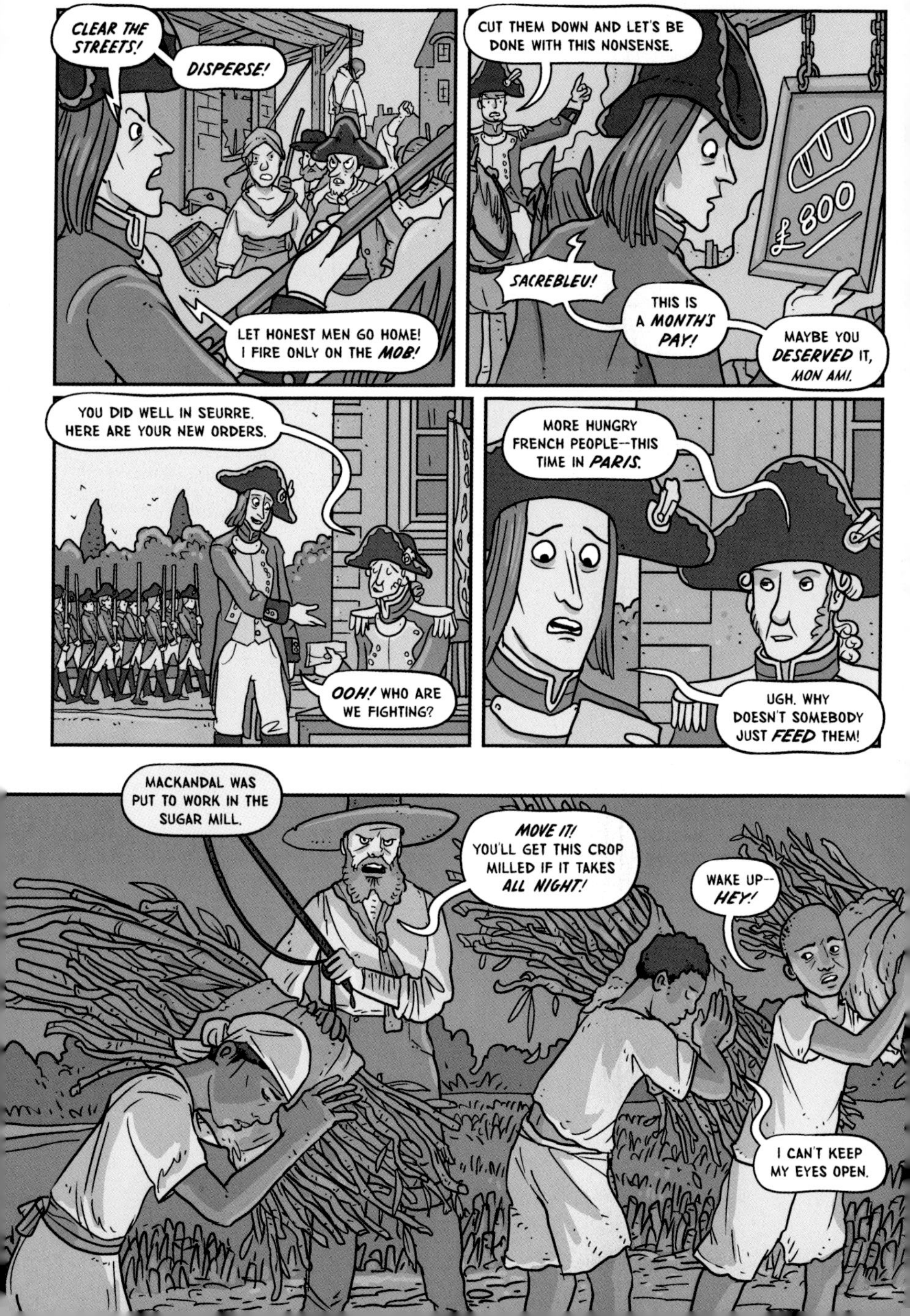
CLEAR THE STREETS!
DISPERSE!
LET HONEST MEN GO HOME! I FIRE ONLY ON THE MOB!
CUT THEM DOWN AND LET'S BE DONE WITH THIS NONSENSE.
£800
SACREBLEU!
THIS IS A MONTH'S PAY!
MAYBE YOU DESERVED IT, MON AMI.
YOU DID WELL IN SEURRE. HERE ARE YOUR NEW ORDERS.
OOH! WHO ARE WE FIGHTING?
MORE HUNGRY FRENCH PEOPLE--THIS TIME IN PARIS.
UGH. WHY DOESN'T SOMEBODY JUST FEED THEM!
MACKANDAL WAS PUT TO WORK IN THE SUGAR MILL.
MOVE IT! YOU'LL GET THIS CROP MILLED IF IT TAKES ALL NIGHT!
WAKE UP-- HEY!
I CAN'T KEEP MY EYES OPEN.

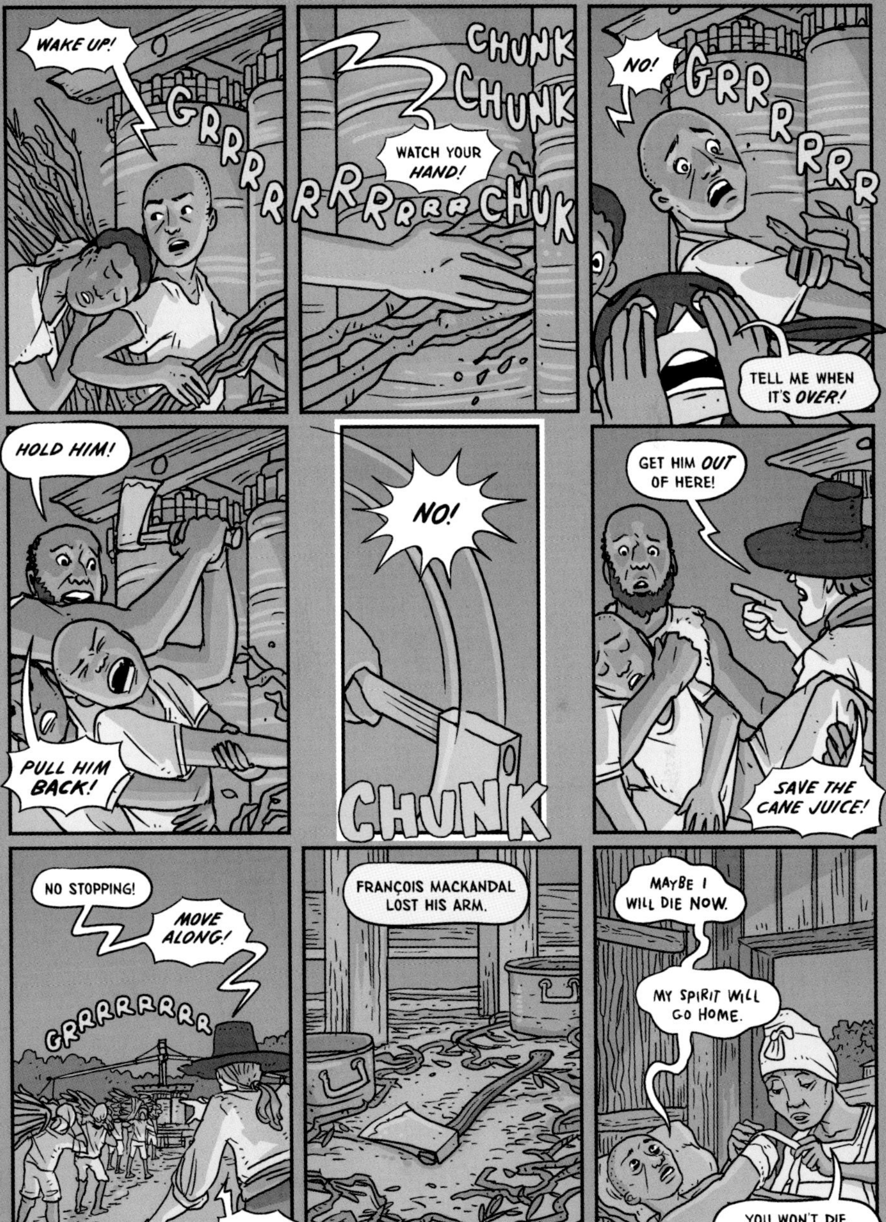
WAKE UP!
GRRRRRRRRRRRRRR
CHUNK
CHUNK
WATCH YOUR HAND!
CHUK
NO!
GRRRRRRR
TELL ME WHEN IT'S OVER!
HOLD HIM!
PULL HIM BACK!
NO!
CHUNK
GET HIM OUT OF HERE!
SAVE THE CANE JUICE!
NO STOPPING!
MOVE ALONG!
GRRRRRRRRR
NEXT!
FRANÇOIS MACKANDAL LOST HIS ARM.
MAYBE I WILL DIE NOW.
MY SPIRIT WILL GO HOME.
YOU WON'T DIE. YOU WON'T GO HOME.

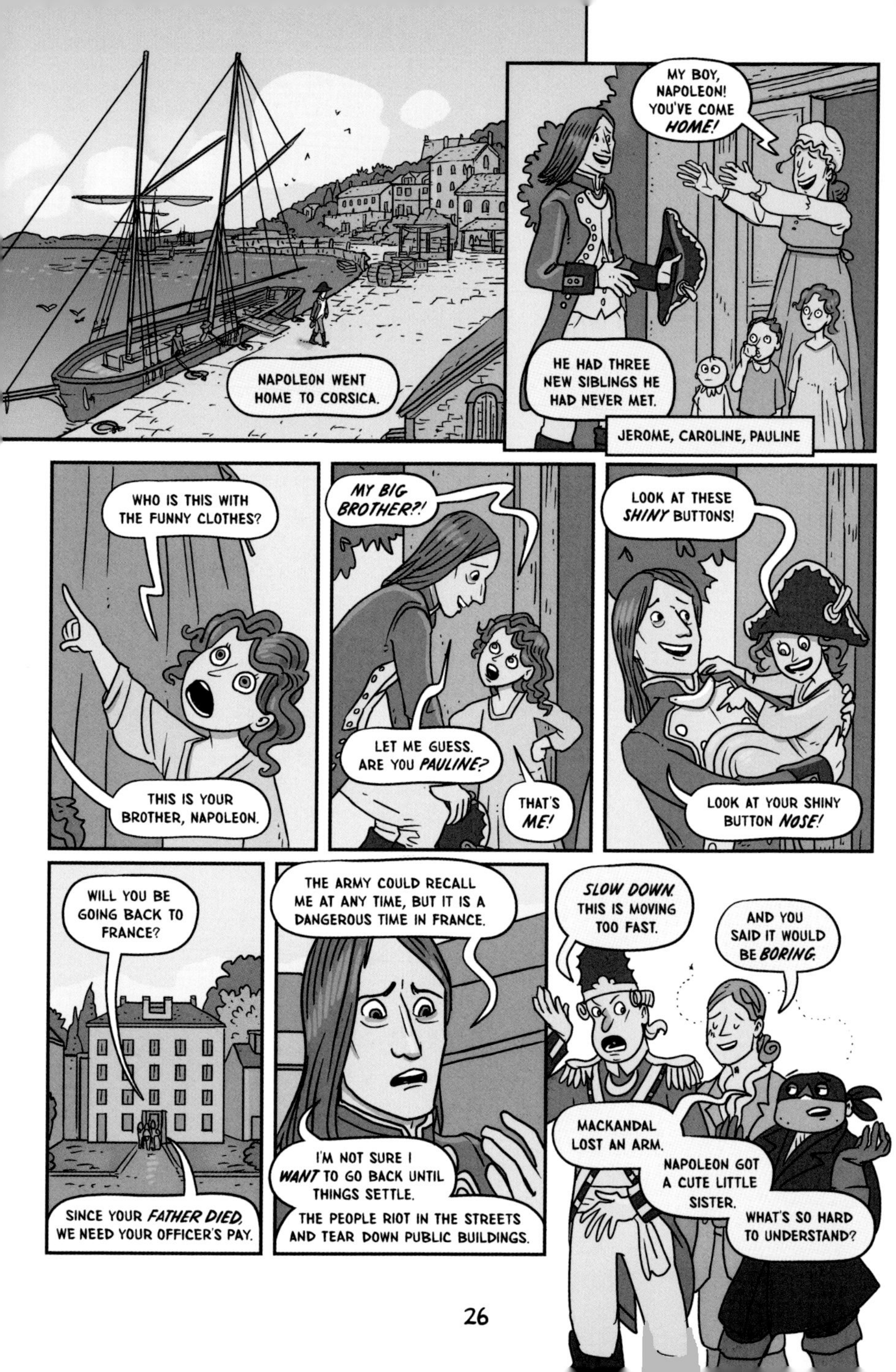
NAPOLEON WENT HOME TO CORSICA.
MY BOY, NAPOLEON! YOU'VE COME HOME!
HE HAD THREE NEW SIBLINGS HE HAD NEVER MET.
JEROME, CAROLINE, PAULINE
WHO IS THIS WITH THE FUNNY CLOTHES?
THIS IS YOUR BROTHER, NAPOLEON.
MY BIG BROTHER?!
LET ME GUESS. ARE YOU PAULINE?
THAT'S ME!
LOOK AT THESE SHINY BUTTONS!
LOOK AT YOUR SHINY BUTTON NOSE!
WILL YOU BE GOING BACK TO FRANCE?
SINCE YOUR FATHER DIED, WE NEED YOUR OFFICER'S PAY.
THE ARMY COULD RECALL ME AT ANY TIME, BUT IT IS A DANGEROUS TIME IN FRANCE.
I'M NOT SURE I WANT TO GO BACK UNTIL THINGS SETTLE.
THE PEOPLE RIOT IN THE STREETS AND TEAR DOWN PUBLIC BUILDINGS.
SLOW DOWN. THIS IS MOVING TOO FAST.
AND YOU SAID IT WOULD BE BORING.
MACKANDAL LOST AN ARM.
NAPOLEON GOT A CUTE LITTLE SISTER.
WHAT'S SO HARD TO UNDERSTAND?

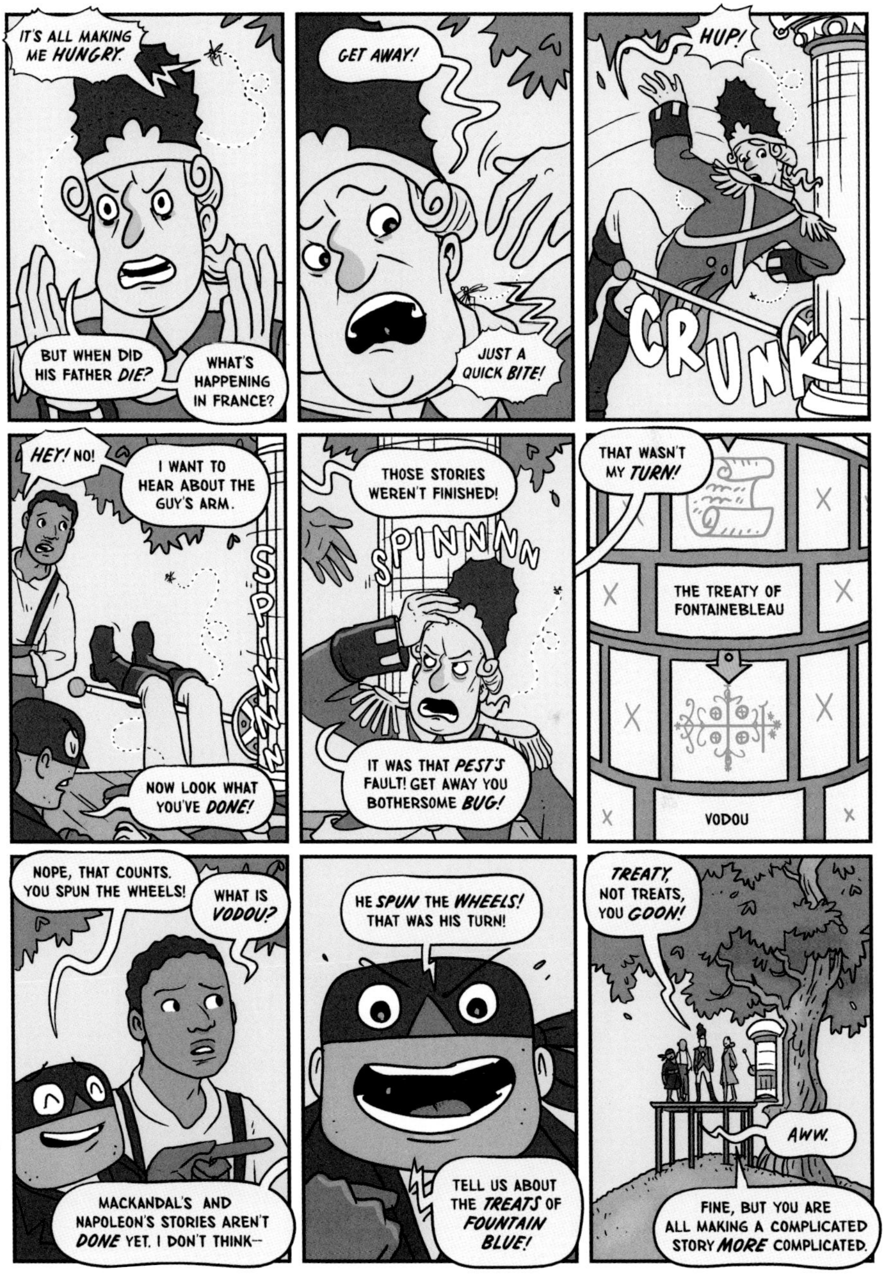
IT'S ALL MAKING ME HUNGRY.
BUT WHEN DID HIS FATHER DIE?
WHAT'S HAPPENING IN FRANCE?
GET AWAY!
JUST A QUICK BITE!
HUP!
CRUNK
HEY! NO!
I WANT TO HEAR ABOUT THE GUY'S ARM.
SPINNNN
NOW LOOK WHAT YOU'VE DONE!
THOSE STORIES WEREN'T FINISHED!
SPINNNNN
IT WAS THAT PEST'S FAULT! GET AWAY YOU BOTHERSOME BUG!
THAT WASN'T MY TURN!
THE TREATY OF FONTAINEBLEAU
VODOU
NOPE, THAT COUNTS. YOU SPUN THE WHEELS!
WHAT IS VODOU?
MACKANDAL'S AND NAPOLEON'S STORIES AREN'T DONE YET. I DON'T THINK—
HE SPUN THE WHEELS! THAT WAS HIS TURN!
TELL US ABOUT THE TREATS OF FOUNTAIN BLUE!
TREATY, NOT TREATS, YOU GOON!
AWW.
FINE, BUT YOU ARE ALL MAKING A COMPLICATED STORY MORE COMPLICATED.

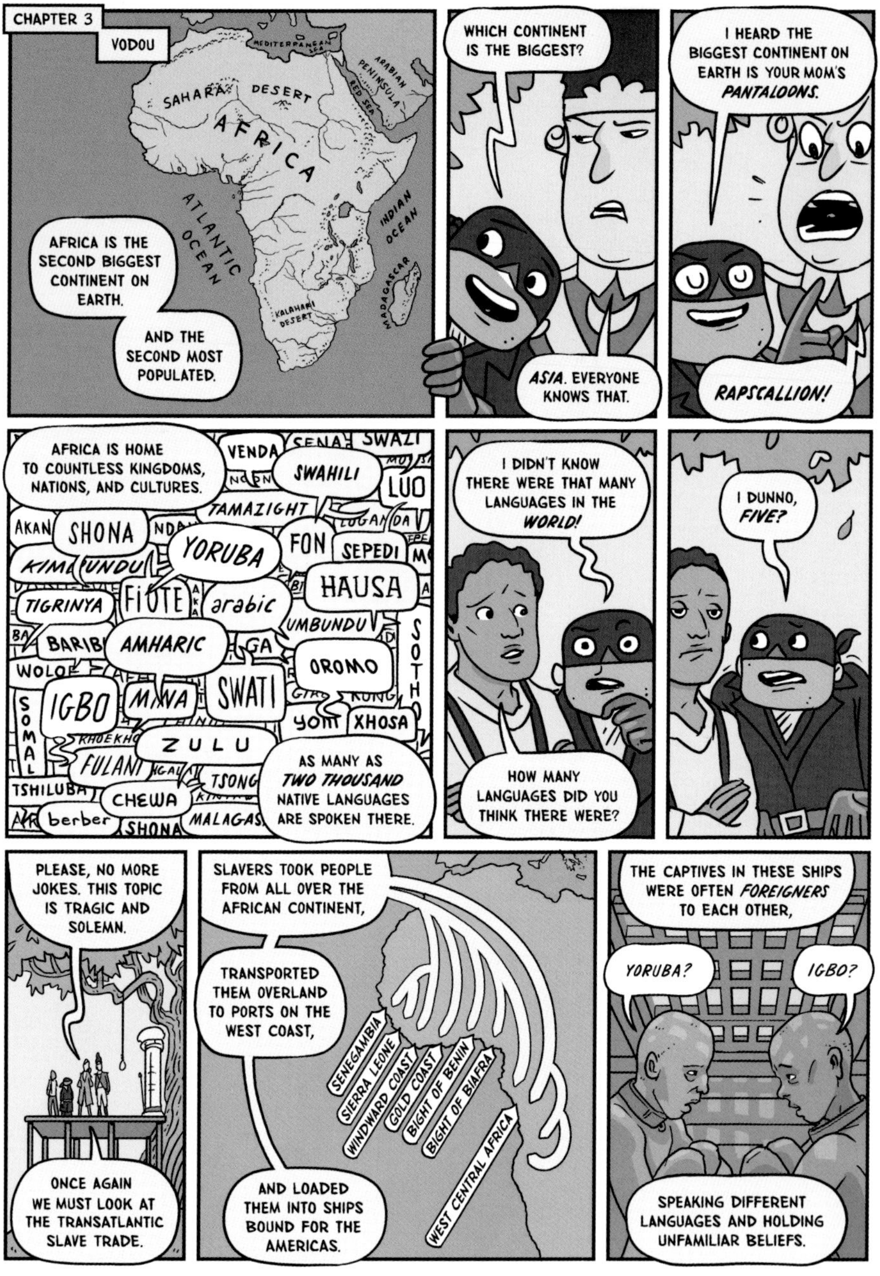
CHAPTER 3
VODOU
MEDITERRANEAN SEA
ARABIAN PENINSULA
RED SEA
SAHARA DESERT
AFRICA
ATLANTIC OCEAN
INDIAN OCEAN
MADAGASCAR
KALAHARI DESERT
AFRICA IS THE SECOND BIGGEST CONTINENT ON EARTH.
AND THE SECOND MOST POPULATED.
WHICH CONTINENT IS THE BIGGEST?
ASIA. EVERYONE KNOWS THAT.
I HEARD THE BIGGEST CONTINENT ON EARTH IS YOUR MOM'S PANTALOONS.
RAPSCALLION!
AFRICA IS HOME TO COUNTLESS KINGDOMS, NATIONS, AND CULTURES.
VENDA
SWAZI
SWAHILI
LUO
TAMAZIGHT
AKAN
SHONA
YORUBA
FON
SEPEDI
HAUSA
FIOTE
arabic
TIGRINYA
UMBUNDU
SOTHO
BARIBA
AMHARIC
GA
OROMO
WOLOF
SOMALI
IGBO
MINA
SWATI
XHOSA
ZULU
FULANI
TSHILUBA
CHEWA
TSONGA
berber
SHONA
MALAGASY
AS MANY AS TWO THOUSAND NATIVE LANGUAGES ARE SPOKEN THERE.
I DIDN'T KNOW THERE WERE THAT MANY LANGUAGES IN THE WORLD!
HOW MANY LANGUAGES DID YOU THINK THERE WERE?
I DUNNO, FIVE?
PLEASE, NO MORE JOKES. THIS TOPIC IS TRAGIC AND SOLEMN.
ONCE AGAIN WE MUST LOOK AT THE TRANSATLANTIC SLAVE TRADE.
SLAVERS TOOK PEOPLE FROM ALL OVER THE AFRICAN CONTINENT,
TRANSPORTED THEM OVERLAND TO PORTS ON THE WEST COAST,
SENEGAMBIA
SIERRA LEONE
WINDWARD COAST
GOLD COAST
BIGHT OF BENIN
BIGHT OF BIAFRA
WEST CENTRAL AFRICA
AND LOADED THEM INTO SHIPS BOUND FOR THE AMERICAS.
THE CAPTIVES IN THESE SHIPS WERE OFTEN FOREIGNERS TO EACH OTHER,
YORUBA?
IGBO?
SPEAKING DIFFERENT LANGUAGES AND HOLDING UNFAMILIAR BELIEFS.

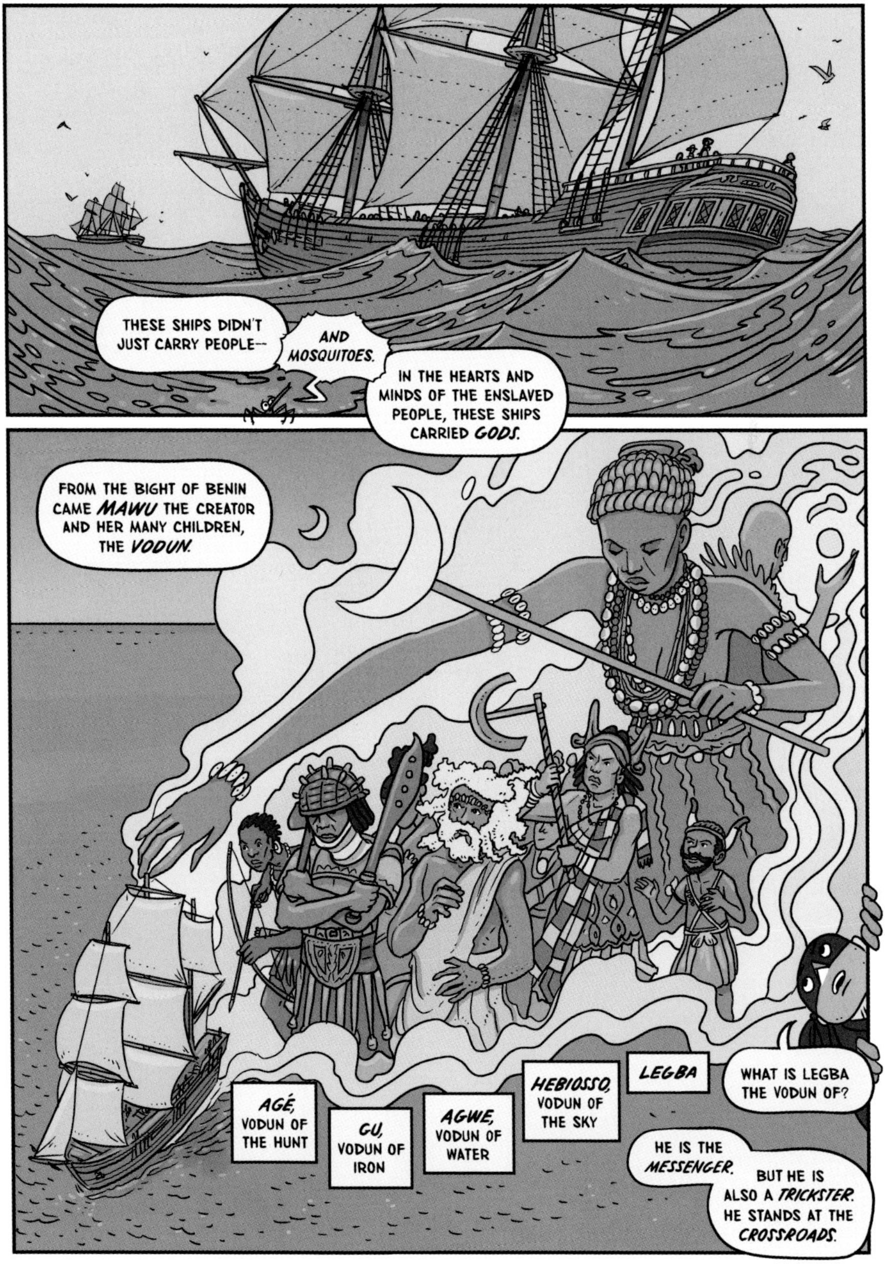
THESE SHIPS DIDN'T JUST CARRY PEOPLE--
AND MOSQUITOES.
IN THE HEARTS AND MINDS OF THE ENSLAVED PEOPLE, THESE SHIPS CARRIED GODS.
FROM THE BIGHT OF BENIN CAME MAWU THE CREATOR AND HER MANY CHILDREN, THE VODUN.
AGÉ, VODUN OF THE HUNT
GU, VODUN OF IRON
AGWE, VODUN OF WATER
HEBIOSSO, VODUN OF THE SKY
LEGBA
WHAT IS LEGBA THE VODUN OF?
HE IS THE MESSENGER.
BUT HE IS ALSO A TRICKSTER. HE STANDS AT THE CROSSROADS.

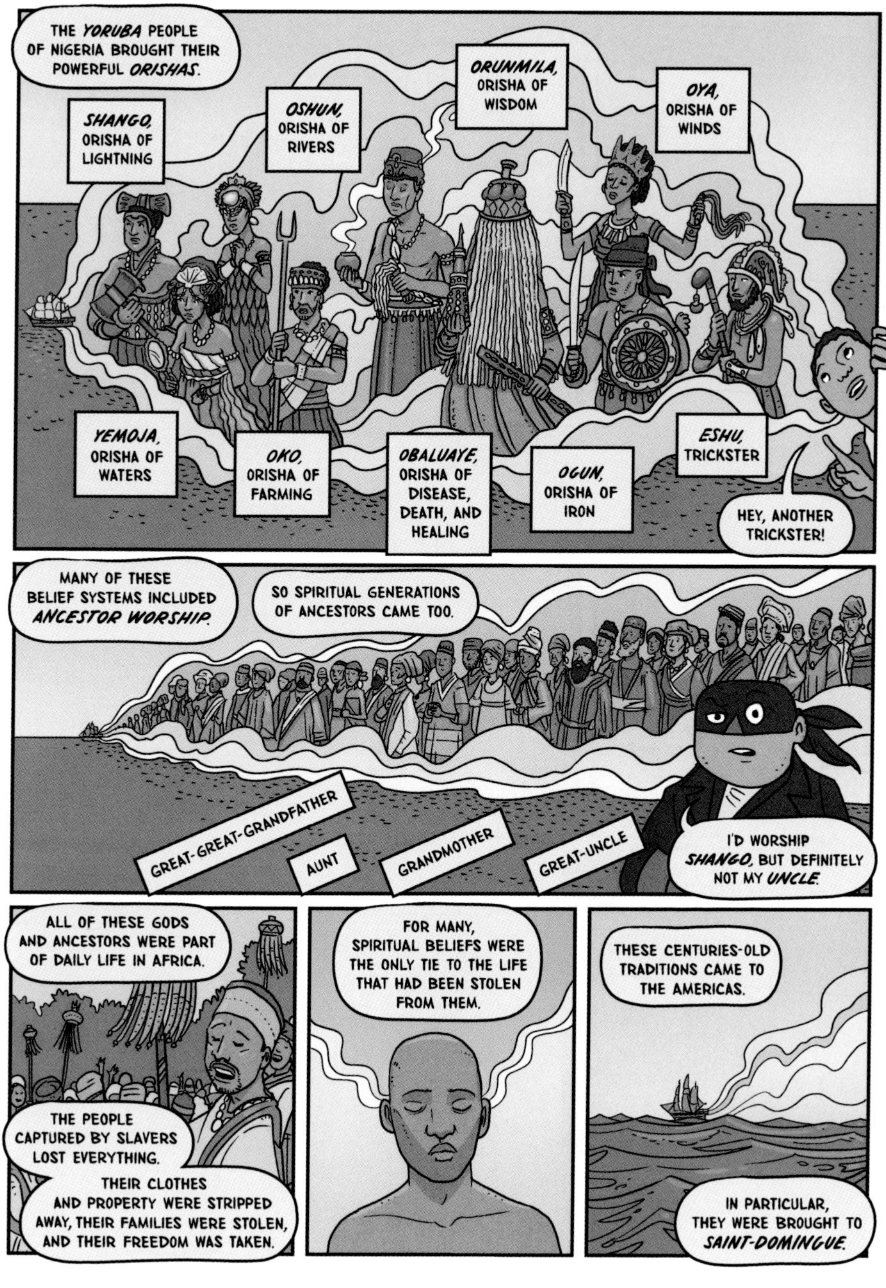
THE *YORUBA* PEOPLE OF NIGERIA BROUGHT THEIR POWERFUL *ORISHAS*.
SHANGO, ORISHA OF LIGHTNING
OSHUN, ORISHA OF RIVERS
ORUNMILA, ORISHA OF WISDOM
OYA, ORISHA OF WINDS
YEMOJA, ORISHA OF WATERS
OKO, ORISHA OF FARMING
OBALUAYE, ORISHA OF DISEASE, DEATH, AND HEALING
OGUN, ORISHA OF IRON
ESHU, TRICKSTER
HEY, ANOTHER TRICKSTER!
MANY OF THESE BELIEF SYSTEMS INCLUDED ***ANCESTOR WORSHIP***.
SO SPIRITUAL GENERATIONS OF ANCESTORS CAME TOO.
GREAT-GREAT-GRANDFATHER
AUNT
GRANDMOTHER
GREAT-UNCLE
I'D WORSHIP *SHANGO*, BUT DEFINITELY NOT MY *UNCLE*.
ALL OF THESE GODS AND ANCESTORS WERE PART OF DAILY LIFE IN AFRICA.
THE PEOPLE CAPTURED BY SLAVERS LOST EVERYTHING.
THEIR CLOTHES AND PROPERTY WERE STRIPPED AWAY, THEIR FAMILIES WERE STOLEN, AND THEIR FREEDOM WAS TAKEN.
FOR MANY, SPIRITUAL BELIEFS WERE THE ONLY TIE TO THE LIFE THAT HAD BEEN STOLEN FROM THEM.
THESE CENTURIES-OLD TRADITIONS CAME TO THE AMERICAS.
IN PARTICULAR, THEY WERE BROUGHT TO *SAINT-DOMINGUE*.

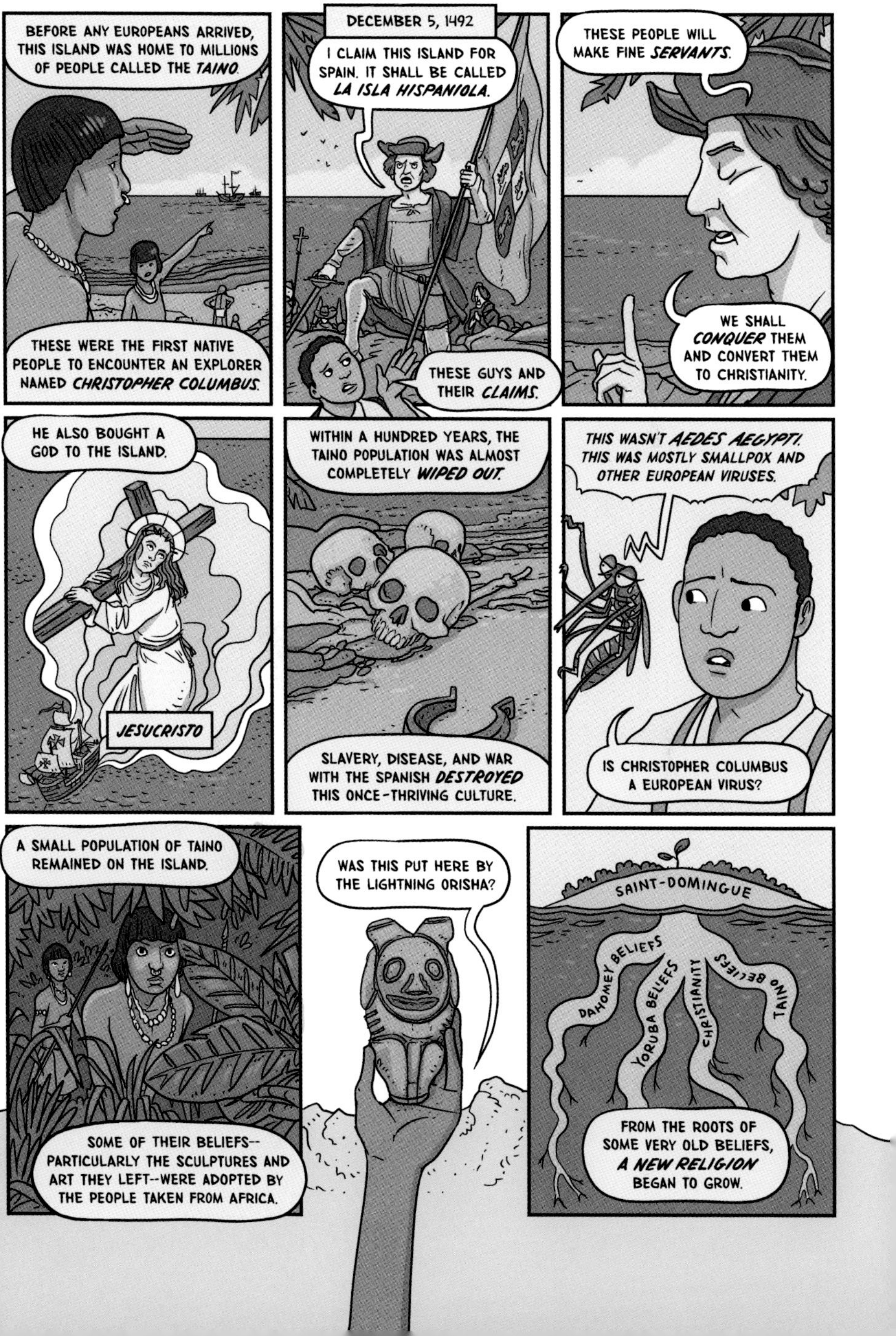
BEFORE ANY EUROPEANS ARRIVED, THIS ISLAND WAS HOME TO MILLIONS OF PEOPLE CALLED THE TAINO.
THESE WERE THE FIRST NATIVE PEOPLE TO ENCOUNTER AN EXPLORER NAMED CHRISTOPHER COLUMBUS.
DECEMBER 5, 1492
I CLAIM THIS ISLAND FOR SPAIN. IT SHALL BE CALLED LA ISLA HISPANIOLA.
THESE GUYS AND THEIR CLAIMS.
THESE PEOPLE WILL MAKE FINE SERVANTS.
WE SHALL CONQUER THEM AND CONVERT THEM TO CHRISTIANITY.
HE ALSO BOUGHT A GOD TO THE ISLAND.
JESUCRISTO
WITHIN A HUNDRED YEARS, THE TAINO POPULATION WAS ALMOST COMPLETELY WIPED OUT.
SLAVERY, DISEASE, AND WAR WITH THE SPANISH DESTROYED THIS ONCE-THRIVING CULTURE.
THIS WASN'T AEDES AEGYPTI. THIS WAS MOSTLY SMALLPOX AND OTHER EUROPEAN VIRUSES.
IS CHRISTOPHER COLUMBUS A EUROPEAN VIRUS?
A SMALL POPULATION OF TAINO REMAINED ON THE ISLAND.
SOME OF THEIR BELIEFS--PARTICULARLY THE SCULPTURES AND ART THEY LEFT--WERE ADOPTED BY THE PEOPLE TAKEN FROM AFRICA.
WAS THIS PUT HERE BY THE LIGHTNING ORISHA?
SAINT-DOMINGUE
DAHOMEY BELIEFS
YORUBA BELIEFS
CHRISTIANITY
TAINO BELIEFS
FROM THE ROOTS OF SOME VERY OLD BELIEFS, A NEW RELIGION BEGAN TO GROW.

THE TREATY OF FONTAINEBLEAU (1762)

HEY, *KING CHARLES III* OF SPAIN-- IT'S YOUR WACKY COUSIN, *KING LOUIS XV* OF FRANCE.

WHAT DO YOU WANT?

I'M GIVING YOU A *LITTLE PRESENT.*

OOOH. WHAT?

THE ENTIRE LOUISIANA TERRITORY!

EEP. THAT'S NOT LITTLE.

FRANCE JUST GAVE THAT LAND TO SPAIN?

THEY DID.

YOU'RE RIGHT. THERE WEREN'T ANY TREATS.

LET'S GET BACK TO VODOU.

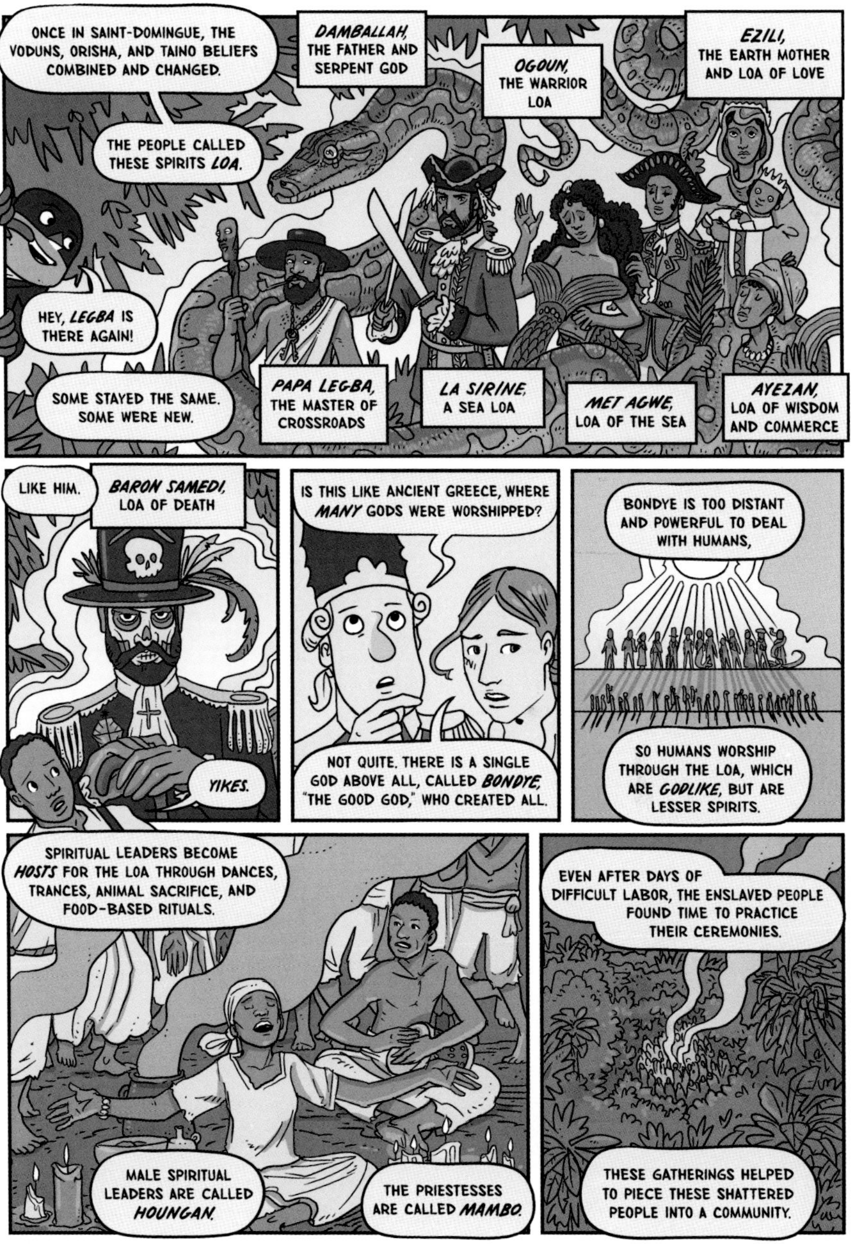
ONCE IN SAINT-DOMINGUE, THE VODUNS, ORISHA, AND TAINO BELIEFS COMBINED AND CHANGED.
THE PEOPLE CALLED THESE SPIRITS *LOA*.
DAMBALLAH, THE FATHER AND SERPENT GOD
OGOUN, THE WARRIOR LOA
EZILI, THE EARTH MOTHER AND LOA OF LOVE
HEY, *LEGBA* IS THERE AGAIN!
SOME STAYED THE SAME. SOME WERE NEW.
PAPA LEGBA, THE MASTER OF CROSSROADS
LA SIRINE, A SEA LOA
MET AGWE, LOA OF THE SEA
AYEZAN, LOA OF WISDOM AND COMMERCE
LIKE HIM.
BARON SAMEDI, LOA OF DEATH
YIKES.
IS THIS LIKE ANCIENT GREECE, WHERE *MANY* GODS WERE WORSHIPPED?
NOT QUITE. THERE IS A SINGLE GOD ABOVE ALL, CALLED *BONDYE,* "THE GOOD GOD," WHO CREATED ALL.
BONDYE IS TOO DISTANT AND POWERFUL TO DEAL WITH HUMANS,
SO HUMANS WORSHIP THROUGH THE LOA, WHICH ARE *GODLIKE*, BUT ARE LESSER SPIRITS.
SPIRITUAL LEADERS BECOME *HOSTS* FOR THE LOA THROUGH DANCES, TRANCES, ANIMAL SACRIFICE, AND FOOD-BASED RITUALS.
MALE SPIRITUAL LEADERS ARE CALLED *HOUNGAN*.
THE PRIESTESSES ARE CALLED *MAMBO*.
EVEN AFTER DAYS OF DIFFICULT LABOR, THE ENSLAVED PEOPLE FOUND TIME TO PRACTICE THEIR CEREMONIES.
THESE GATHERINGS HELPED TO PIECE THESE SHATTERED PEOPLE INTO A COMMUNITY.

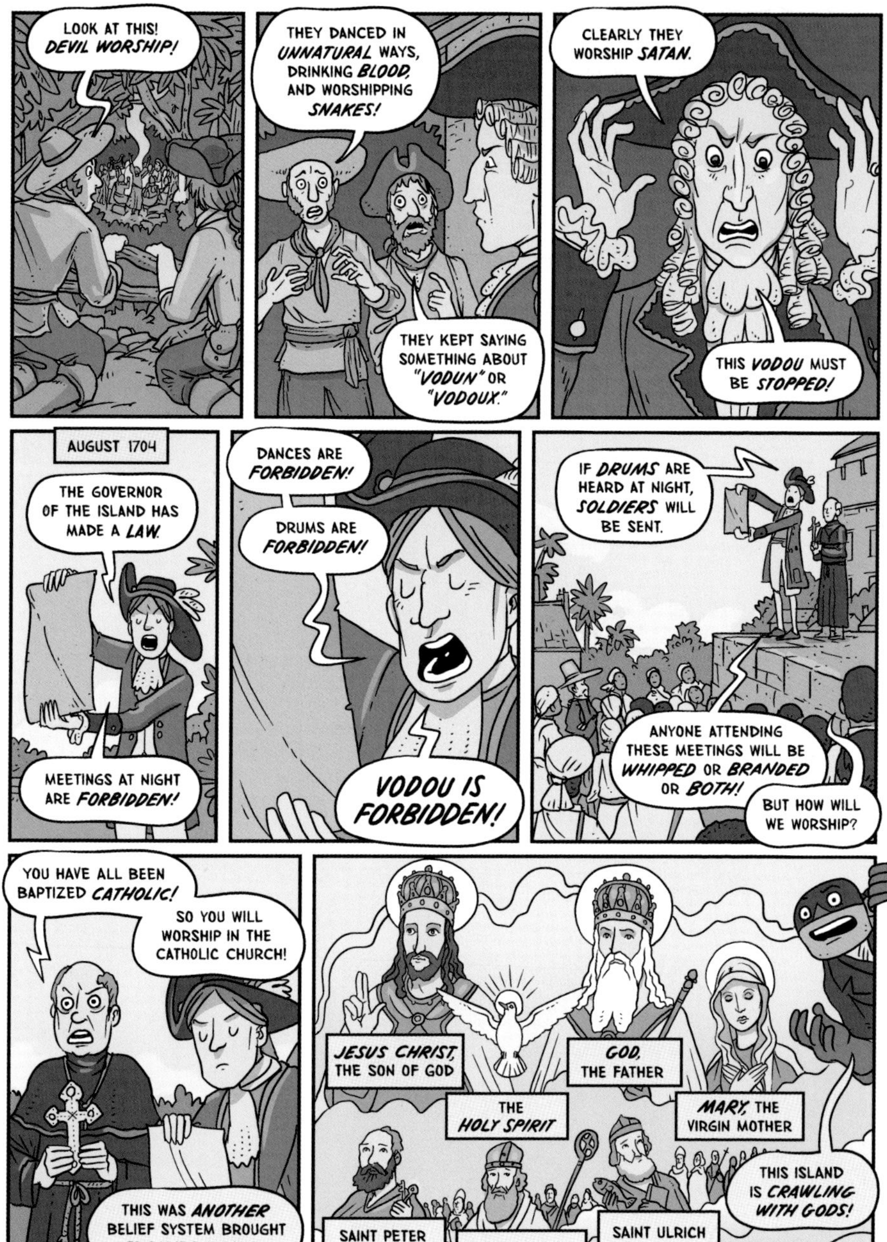
LOOK AT THIS! DEVIL WORSHIP!
THEY DANCED IN UNNATURAL WAYS, DRINKING BLOOD, AND WORSHIPPING SNAKES!
THEY KEPT SAYING SOMETHING ABOUT "VODUN" OR "VODOUX."
CLEARLY THEY WORSHIP SATAN.
THIS VODOU MUST BE STOPPED!
AUGUST 1704
THE GOVERNOR OF THE ISLAND HAS MADE A LAW.
MEETINGS AT NIGHT ARE FORBIDDEN!
DANCES ARE FORBIDDEN!
DRUMS ARE FORBIDDEN!
VODOU IS FORBIDDEN!
IF DRUMS ARE HEARD AT NIGHT, SOLDIERS WILL BE SENT.
ANYONE ATTENDING THESE MEETINGS WILL BE WHIPPED OR BRANDED OR BOTH!
BUT HOW WILL WE WORSHIP?
YOU HAVE ALL BEEN BAPTIZED CATHOLIC!
SO YOU WILL WORSHIP IN THE CATHOLIC CHURCH!
THIS WAS ANOTHER BELIEF SYSTEM BROUGHT TO SAINT-DOMINGUE.
JESUS CHRIST, THE SON OF GOD
GOD, THE FATHER
THE HOLY SPIRIT
MARY, THE VIRGIN MOTHER
SAINT PETER
SAINT PATRICK
SAINT ULRICH
THIS ISLAND IS CRAWLING WITH GODS!

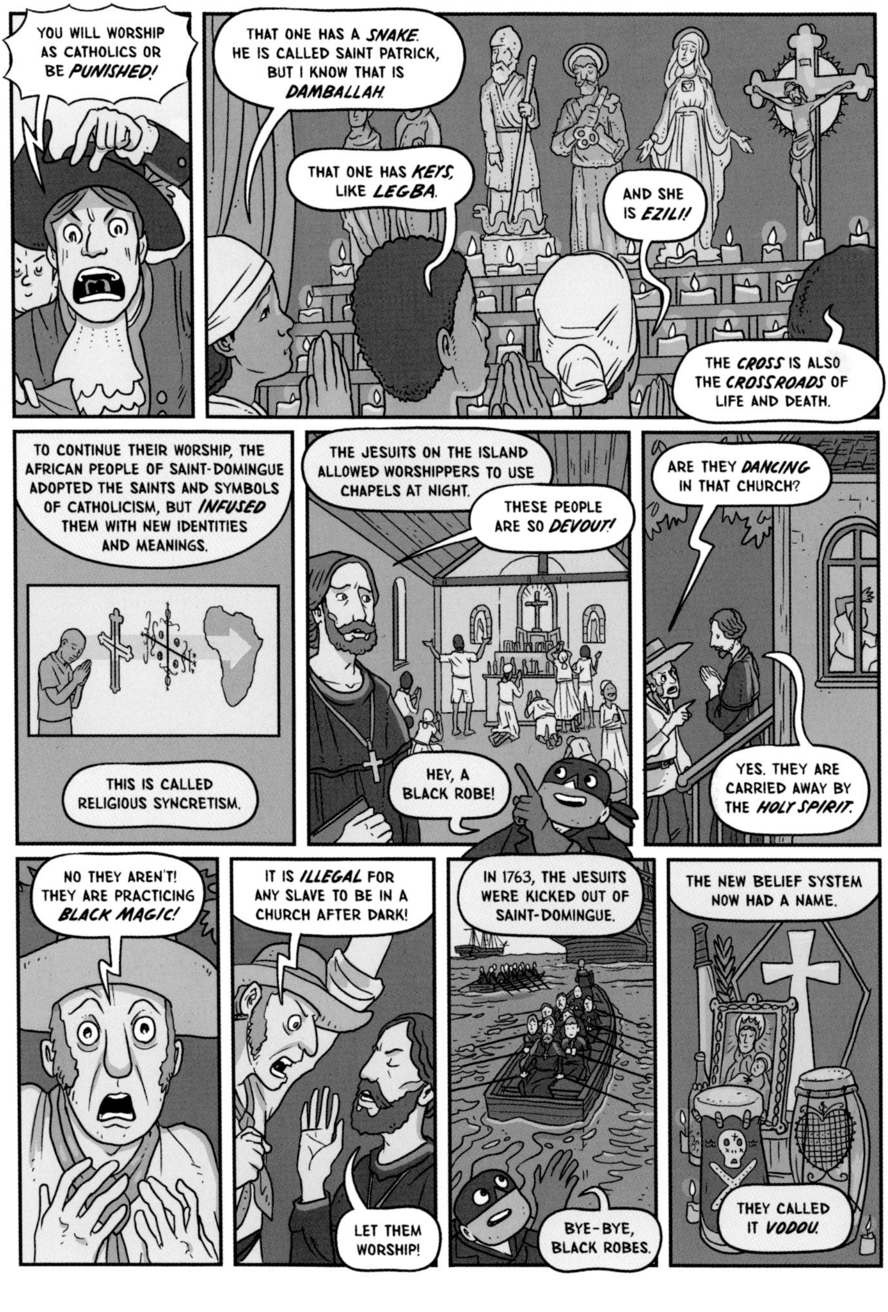
YOU WILL WORSHIP AS CATHOLICS OR BE PUNISHED!
THAT ONE HAS A SNAKE. HE IS CALLED SAINT PATRICK, BUT I KNOW THAT IS DAMBALLAH.
THAT ONE HAS KEYS, LIKE LEGBA.
AND SHE IS EZILI!
THE CROSS IS ALSO THE CROSSROADS OF LIFE AND DEATH.
TO CONTINUE THEIR WORSHIP, THE AFRICAN PEOPLE OF SAINT-DOMINGUE ADOPTED THE SAINTS AND SYMBOLS OF CATHOLICISM, BUT INFUSED THEM WITH NEW IDENTITIES AND MEANINGS.
THIS IS CALLED RELIGIOUS SYNCRETISM.
THE JESUITS ON THE ISLAND ALLOWED WORSHIPPERS TO USE CHAPELS AT NIGHT.
THESE PEOPLE ARE SO DEVOUT!
HEY, A BLACK ROBE!
ARE THEY DANCING IN THAT CHURCH?
YES. THEY ARE CARRIED AWAY BY THE HOLY SPIRIT.
NO THEY AREN'T! THEY ARE PRACTICING BLACK MAGIC!
IT IS ILLEGAL FOR ANY SLAVE TO BE IN A CHURCH AFTER DARK!
LET THEM WORSHIP!
IN 1763, THE JESUITS WERE KICKED OUT OF SAINT-DOMINGUE.
BYE-BYE, BLACK ROBES.
THE NEW BELIEF SYSTEM NOW HAD A NAME.
THEY CALLED IT VODOU.

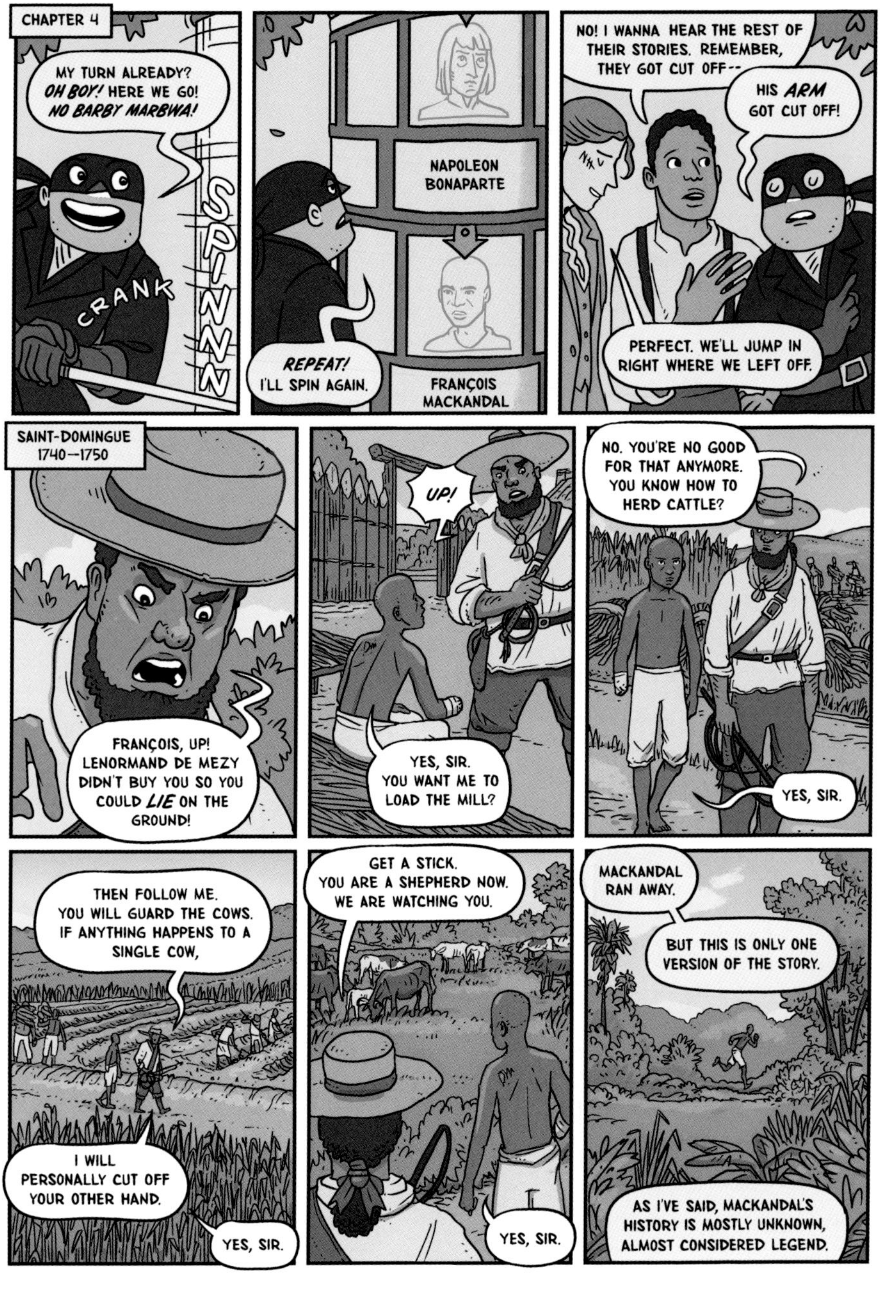
CHAPTER 4
MY TURN ALREADY? OH BOY! HERE WE GO! NO BARBY MARBWA!
CRANK
SPINNN
NAPOLEON BONAPARTE
FRANÇOIS MACKANDAL
REPEAT! I'LL SPIN AGAIN.
NO! I WANNA HEAR THE REST OF THEIR STORIES. REMEMBER, THEY GOT CUT OFF--
HIS ARM GOT CUT OFF!
PERFECT. WE'LL JUMP IN RIGHT WHERE WE LEFT OFF.
SAINT-DOMINGUE 1740--1750
FRANÇOIS, UP! LENORMAND DE MEZY DIDN'T BUY YOU SO YOU COULD LIE ON THE GROUND!
UP!
YES, SIR. YOU WANT ME TO LOAD THE MILL?
NO. YOU'RE NO GOOD FOR THAT ANYMORE. YOU KNOW HOW TO HERD CATTLE?
YES, SIR.
THEN FOLLOW ME. YOU WILL GUARD THE COWS. IF ANYTHING HAPPENS TO A SINGLE COW,
I WILL PERSONALLY CUT OFF YOUR OTHER HAND.
YES, SIR.
GET A STICK. YOU ARE A SHEPHERD NOW. WE ARE WATCHING YOU.
YES, SIR.
MACKANDAL RAN AWAY.
BUT THIS IS ONLY ONE VERSION OF THE STORY.
AS I'VE SAID, MACKANDAL'S HISTORY IS MOSTLY UNKNOWN, ALMOST CONSIDERED LEGEND.

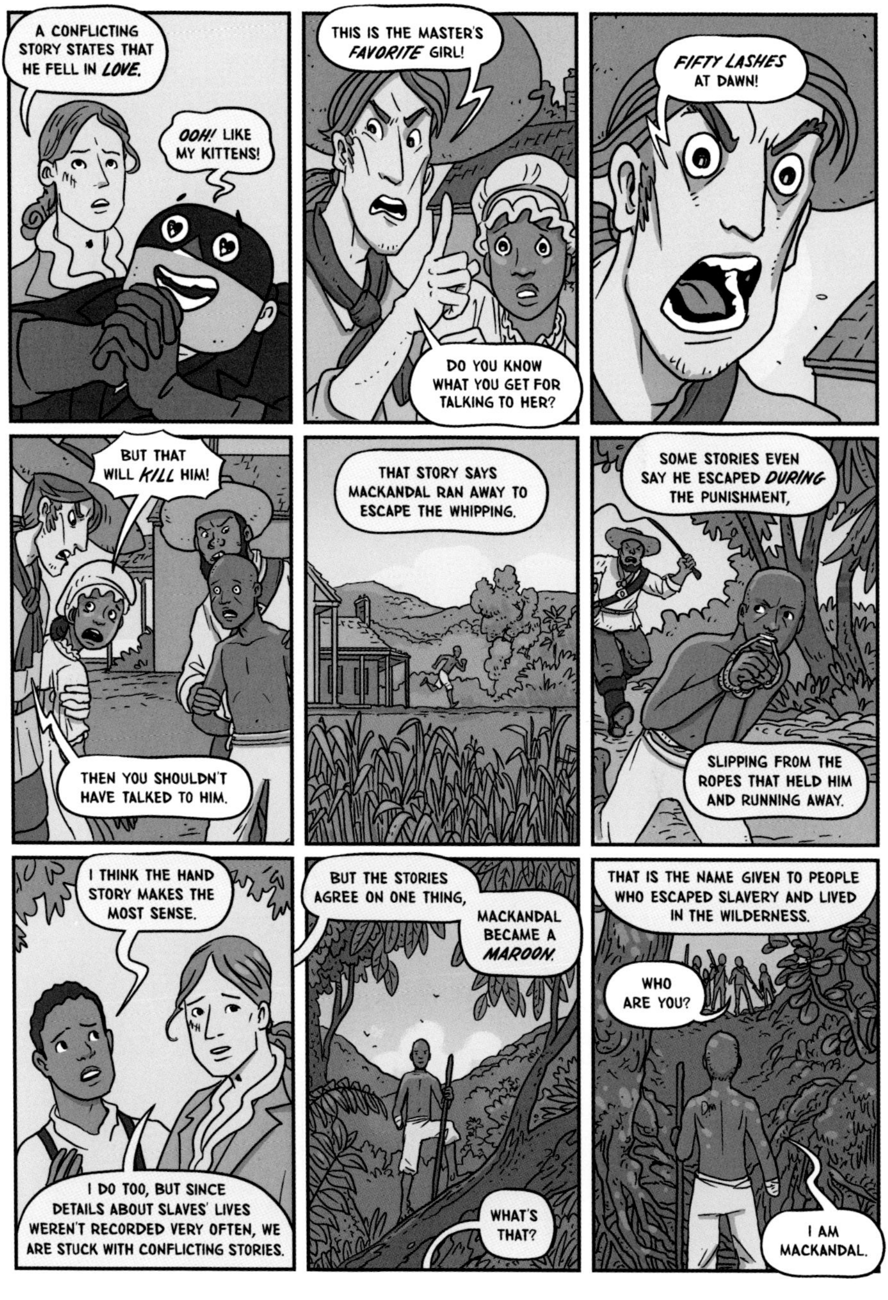
A CONFLICTING STORY STATES THAT HE FELL IN *LOVE*.
OOH! LIKE MY KITTENS!
THIS IS THE MASTER'S *FAVORITE* GIRL!
DO YOU KNOW WHAT YOU GET FOR TALKING TO HER?
FIFTY LASHES AT DAWN!
BUT THAT WILL *KILL* HIM!
THEN YOU SHOULDN'T HAVE TALKED TO HIM.
THAT STORY SAYS MACKANDAL RAN AWAY TO ESCAPE THE WHIPPING.
SOME STORIES EVEN SAY HE ESCAPED *DURING* THE PUNISHMENT,
SLIPPING FROM THE ROPES THAT HELD HIM AND RUNNING AWAY.
I THINK THE HAND STORY MAKES THE MOST SENSE.
I DO TOO, BUT SINCE DETAILS ABOUT SLAVES' LIVES WEREN'T RECORDED VERY OFTEN, WE ARE STUCK WITH CONFLICTING STORIES.
BUT THE STORIES AGREE ON ONE THING,
MACKANDAL BECAME A *MAROON*.
WHAT'S THAT?
THAT IS THE NAME GIVEN TO PEOPLE WHO ESCAPED SLAVERY AND LIVED IN THE WILDERNESS.
WHO ARE YOU?
I AM MACKANDAL.

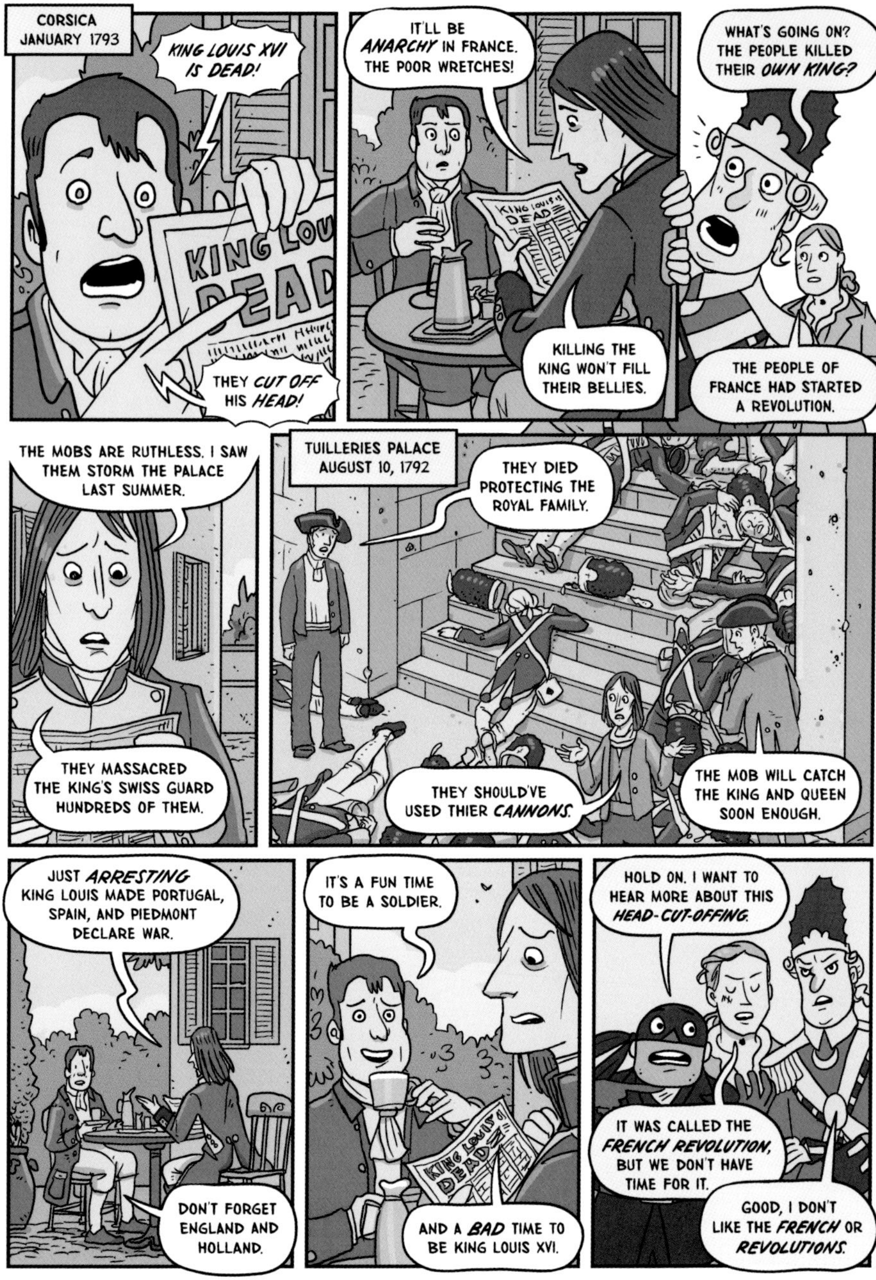
CORSICA
JANUARY 1793
KING LOUIS XVI IS DEAD!
KING LOUIS DEAD
THEY CUT OFF HIS HEAD!
IT'LL BE ANARCHY IN FRANCE. THE POOR WRETCHES!
KING LOUIS IS DEAD
KILLING THE KING WON'T FILL THEIR BELLIES.
WHAT'S GOING ON? THE PEOPLE KILLED THEIR OWN KING?
THE PEOPLE OF FRANCE HAD STARTED A REVOLUTION.
THE MOBS ARE RUTHLESS. I SAW THEM STORM THE PALACE LAST SUMMER.
THEY MASSACRED THE KING'S SWISS GUARD HUNDREDS OF THEM.
TUILLERIES PALACE
AUGUST 10, 1792
THEY DIED PROTECTING THE ROYAL FAMILY.
THEY SHOULD'VE USED THIER CANNONS.
THE MOB WILL CATCH THE KING AND QUEEN SOON ENOUGH.
JUST ARRESTING KING LOUIS MADE PORTUGAL, SPAIN, AND PIEDMONT DECLARE WAR.
DON'T FORGET ENGLAND AND HOLLAND.
IT'S A FUN TIME TO BE A SOLDIER.
KING LOUIS IS DEAD
AND A BAD TIME TO BE KING LOUIS XVI.
HOLD ON. I WANT TO HEAR MORE ABOUT THIS HEAD-CUT-OFFING.
IT WAS CALLED THE FRENCH REVOLUTION, BUT WE DON'T HAVE TIME FOR IT.
GOOD, I DON'T LIKE THE FRENCH OR REVOLUTIONS.

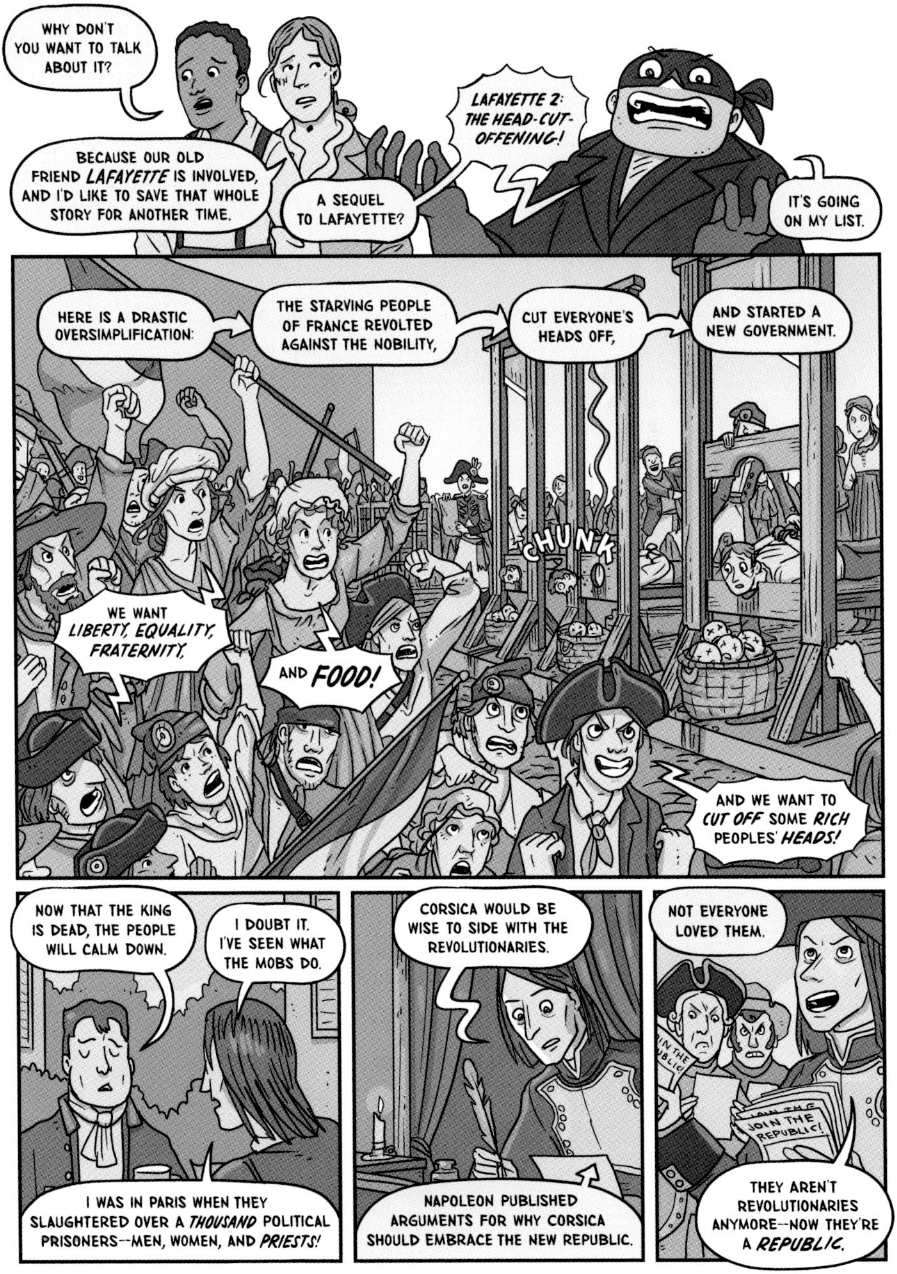
WHY DON'T YOU WANT TO TALK ABOUT IT?
BECAUSE OUR OLD FRIEND LAFAYETTE IS INVOLVED, AND I'D LIKE TO SAVE THAT WHOLE STORY FOR ANOTHER TIME.
A SEQUEL TO LAFAYETTE?
LAFAYETTE 2: THE HEAD-CUT-OFFENING!
IT'S GOING ON MY LIST.
HERE IS A DRASTIC OVERSIMPLIFICATION:
THE STARVING PEOPLE OF FRANCE REVOLTED AGAINST THE NOBILITY,
CUT EVERYONE'S HEADS OFF,
AND STARTED A NEW GOVERNMENT.
CHUNK
WE WANT LIBERTY, EQUALITY, FRATERNITY,
AND FOOD!
AND WE WANT TO CUT OFF SOME RICH PEOPLES' HEADS!
NOW THAT THE KING IS DEAD, THE PEOPLE WILL CALM DOWN.
I DOUBT IT. I'VE SEEN WHAT THE MOBS DO.
I WAS IN PARIS WHEN THEY SLAUGHTERED OVER A THOUSAND POLITICAL PRISONERS--MEN, WOMEN, AND PRIESTS!
CORSICA WOULD BE WISE TO SIDE WITH THE REVOLUTIONARIES.
NAPOLEON PUBLISHED ARGUMENTS FOR WHY CORSICA SHOULD EMBRACE THE NEW REPUBLIC.
NOT EVERYONE LOVED THEM.
JOIN THE REPUBLIC!
THEY AREN'T REVOLUTIONARIES ANYMORE--NOW THEY'RE A REPUBLIC.

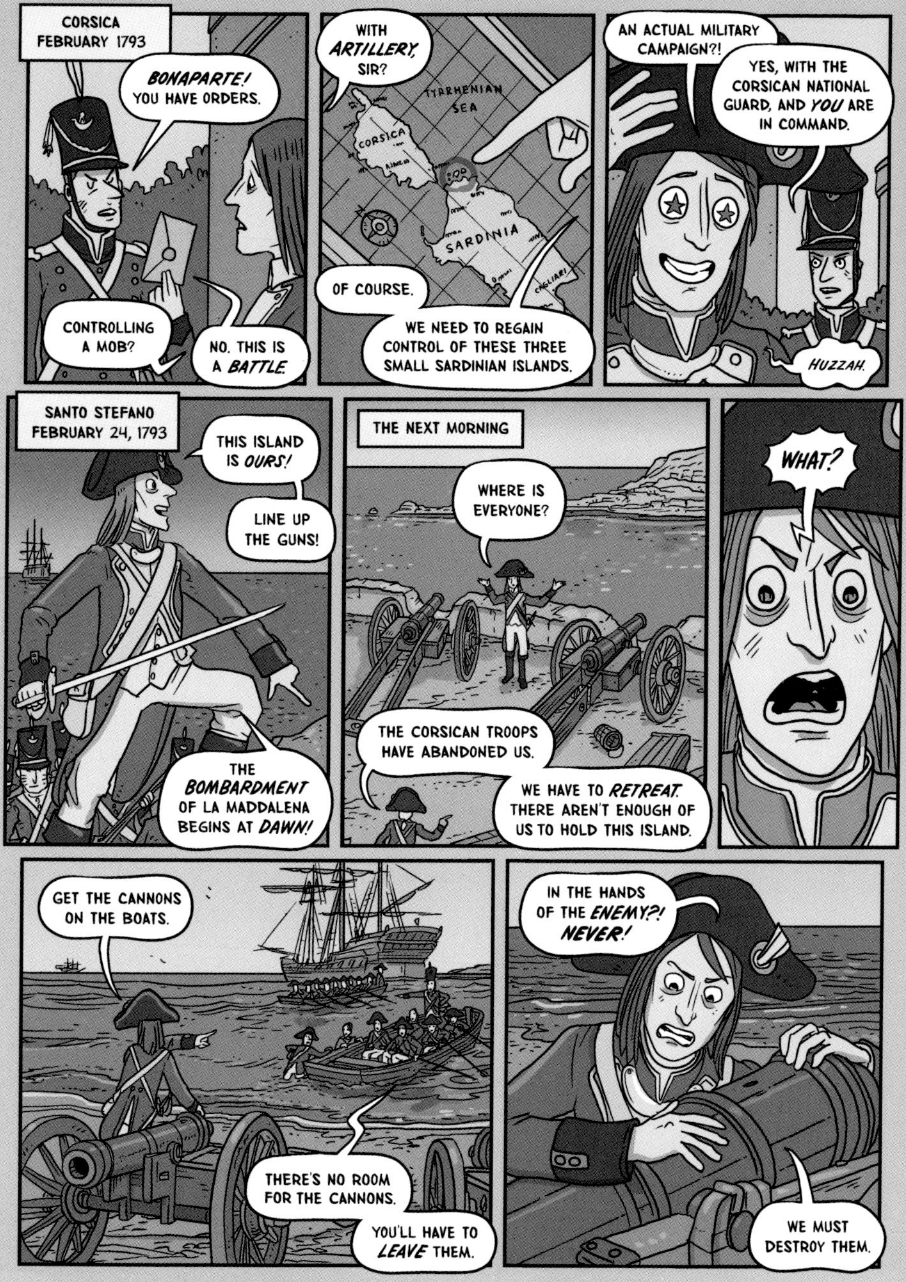
CORSICA
FEBRUARY 1793
BONAPARTE! YOU HAVE ORDERS.
CONTROLLING A MOB?
NO. THIS IS A BATTLE.
WITH ARTILLERY, SIR?
TYRRHENIAN SEA
CORSICA
SARDINIA
CAGLIARI
OF COURSE.
WE NEED TO REGAIN CONTROL OF THESE THREE SMALL SARDINIAN ISLANDS.
AN ACTUAL MILITARY CAMPAIGN?!
YES, WITH THE CORSICAN NATIONAL GUARD, AND YOU ARE IN COMMAND.
HUZZAH.
SANTO STEFANO
FEBRUARY 24, 1793
THIS ISLAND IS OURS!
LINE UP THE GUNS!
THE BOMBARDMENT OF LA MADDALENA BEGINS AT DAWN!
THE NEXT MORNING
WHERE IS EVERYONE?
THE CORSICAN TROOPS HAVE ABANDONED US.
WE HAVE TO RETREAT. THERE AREN'T ENOUGH OF US TO HOLD THIS ISLAND.
WHAT?
GET THE CANNONS ON THE BOATS.
THERE'S NO ROOM FOR THE CANNONS.
YOU'LL HAVE TO LEAVE THEM.
IN THE HANDS OF THE ENEMY?! NEVER!
WE MUST DESTROY THEM.

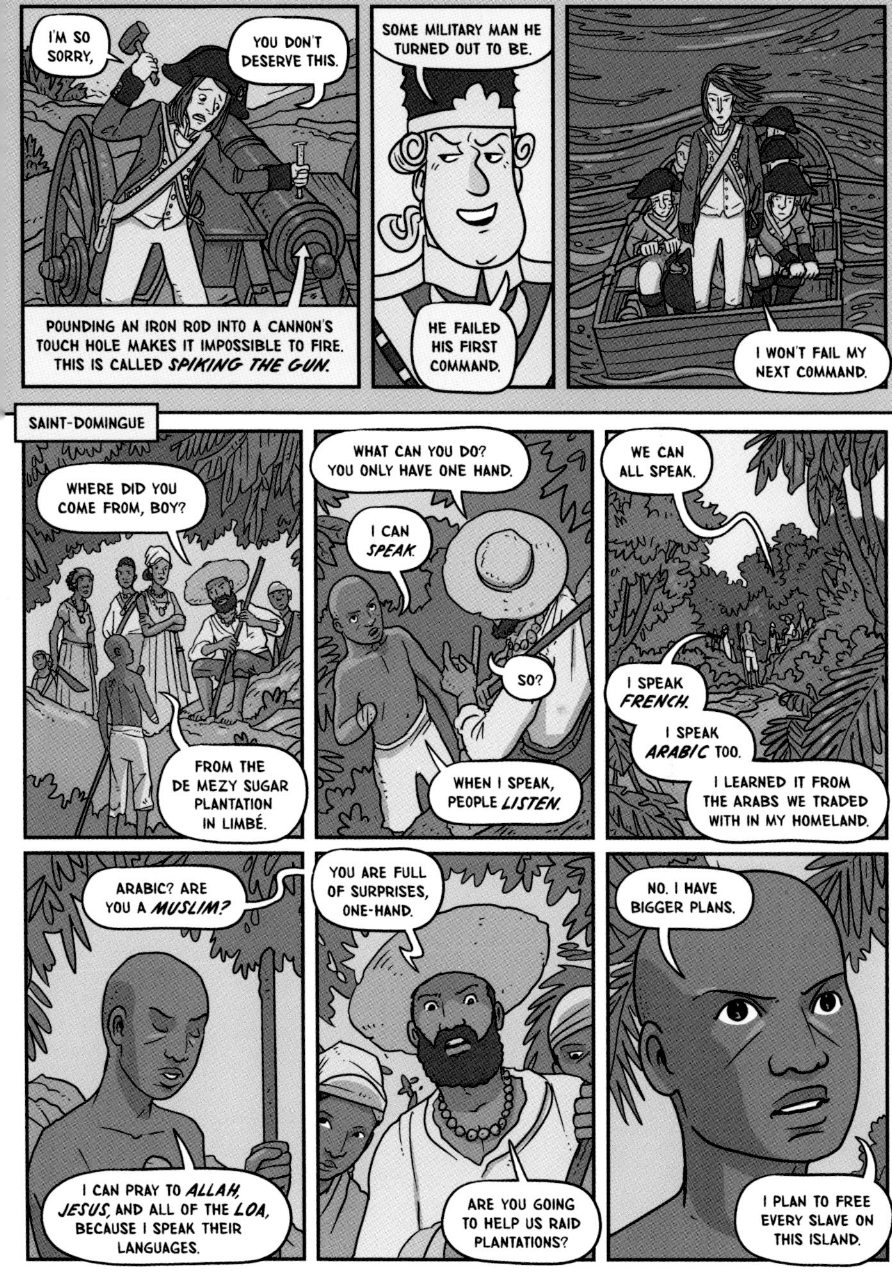
I'M SO SORRY,
YOU DON'T DESERVE THIS.
POUNDING AN IRON ROD INTO A CANNON'S TOUCH HOLE MAKES IT IMPOSSIBLE TO FIRE. THIS IS CALLED *SPIKING THE GUN.*
SOME MILITARY MAN HE TURNED OUT TO BE.
HE FAILED HIS FIRST COMMAND.
I WON'T FAIL MY NEXT COMMAND.
SAINT-DOMINGUE
WHERE DID YOU COME FROM, BOY?
FROM THE DE MEZY SUGAR PLANTATION IN LIMBÉ.
WHAT CAN YOU DO? YOU ONLY HAVE ONE HAND.
I CAN *SPEAK.*
SO?
WHEN I SPEAK, PEOPLE *LISTEN.*
WE CAN ALL SPEAK.
I SPEAK *FRENCH.*
I SPEAK *ARABIC* TOO.
I LEARNED IT FROM THE ARABS WE TRADED WITH IN MY HOMELAND.
ARABIC? ARE YOU A *MUSLIM?*
I CAN PRAY TO *ALLAH, JESUS,* AND ALL OF THE *LOA,* BECAUSE I SPEAK THEIR LANGUAGES.
YOU ARE FULL OF SURPRISES, ONE-HAND.
ARE YOU GOING TO HELP US RAID PLANTATIONS?
NO. I HAVE BIGGER PLANS.
I PLAN TO FREE EVERY SLAVE ON THIS ISLAND.

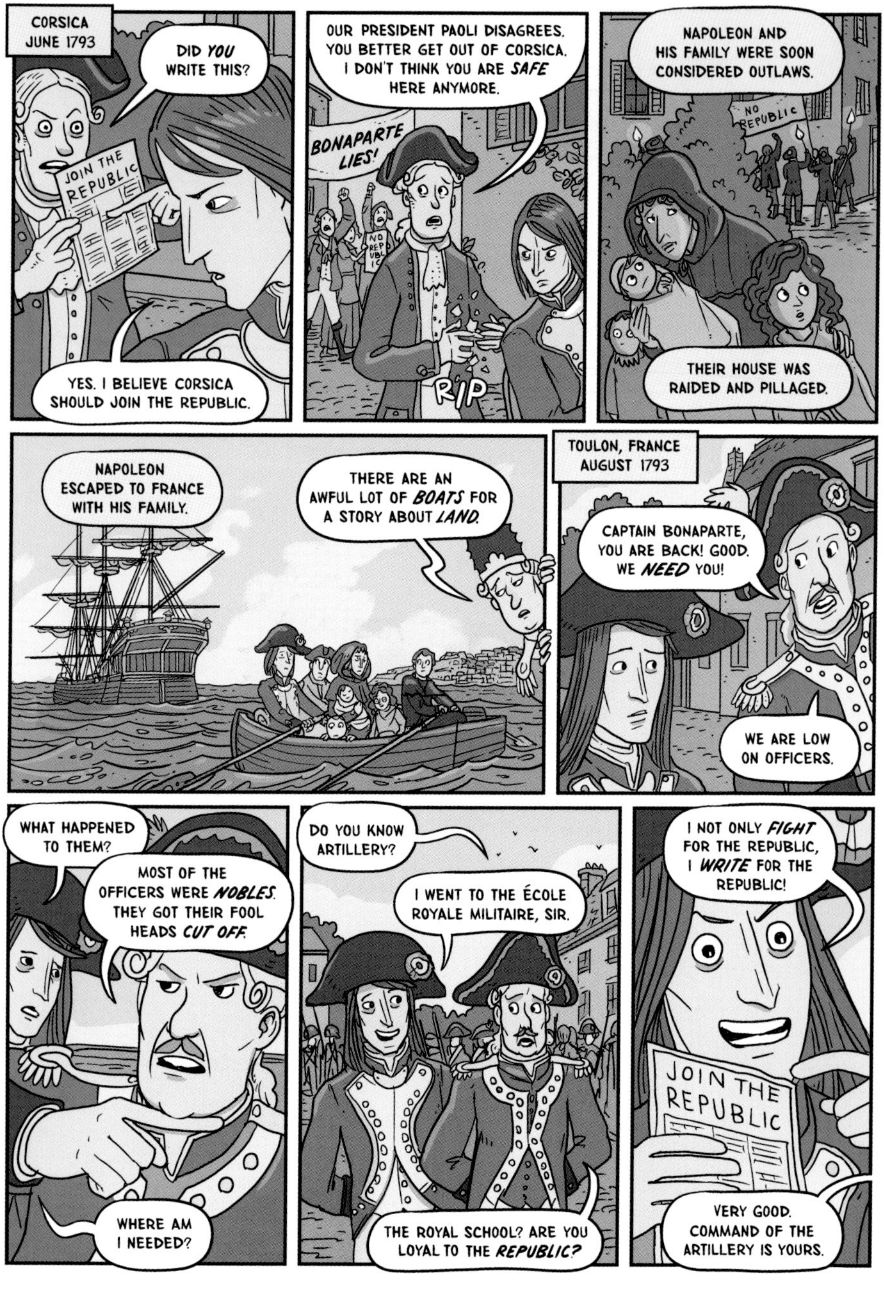
CORSICA
JUNE 1793
DID YOU WRITE THIS?
JOIN THE REPUBLIC
YES. I BELIEVE CORSICA SHOULD JOIN THE REPUBLIC.
OUR PRESIDENT PAOLI DISAGREES. YOU BETTER GET OUT OF CORSICA. I DON'T THINK YOU ARE SAFE HERE ANYMORE.
BONAPARTE LIES!
NO REPUBLIC
RIP
NAPOLEON AND HIS FAMILY WERE SOON CONSIDERED OUTLAWS.
NO REPUBLIC
THEIR HOUSE WAS RAIDED AND PILLAGED.
NAPOLEON ESCAPED TO FRANCE WITH HIS FAMILY.
THERE ARE AN AWFUL LOT OF BOATS FOR A STORY ABOUT LAND.
TOULON, FRANCE
AUGUST 1793
CAPTAIN BONAPARTE, YOU ARE BACK! GOOD. WE NEED YOU!
WE ARE LOW ON OFFICERS.
WHAT HAPPENED TO THEM?
MOST OF THE OFFICERS WERE NOBLES. THEY GOT THEIR FOOL HEADS CUT OFF.
WHERE AM I NEEDED?
DO YOU KNOW ARTILLERY?
I WENT TO THE ÉCOLE ROYALE MILITAIRE, SIR.
THE ROYAL SCHOOL? ARE YOU LOYAL TO THE REPUBLIC?
I NOT ONLY FIGHT FOR THE REPUBLIC, I WRITE FOR THE REPUBLIC!
JOIN THE REPUBLIC
VERY GOOD. COMMAND OF THE ARTILLERY IS YOURS.

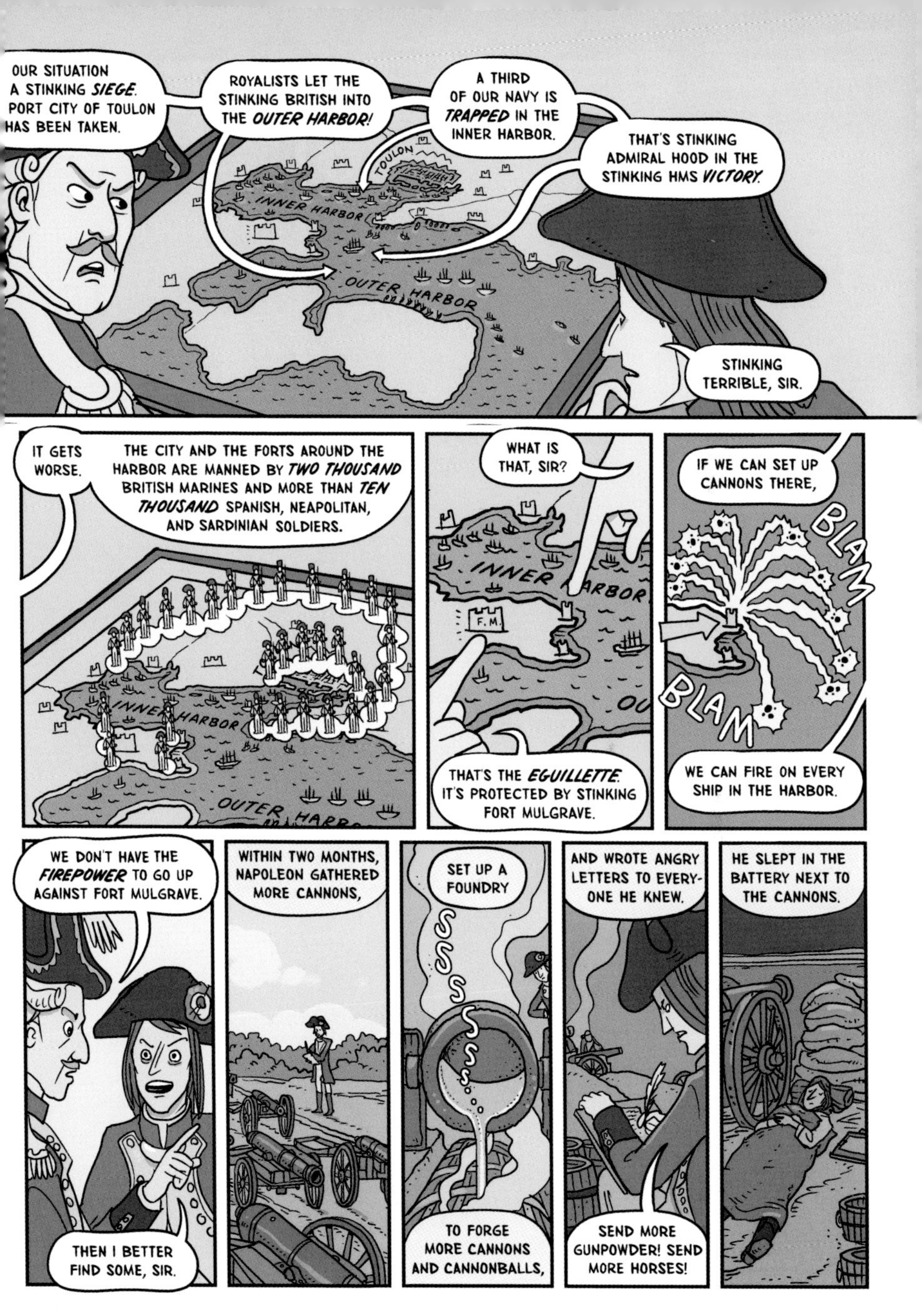
OUR SITUATION A STINKING SIEGE. PORT CITY OF TOULON HAS BEEN TAKEN.
ROYALISTS LET THE STINKING BRITISH INTO THE OUTER HARBOR!
A THIRD OF OUR NAVY IS TRAPPED IN THE INNER HARBOR.
THAT'S STINKING ADMIRAL HOOD IN THE STINKING HMS VICTORY.
TOULON
INNER HARBOR
OUTER HARBOR
STINKING TERRIBLE, SIR.
IT GETS WORSE.
THE CITY AND THE FORTS AROUND THE HARBOR ARE MANNED BY TWO THOUSAND BRITISH MARINES AND MORE THAN TEN THOUSAND SPANISH, NEAPOLITAN, AND SARDINIAN SOLDIERS.
INNER HARBOR
WHAT IS THAT, SIR?
INNER HARBOR
F.M.
THAT'S THE EGUILLETTE. IT'S PROTECTED BY STINKING FORT MULGRAVE.
IF WE CAN SET UP CANNONS THERE,
BLAM
BLAM
WE CAN FIRE ON EVERY SHIP IN THE HARBOR.
WE DON'T HAVE THE FIREPOWER TO GO UP AGAINST FORT MULGRAVE.
THEN I BETTER FIND SOME, SIR.
WITHIN TWO MONTHS, NAPOLEON GATHERED MORE CANNONS,
SET UP A FOUNDRY
SSSSSS
TO FORGE MORE CANNONS AND CANNONBALLS,
AND WROTE ANGRY LETTERS TO EVERYONE HE KNEW.
SEND MORE GUNPOWDER! SEND MORE HORSES!
HE SLEPT IN THE BATTERY NEXT TO THE CANNONS.

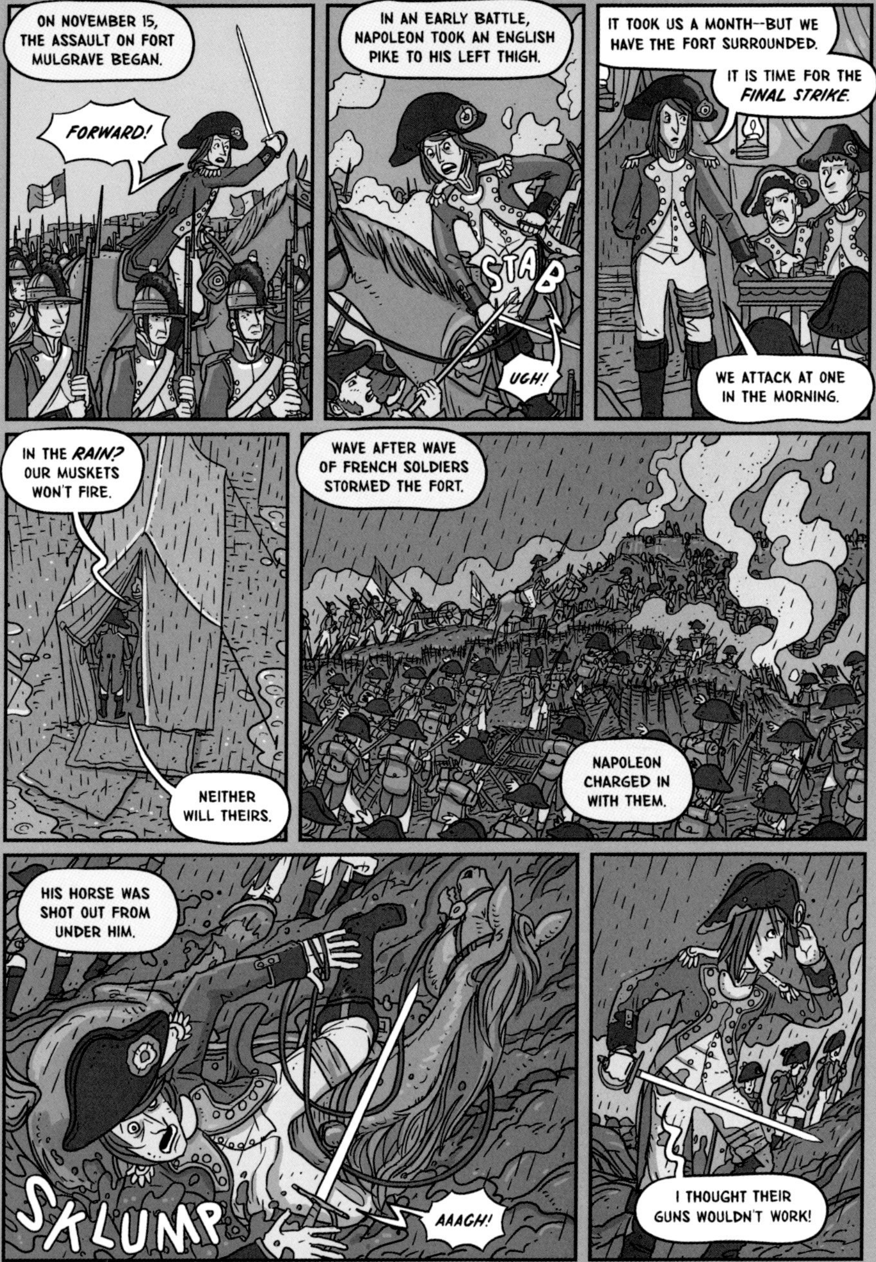

ON NOVEMBER 15, THE ASSAULT ON FORT MULGRAVE BEGAN.
FORWARD!
IN AN EARLY BATTLE, NAPOLEON TOOK AN ENGLISH PIKE TO HIS LEFT THIGH.
STAB
UGH!
IT TOOK US A MONTH--BUT WE HAVE THE FORT SURROUNDED.
IT IS TIME FOR THE FINAL STRIKE.
WE ATTACK AT ONE IN THE MORNING.
IN THE RAIN? OUR MUSKETS WON'T FIRE.
NEITHER WILL THEIRS.
WAVE AFTER WAVE OF FRENCH SOLDIERS STORMED THE FORT.
NAPOLEON CHARGED IN WITH THEM.
HIS HORSE WAS SHOT OUT FROM UNDER HIM.
SKLUMP
AAAGH!
I THOUGHT THEIR GUNS WOULDN'T WORK!

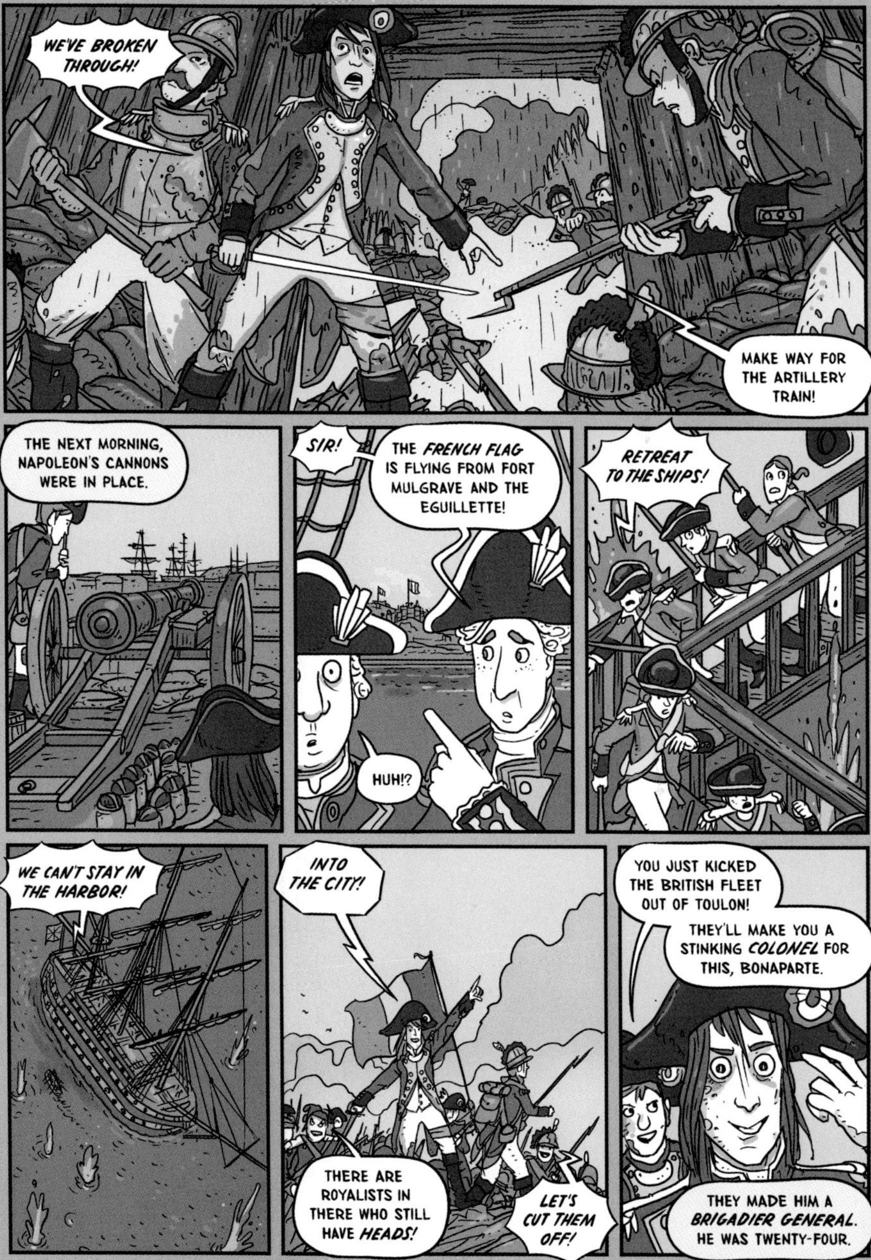
WE'VE BROKEN THROUGH!
MAKE WAY FOR THE ARTILLERY TRAIN!
THE NEXT MORNING, NAPOLEON'S CANNONS WERE IN PLACE.
SIR!
THE FRENCH FLAG IS FLYING FROM FORT MULGRAVE AND THE EGUILLETTE!
HUH!?
RETREAT TO THE SHIPS!
WE CAN'T STAY IN THE HARBOR!
INTO THE CITY!
THERE ARE ROYALISTS IN THERE WHO STILL HAVE HEADS!
LET'S CUT THEM OFF!
YOU JUST KICKED THE BRITISH FLEET OUT OF TOULON!
THEY'LL MAKE YOU A STINKING COLONEL FOR THIS, BONAPARTE.
THEY MADE HIM A BRIGADIER GENERAL. HE WAS TWENTY-FOUR.

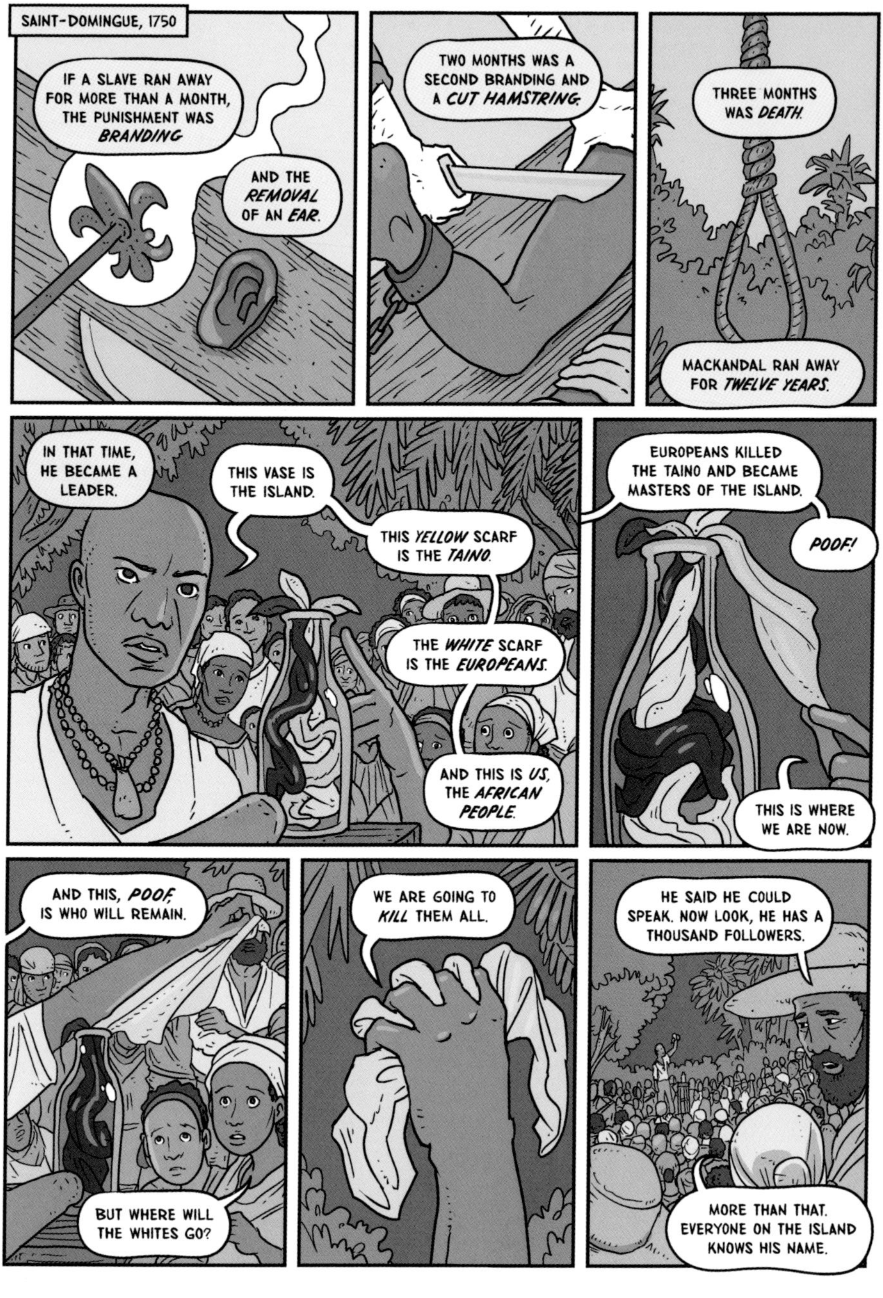
SAINT-DOMINGUE, 1750
IF A SLAVE RAN AWAY FOR MORE THAN A MONTH, THE PUNISHMENT WAS BRANDING
AND THE REMOVAL OF AN EAR.
TWO MONTHS WAS A SECOND BRANDING AND A CUT HAMSTRING.
THREE MONTHS WAS DEATH.
MACKANDAL RAN AWAY FOR TWELVE YEARS.
IN THAT TIME, HE BECAME A LEADER.
THIS VASE IS THE ISLAND.
THIS YELLOW SCARF IS THE TAINO.
THE WHITE SCARF IS THE EUROPEANS.
AND THIS IS US, THE AFRICAN PEOPLE.
EUROPEANS KILLED THE TAINO AND BECAME MASTERS OF THE ISLAND.
POOF!
THIS IS WHERE WE ARE NOW.
AND THIS, POOF, IS WHO WILL REMAIN.
BUT WHERE WILL THE WHITES GO?
WE ARE GOING TO KILL THEM ALL.
HE SAID HE COULD SPEAK. NOW LOOK, HE HAS A THOUSAND FOLLOWERS.
MORE THAN THAT. EVERYONE ON THE ISLAND KNOWS HIS NAME.

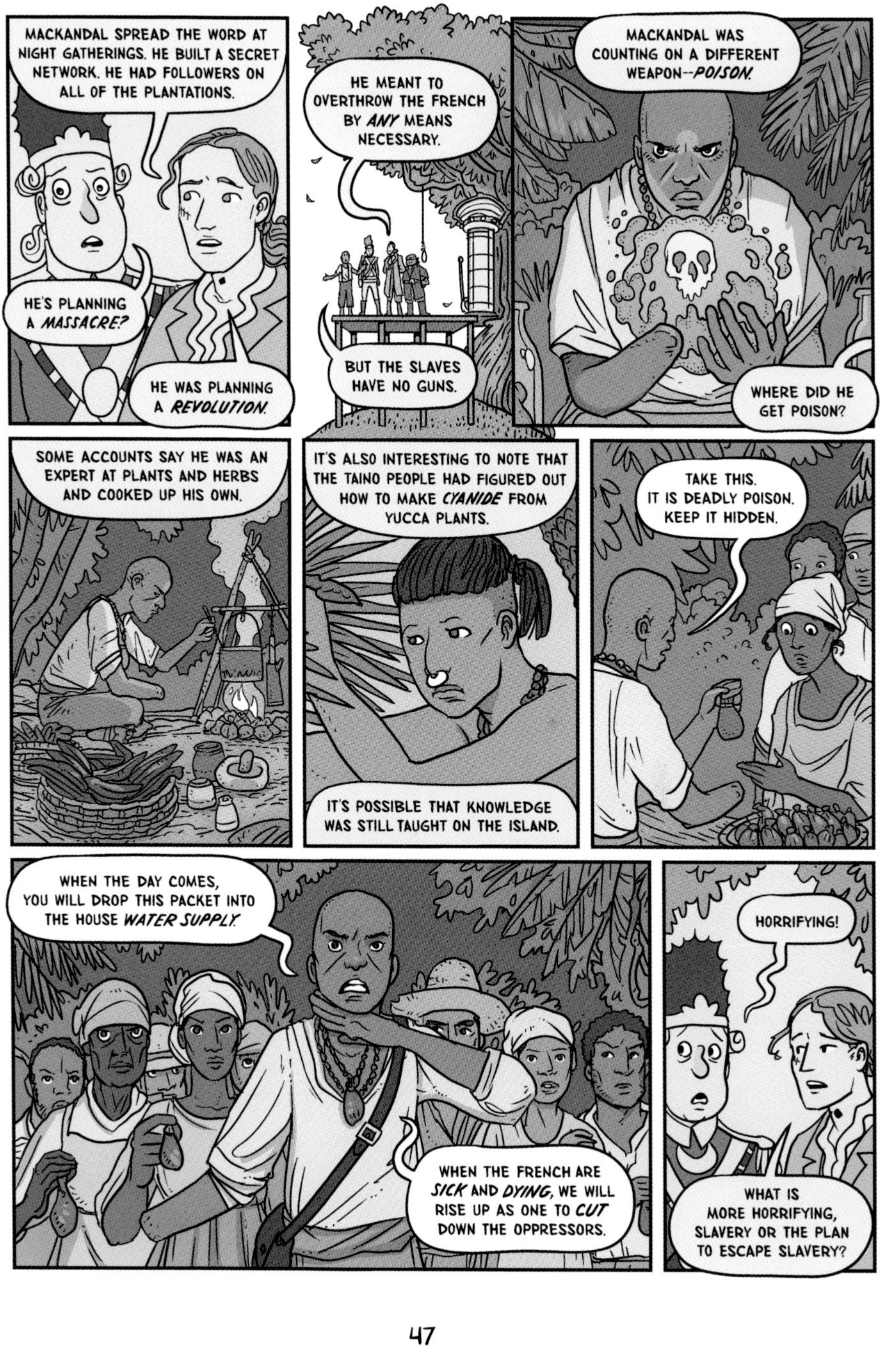
MACKANDAL SPREAD THE WORD AT NIGHT GATHERINGS. HE BUILT A SECRET NETWORK. HE HAD FOLLOWERS ON ALL OF THE PLANTATIONS.
HE'S PLANNING A *MASSACRE?*
HE WAS PLANNING A *REVOLUTION.*
HE MEANT TO OVERTHROW THE FRENCH BY *ANY* MEANS NECESSARY.
BUT THE SLAVES HAVE NO GUNS.
MACKANDAL WAS COUNTING ON A DIFFERENT WEAPON--*POISON.*
WHERE DID HE GET POISON?
SOME ACCOUNTS SAY HE WAS AN EXPERT AT PLANTS AND HERBS AND COOKED UP HIS OWN.
IT'S ALSO INTERESTING TO NOTE THAT THE TAINO PEOPLE HAD FIGURED OUT HOW TO MAKE *CYANIDE* FROM YUCCA PLANTS.
IT'S POSSIBLE THAT KNOWLEDGE WAS STILL TAUGHT ON THE ISLAND.
TAKE THIS. IT IS DEADLY POISON. KEEP IT HIDDEN.
WHEN THE DAY COMES, YOU WILL DROP THIS PACKET INTO THE HOUSE *WATER SUPPLY.*
WHEN THE FRENCH ARE *SICK* AND *DYING*, WE WILL RISE UP AS ONE TO *CUT* DOWN THE OPPRESSORS.
HORRIFYING!
WHAT IS MORE HORRIFYING, SLAVERY OR THE PLAN TO ESCAPE SLAVERY?

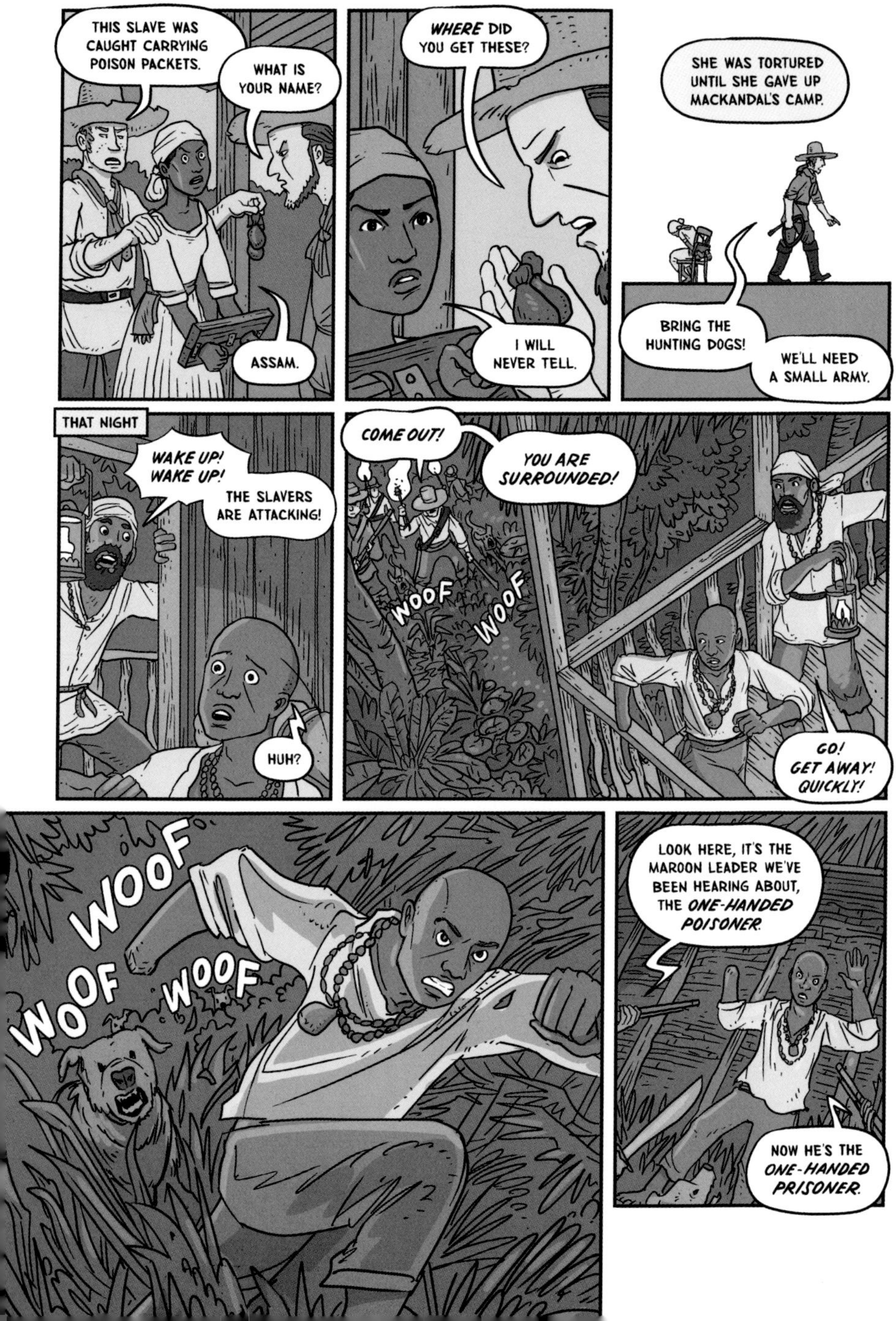
THIS SLAVE WAS CAUGHT CARRYING POISON PACKETS.
WHAT IS YOUR NAME?
ASSAM.
WHERE DID YOU GET THESE?
I WILL NEVER TELL.
SHE WAS TORTURED UNTIL SHE GAVE UP MACKANDAL'S CAMP.
BRING THE HUNTING DOGS!
WE'LL NEED A SMALL ARMY.
THAT NIGHT
WAKE UP! WAKE UP!
THE SLAVERS ARE ATTACKING!
HUH?
COME OUT!
YOU ARE SURROUNDED!
WOOF
WOOF
GO! GET AWAY! QUICKLY!
WOOF
WOOF
WOOF
LOOK HERE, IT'S THE MAROON LEADER WE'VE BEEN HEARING ABOUT, THE *ONE-HANDED POISONER.*
NOW HE'S THE *ONE-HANDED PRISONER.*

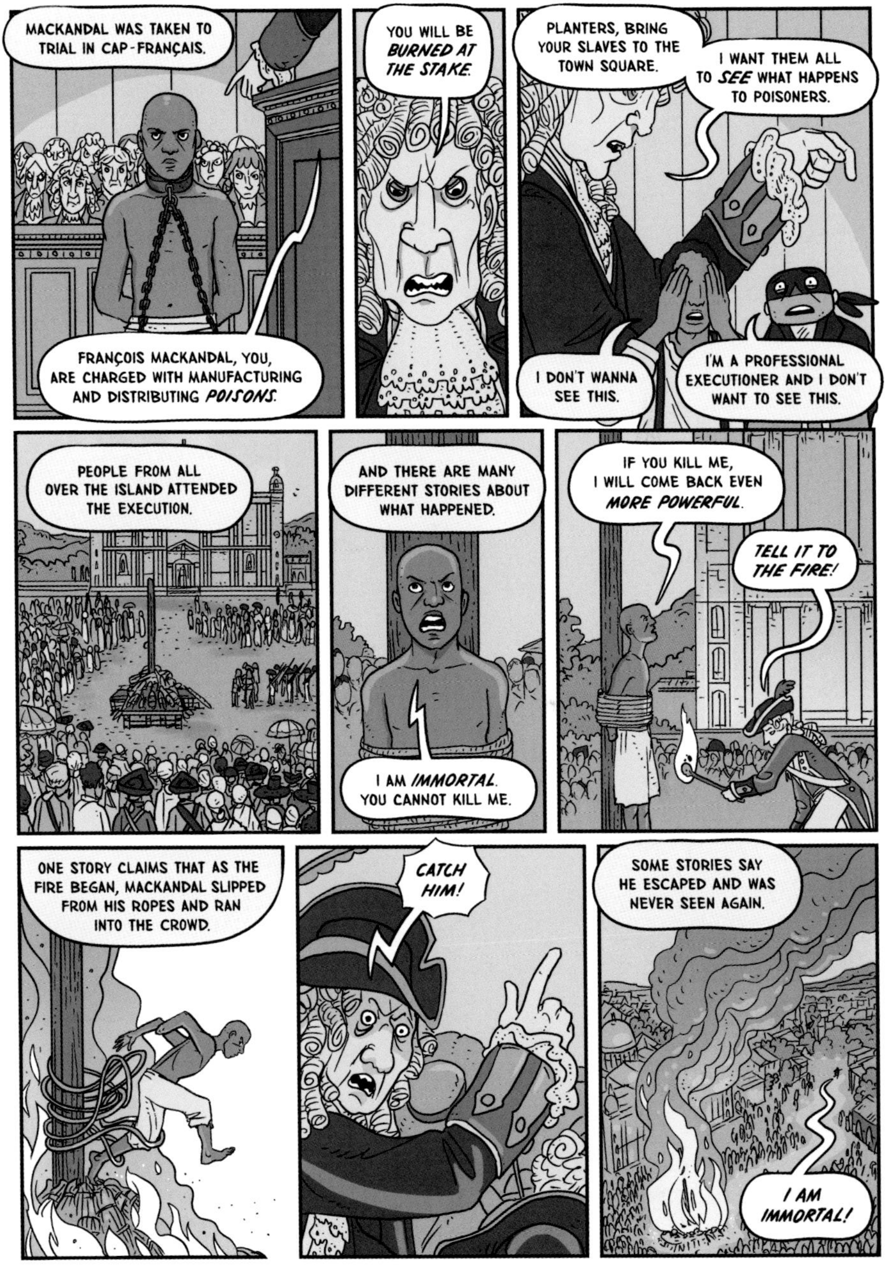
MACKANDAL WAS TAKEN TO TRIAL IN CAP-FRANÇAIS.
FRANÇOIS MACKANDAL, YOU, ARE CHARGED WITH MANUFACTURING AND DISTRIBUTING POISONS.
YOU WILL BE BURNED AT THE STAKE.
PLANTERS, BRING YOUR SLAVES TO THE TOWN SQUARE.
I WANT THEM ALL TO SEE WHAT HAPPENS TO POISONERS.
I DON'T WANNA SEE THIS.
I'M A PROFESSIONAL EXECUTIONER AND I DON'T WANT TO SEE THIS.
PEOPLE FROM ALL OVER THE ISLAND ATTENDED THE EXECUTION.
AND THERE ARE MANY DIFFERENT STORIES ABOUT WHAT HAPPENED.
I AM IMMORTAL. YOU CANNOT KILL ME.
IF YOU KILL ME, I WILL COME BACK EVEN MORE POWERFUL.
TELL IT TO THE FIRE!
ONE STORY CLAIMS THAT AS THE FIRE BEGAN, MACKANDAL SLIPPED FROM HIS ROPES AND RAN INTO THE CROWD.
CATCH HIM!
SOME STORIES SAY HE ESCAPED AND WAS NEVER SEEN AGAIN.
I AM IMMORTAL!

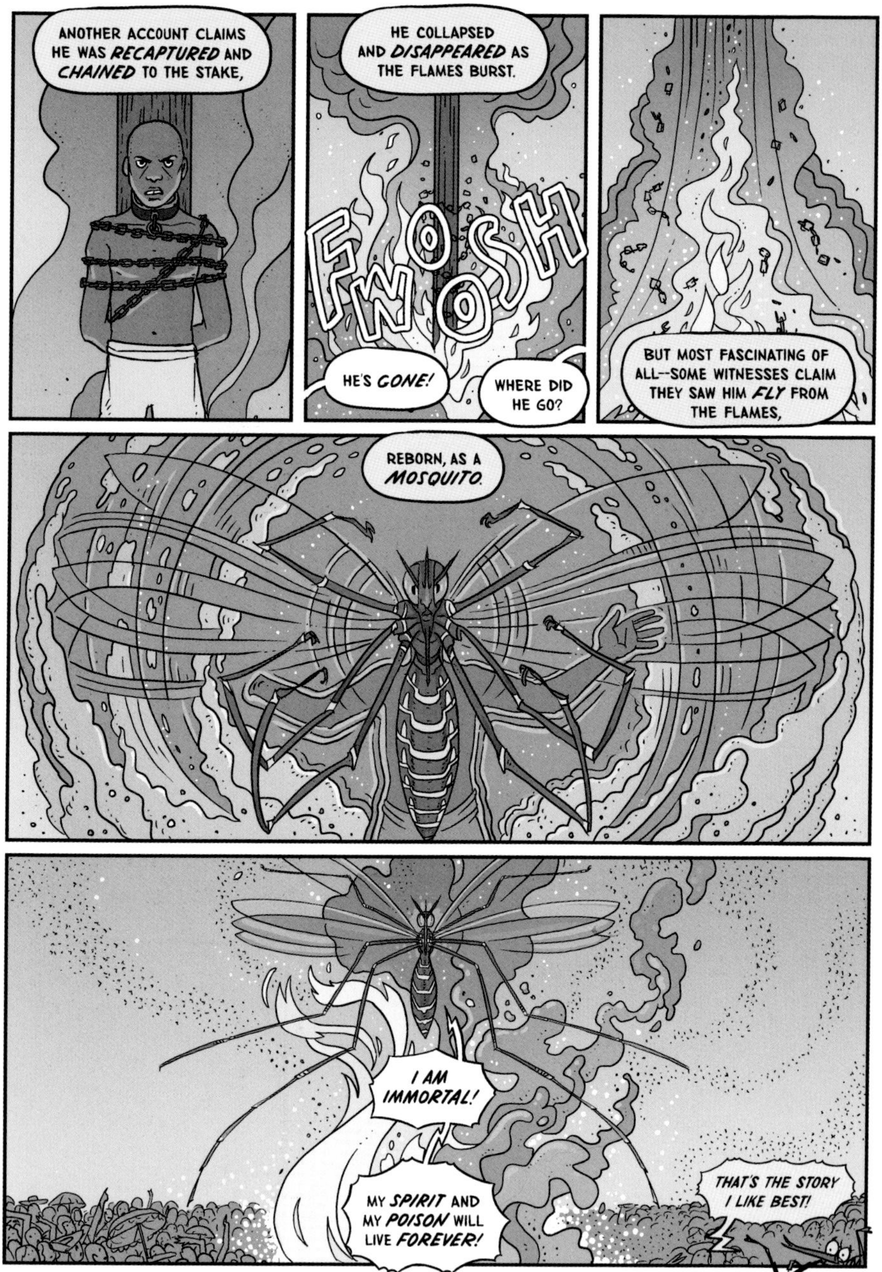
ANOTHER ACCOUNT CLAIMS HE WAS RECAPTURED AND CHAINED TO THE STAKE,
HE COLLAPSED AND DISAPPEARED AS THE FLAMES BURST.
FWOOSH
HE'S GONE!
WHERE DID HE GO?
BUT MOST FASCINATING OF ALL--SOME WITNESSES CLAIM THEY SAW HIM FLY FROM THE FLAMES,
REBORN, AS A MOSQUITO.
I AM IMMORTAL!
MY SPIRIT AND MY POISON WILL LIVE FOREVER!
THAT'S THE STORY I LIKE BEST!

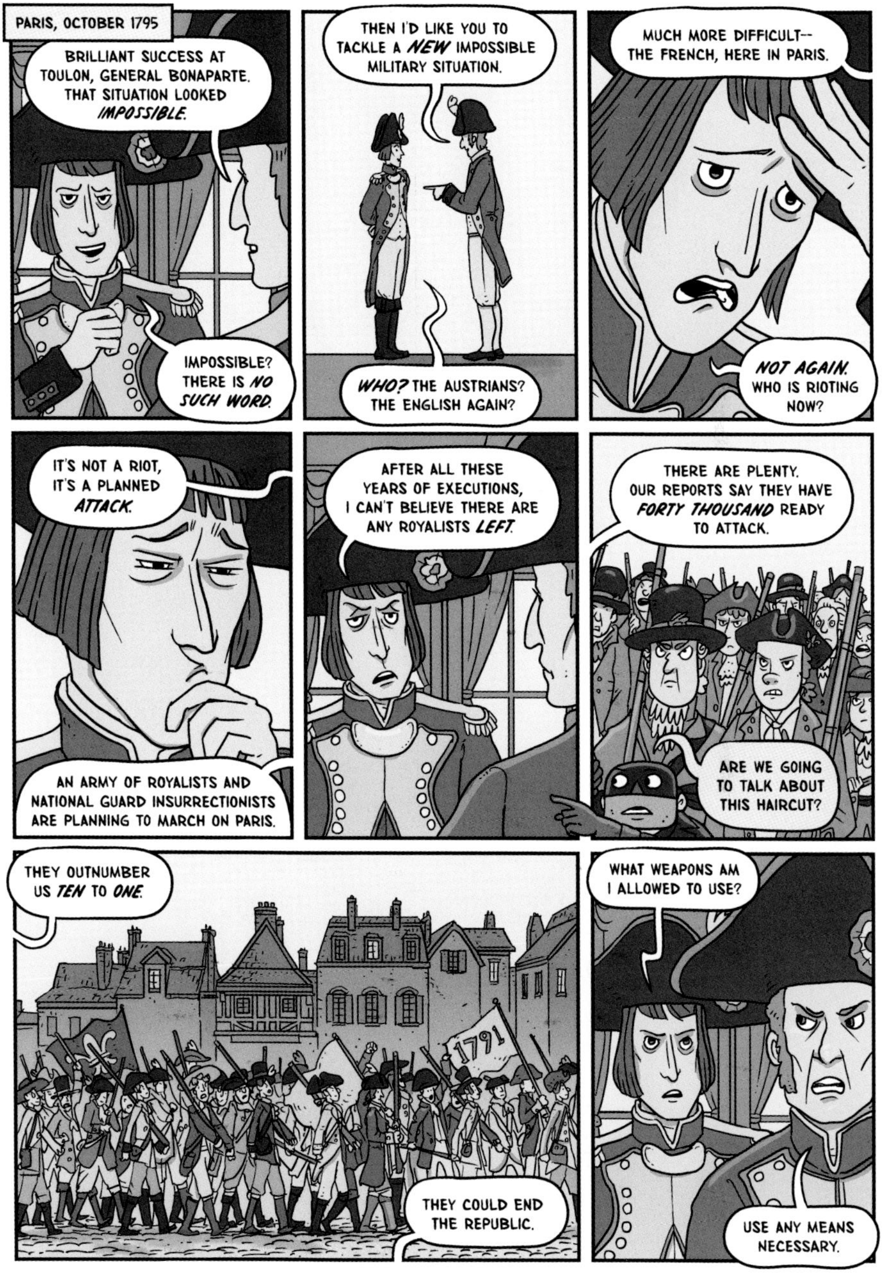
PARIS, OCTOBER 1795
BRILLIANT SUCCESS AT TOULON, GENERAL BONAPARTE. THAT SITUATION LOOKED *IMPOSSIBLE*.
IMPOSSIBLE? THERE IS *NO SUCH WORD*.
THEN I'D LIKE YOU TO TACKLE A *NEW* IMPOSSIBLE MILITARY SITUATION.
WHO? THE AUSTRIANS? THE ENGLISH AGAIN?
MUCH MORE DIFFICULT-- THE FRENCH, HERE IN PARIS.
NOT AGAIN. WHO IS RIOTING NOW?
IT'S NOT A RIOT, IT'S A PLANNED *ATTACK*.
AN ARMY OF ROYALISTS AND NATIONAL GUARD INSURRECTIONISTS ARE PLANNING TO MARCH ON PARIS.
AFTER ALL THESE YEARS OF EXECUTIONS, I CAN'T BELIEVE THERE ARE ANY ROYALISTS *LEFT*.
THERE ARE PLENTY. OUR REPORTS SAY THEY HAVE *FORTY THOUSAND* READY TO ATTACK.
ARE WE GOING TO TALK ABOUT THIS HAIRCUT?
THEY OUTNUMBER US *TEN* TO *ONE*.
1791
THEY COULD END THE REPUBLIC.
WHAT WEAPONS AM I ALLOWED TO USE?
USE ANY MEANS NECESSARY.

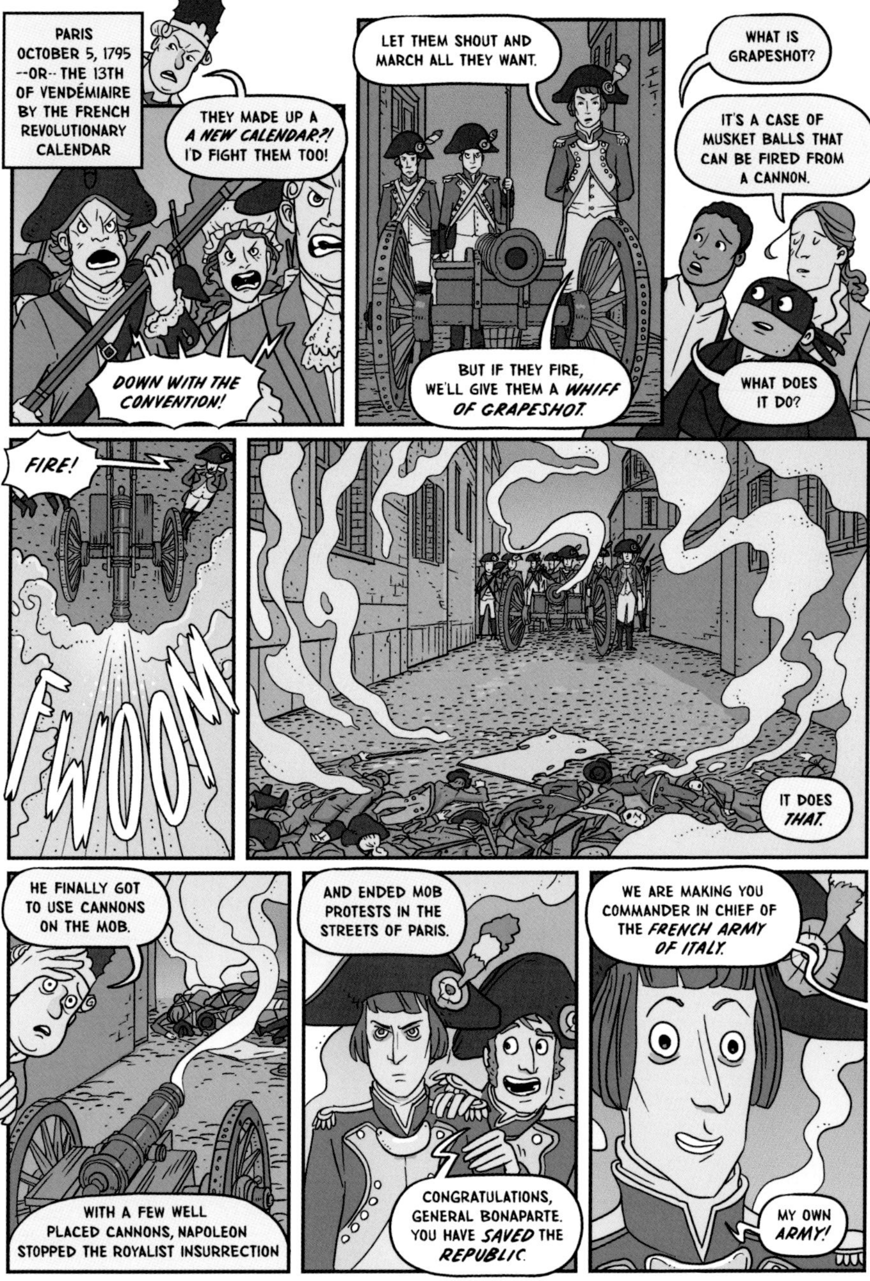
PARIS OCTOBER 5, 1795 --OR-- THE 13TH OF VENDÉMIAIRE BY THE FRENCH REVOLUTIONARY CALENDAR
THEY MADE UP A A NEW CALENDAR?! I'D FIGHT THEM TOO!
DOWN WITH THE CONVENTION!
LET THEM SHOUT AND MARCH ALL THEY WANT.
BUT IF THEY FIRE, WE'LL GIVE THEM A WHIFF OF GRAPESHOT.
WHAT IS GRAPESHOT?
IT'S A CASE OF MUSKET BALLS THAT CAN BE FIRED FROM A CANNON.
WHAT DOES IT DO?
FIRE!
FWOOM
IT DOES THAT.
HE FINALLY GOT TO USE CANNONS ON THE MOB.
WITH A FEW WELL PLACED CANNONS, NAPOLEON STOPPED THE ROYALIST INSURRECTION
AND ENDED MOB PROTESTS IN THE STREETS OF PARIS.
CONGRATULATIONS, GENERAL BONAPARTE. YOU HAVE SAVED THE REPUBLIC.
WE ARE MAKING YOU COMMANDER IN CHIEF OF THE FRENCH ARMY OF ITALY.
MY OWN ARMY!

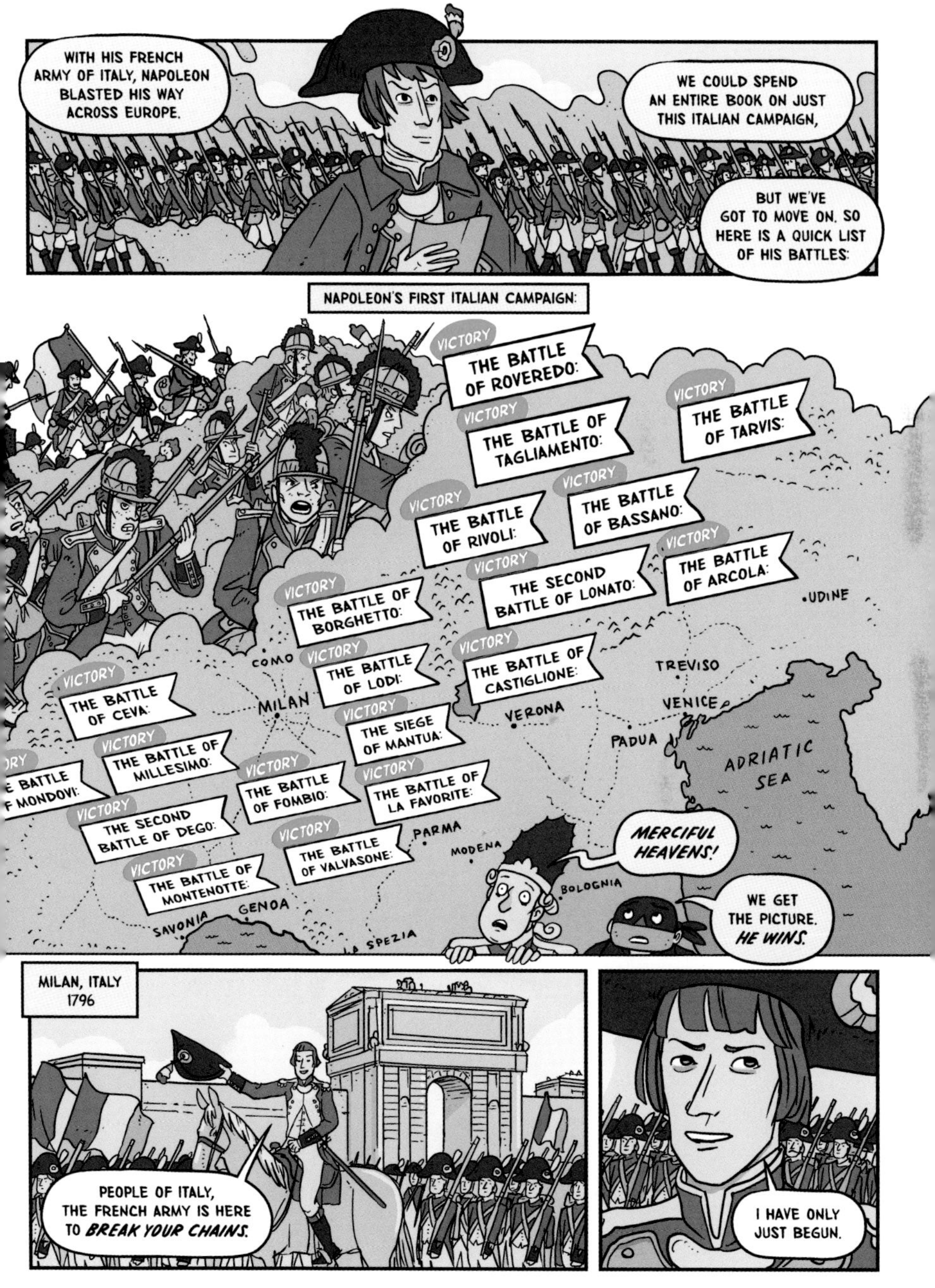

WITH HIS FRENCH ARMY OF ITALY, NAPOLEON BLASTED HIS WAY ACROSS EUROPE.
WE COULD SPEND AN ENTIRE BOOK ON JUST THIS ITALIAN CAMPAIGN,
BUT WE'VE GOT TO MOVE ON, SO HERE IS A QUICK LIST OF HIS BATTLES:
NAPOLEON'S FIRST ITALIAN CAMPAIGN:
VICTORY THE BATTLE OF ROVEREDO:
VICTORY THE BATTLE OF TAGLIAMENTO:
VICTORY THE BATTLE OF TARVIS:
VICTORY THE BATTLE OF RIVOLI:
VICTORY THE BATTLE OF BASSANO:
VICTORY THE SECOND BATTLE OF LONATO:
VICTORY THE BATTLE OF ARCOLA:
VICTORY THE BATTLE OF BORGHETTO:
VICTORY THE BATTLE OF LODI:
VICTORY THE BATTLE OF CASTIGLIONE:
VICTORY THE BATTLE OF CEVA:
VICTORY THE SIEGE OF MANTUA:
VICTORY THE BATTLE OF MILLESIMO:
E BATTLE F MONDOVI:
VICTORY THE BATTLE OF FOMBIO:
VICTORY THE BATTLE OF LA FAVORITE:
VICTORY THE SECOND BATTLE OF DEGO:
VICTORY THE BATTLE OF VALVASONE:
VICTORY THE BATTLE OF MONTENOTTE:
COMO
MILAN
VERONA
TREVISO
VENICE
PADUA
UDINE
ADRIATIC SEA
PARMA
MODENA
BOLOGNIA
GENOA
SAVONIA
LA SPEZIA
MERCIFUL HEAVENS!
WE GET THE PICTURE. HE WINS.
MILAN, ITALY 1796
PEOPLE OF ITALY, THE FRENCH ARMY IS HERE TO BREAK YOUR CHAINS.
I HAVE ONLY JUST BEGUN.

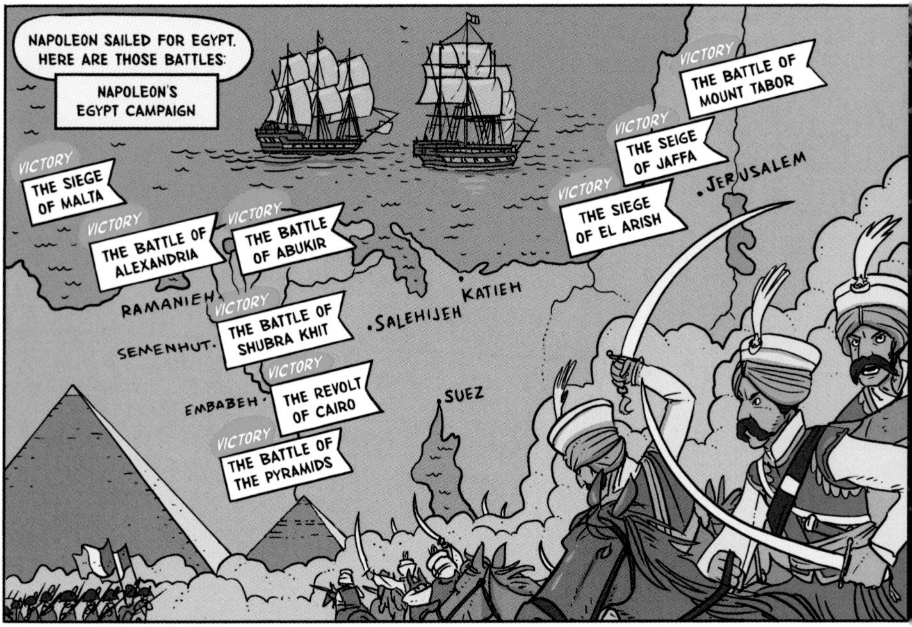
NAPOLEON SAILED FOR EGYPT. HERE ARE THOSE BATTLES:
NAPOLEON'S EGYPT CAMPAIGN
VICTORY
THE SIEGE OF MALTA
VICTORY
THE BATTLE OF ALEXANDRIA
VICTORY
THE BATTLE OF ABUKIR
VICTORY
THE BATTLE OF SHUBRA KHIT
VICTORY
THE REVOLT OF CAIRO
VICTORY
THE BATTLE OF THE PYRAMIDS
VICTORY
THE SIEGE OF EL ARISH
VICTORY
THE SEIGE OF JAFFA
VICTORY
THE BATTLE OF MOUNT TABOR
JERUSALEM
RAMANIEH
SEMENHUT
EMBABEH
SALEHIJEH
KATIEH
SUEZ

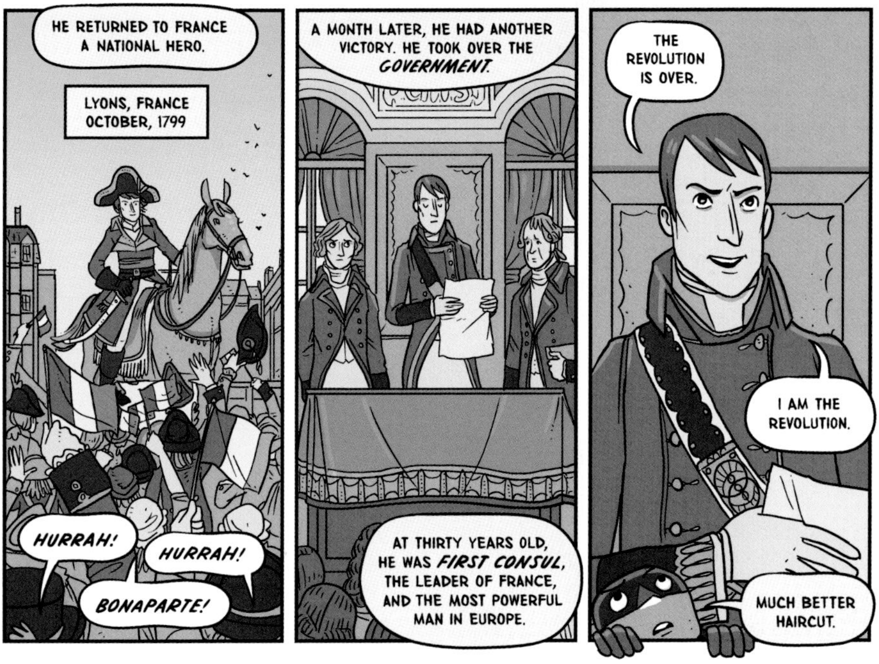
HE RETURNED TO FRANCE A NATIONAL HERO.
LYONS, FRANCE OCTOBER, 1799
HURRAH!
HURRAH!
BONAPARTE!
A MONTH LATER, HE HAD ANOTHER VICTORY. HE TOOK OVER THE GOVERNMENT.
AT THIRTY YEARS OLD, HE WAS FIRST CONSUL, THE LEADER OF FRANCE, AND THE MOST POWERFUL MAN IN EUROPE.
THE REVOLUTION IS OVER.
I AM THE REVOLUTION.
MUCH BETTER HAIRCUT.

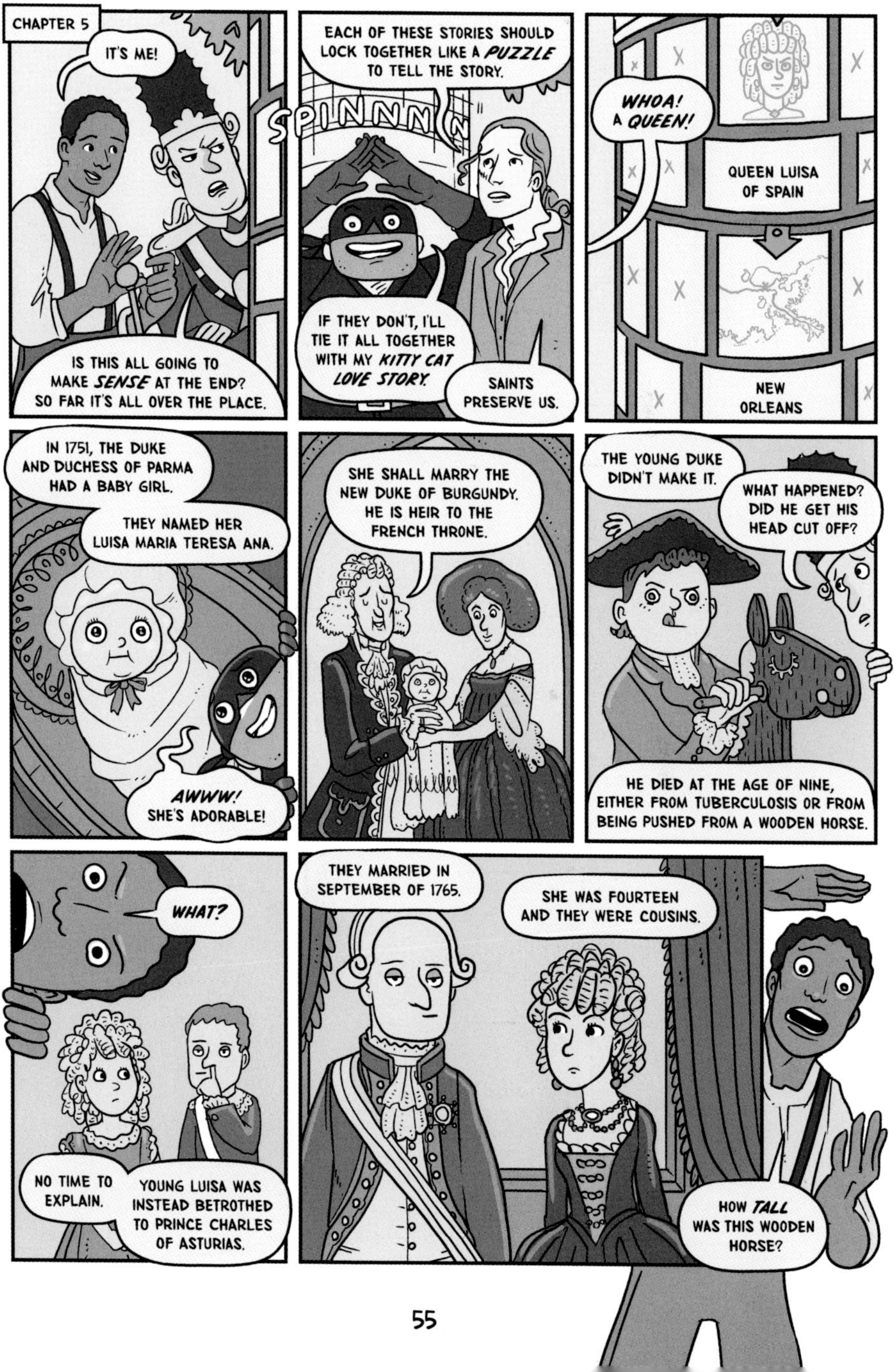
CHAPTER 5
IT'S ME!
IS THIS ALL GOING TO MAKE *SENSE* AT THE END? SO FAR IT'S ALL OVER THE PLACE.
EACH OF THESE STORIES SHOULD LOCK TOGETHER LIKE A *PUZZLE* TO TELL THE STORY.
SPINNNN
IF THEY DON'T, I'LL TIE IT ALL TOGETHER WITH MY *KITTY CAT LOVE STORY.*
SAINTS PRESERVE US.
WHOA! A *QUEEN!*
QUEEN LUISA OF SPAIN
NEW ORLEANS
IN 1751, THE DUKE AND DUCHESS OF PARMA HAD A BABY GIRL.
THEY NAMED HER LUISA MARIA TERESA ANA.
AWWW! SHE'S ADORABLE!
SHE SHALL MARRY THE NEW DUKE OF BURGUNDY. HE IS HEIR TO THE FRENCH THRONE.
THE YOUNG DUKE DIDN'T MAKE IT.
WHAT HAPPENED? DID HE GET HIS HEAD CUT OFF?
HE DIED AT THE AGE OF NINE, EITHER FROM TUBERCULOSIS OR FROM BEING PUSHED FROM A WOODEN HORSE.
WHAT?
NO TIME TO EXPLAIN.
YOUNG LUISA WAS INSTEAD BETROTHED TO PRINCE CHARLES OF ASTURIAS.
THEY MARRIED IN SEPTEMBER OF 1765.
SHE WAS FOURTEEN AND THEY WERE COUSINS.
HOW *TALL* WAS THIS WOODEN HORSE?

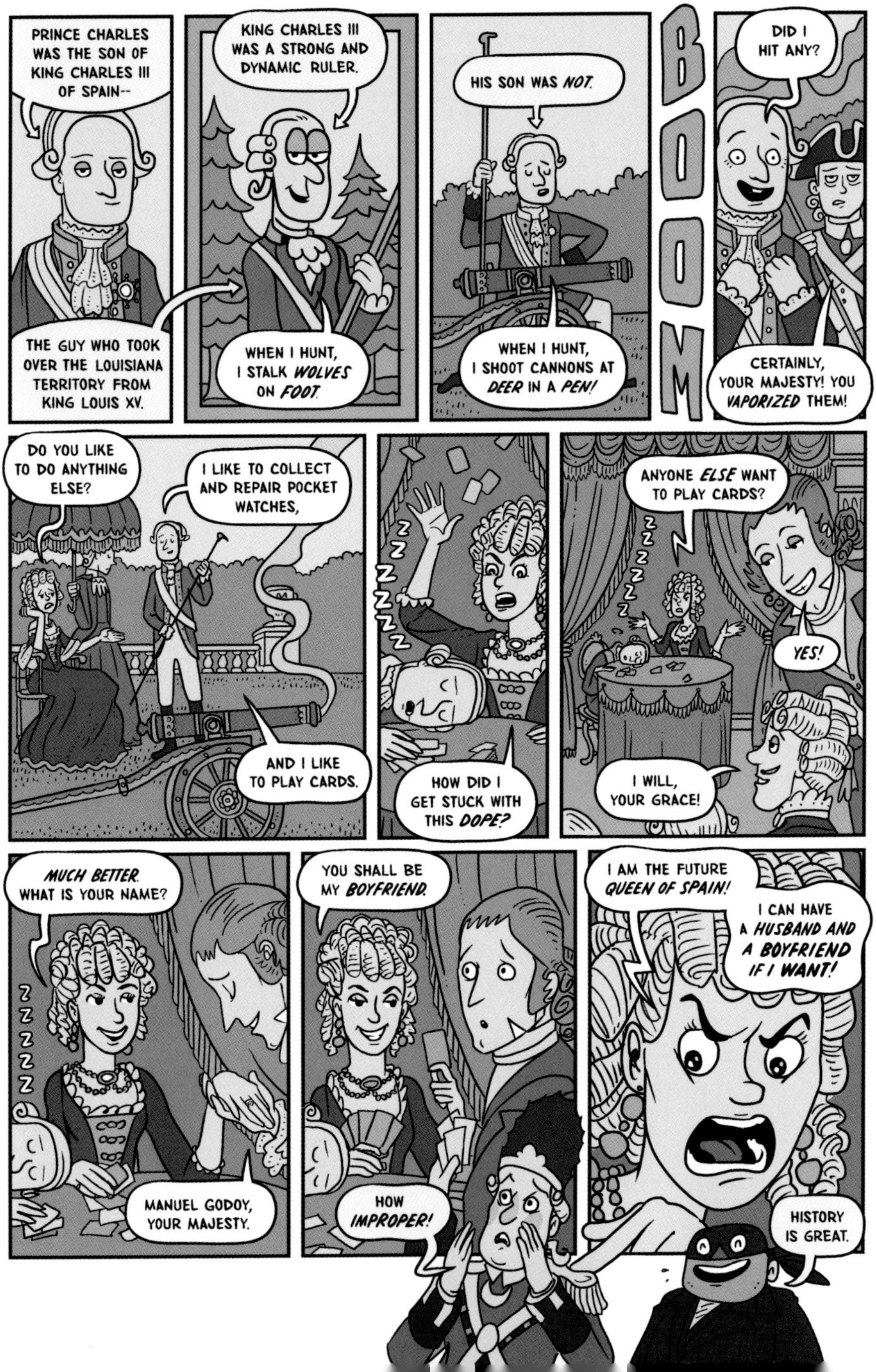

PRINCE CHARLES WAS THE SON OF KING CHARLES III OF SPAIN--
THE GUY WHO TOOK OVER THE LOUISIANA TERRITORY FROM KING LOUIS XV.
KING CHARLES III WAS A STRONG AND DYNAMIC RULER.
WHEN I HUNT, I STALK *WOLVES* ON *FOOT*.
HIS SON WAS *NOT*.
WHEN I HUNT, I SHOOT CANNONS AT *DEER* IN A *PEN!*
BOOOM
DID I HIT ANY?
CERTAINLY, YOUR MAJESTY! YOU *VAPORIZED* THEM!
DO YOU LIKE TO DO ANYTHING ELSE?
I LIKE TO COLLECT AND REPAIR POCKET WATCHES,
AND I LIKE TO PLAY CARDS.
Z Z Z Z Z Z
HOW DID I GET STUCK WITH THIS *DOPE?*
Z Z Z Z Z Z Z
ANYONE *ELSE* WANT TO PLAY CARDS?
YES!
I WILL, YOUR GRACE!
MUCH BETTER. WHAT IS YOUR NAME?
Z Z Z Z Z
MANUEL GODOY, YOUR MAJESTY.
YOU SHALL BE MY *BOYFRIEND.*
HOW *IMPROPER!*
I AM THE FUTURE *QUEEN OF SPAIN!*
I CAN HAVE A *HUSBAND AND A BOYFRIEND IF I WANT!*
HISTORY IS GREAT.

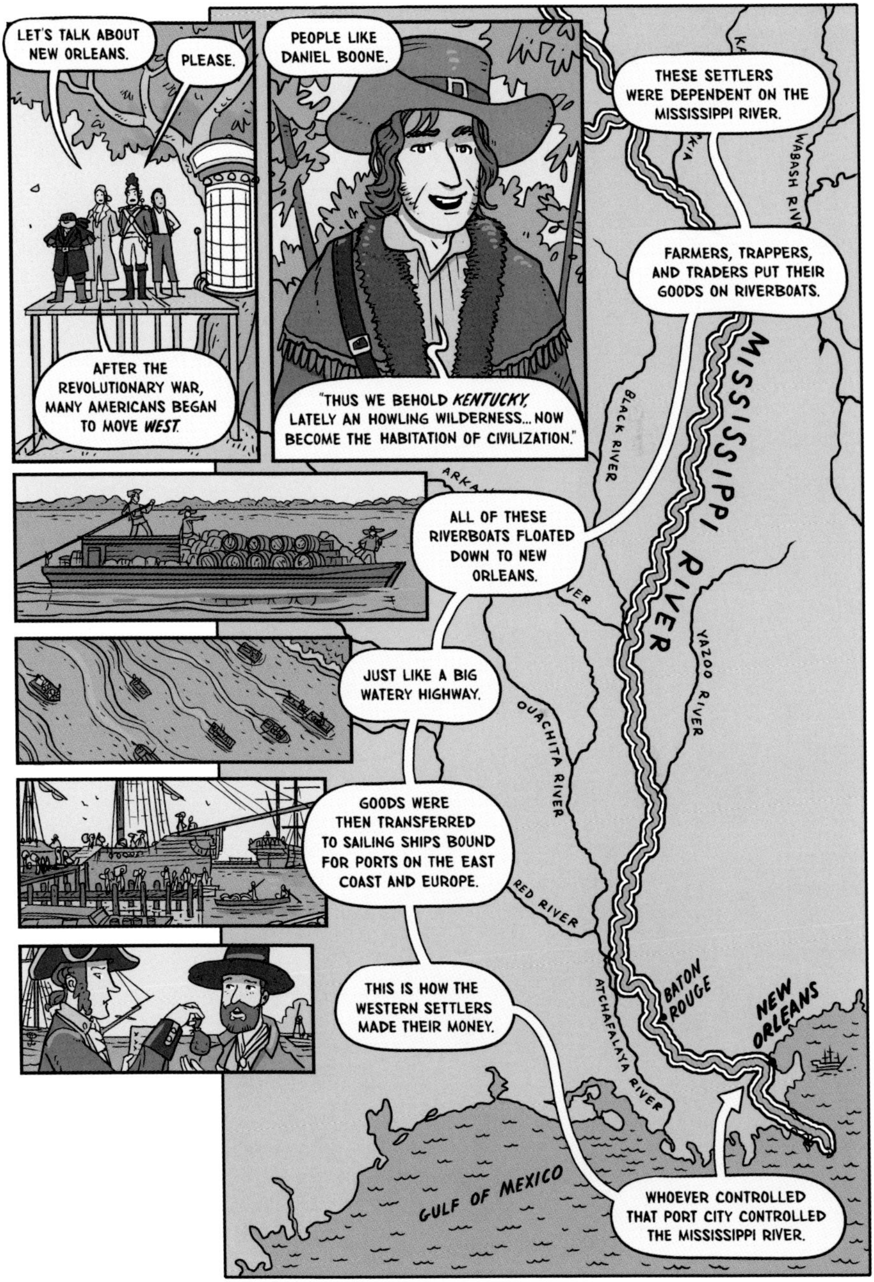

LET'S TALK ABOUT NEW ORLEANS.
PLEASE.
AFTER THE REVOLUTIONARY WAR, MANY AMERICANS BEGAN TO MOVE *WEST*.
PEOPLE LIKE DANIEL BOONE.
"THUS WE BEHOLD *KENTUCKY*, LATELY AN HOWLING WILDERNESS... NOW BECOME THE HABITATION OF CIVILIZATION."
THESE SETTLERS WERE DEPENDENT ON THE MISSISSIPPI RIVER.
FARMERS, TRAPPERS, AND TRADERS PUT THEIR GOODS ON RIVERBOATS.
ALL OF THESE RIVERBOATS FLOATED DOWN TO NEW ORLEANS.
JUST LIKE A BIG WATERY HIGHWAY.
GOODS WERE THEN TRANSFERRED TO SAILING SHIPS BOUND FOR PORTS ON THE EAST COAST AND EUROPE.
THIS IS HOW THE WESTERN SETTLERS MADE THEIR MONEY.
WHOEVER CONTROLLED THAT PORT CITY CONTROLLED THE MISSISSIPPI RIVER.
MISSISSIPPI RIVER
WABASH RIV
BLACK RIVER
YAZOO RIVER
OUACHITA RIVER
RED RIVER
ATCHAFALAYA RIVER
BATON ROUGE
NEW ORLEANS
GULF OF MEXICO

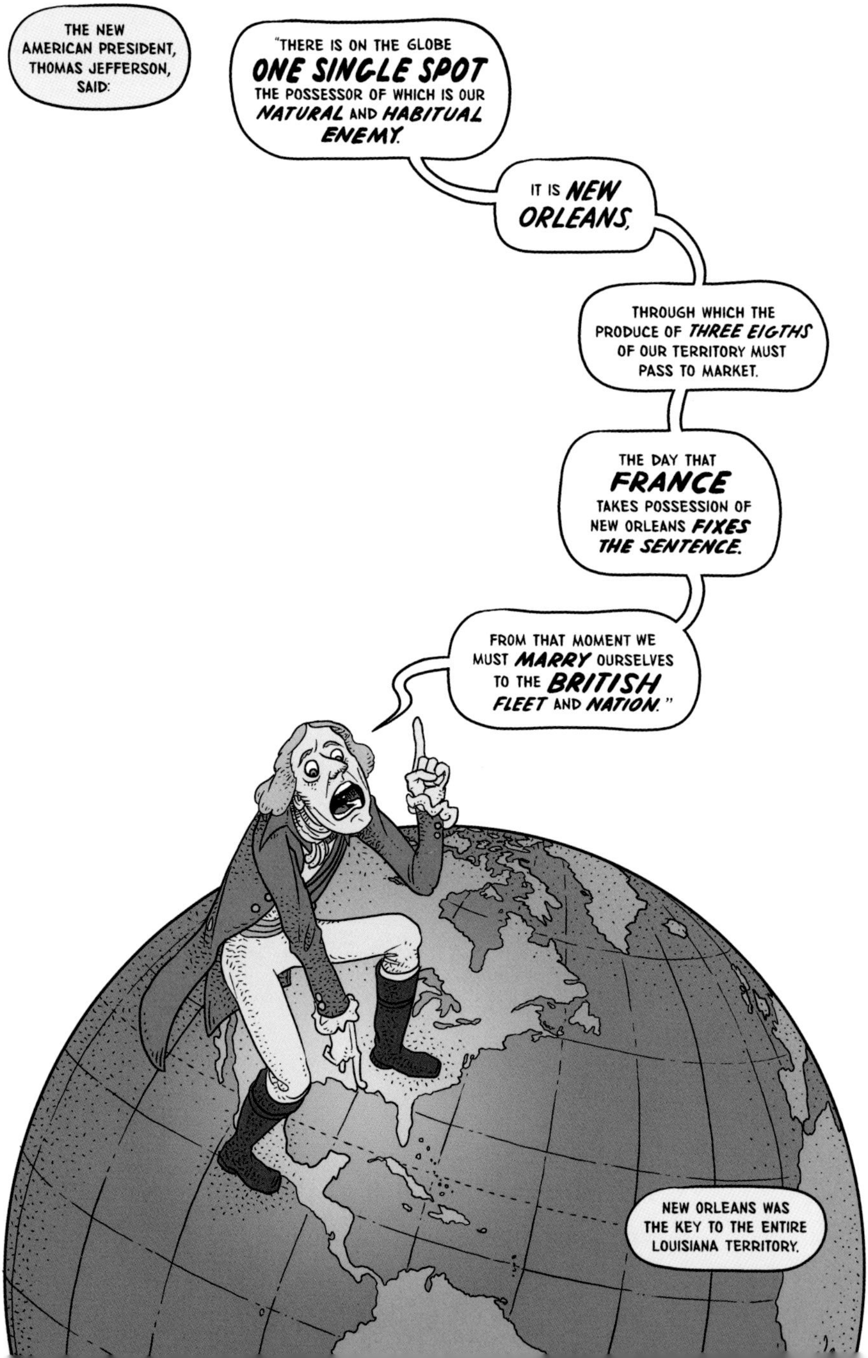
THE NEW AMERICAN PRESIDENT, THOMAS JEFFERSON, SAID:
"THERE IS ON THE GLOBE ONE SINGLE SPOT THE POSSESSOR OF WHICH IS OUR NATURAL AND HABITUAL ENEMY.
IT IS NEW ORLEANS,
THROUGH WHICH THE PRODUCE OF THREE EIGTHS OF OUR TERRITORY MUST PASS TO MARKET.
THE DAY THAT FRANCE TAKES POSSESSION OF NEW ORLEANS FIXES THE SENTENCE.
FROM THAT MOMENT WE MUST MARRY OURSELVES TO THE BRITISH FLEET AND NATION."
NEW ORLEANS WAS THE KEY TO THE ENTIRE LOUISIANA TERRITORY.

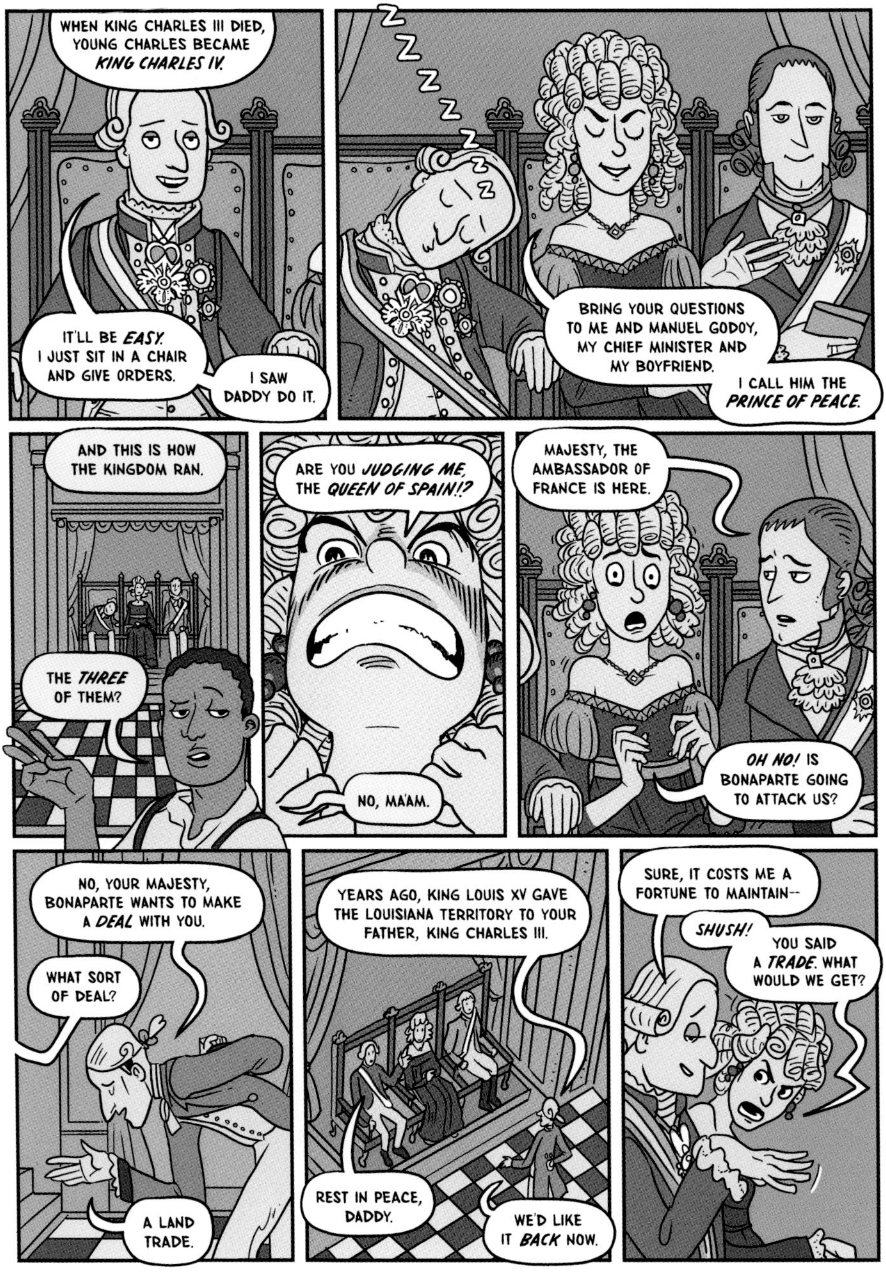
WHEN KING CHARLES III DIED, YOUNG CHARLES BECAME *KING CHARLES IV.*
IT'LL BE *EASY.* I JUST SIT IN A CHAIR AND GIVE ORDERS.
I SAW DADDY DO IT.
Z Z Z Z Z Z Z
BRING YOUR QUESTIONS TO ME AND MANUEL GODOY, MY CHIEF MINISTER AND MY BOYFRIEND.
I CALL HIM THE *PRINCE OF PEACE.*
AND THIS IS HOW THE KINGDOM RAN.
THE *THREE* OF THEM?
ARE YOU *JUDGING ME,* THE *QUEEN OF SPAIN!?*
NO, MA'AM.
MAJESTY, THE AMBASSADOR OF FRANCE IS HERE.
OH NO! IS BONAPARTE GOING TO ATTACK US?
NO, YOUR MAJESTY, BONAPARTE WANTS TO MAKE A *DEAL* WITH YOU.
WHAT SORT OF DEAL?
A LAND TRADE.
YEARS AGO, KING LOUIS XV GAVE THE LOUISIANA TERRITORY TO YOUR FATHER, KING CHARLES III.
REST IN PEACE, DADDY.
WE'D LIKE IT *BACK* NOW.
SURE, IT COSTS ME A FORTUNE TO MAINTAIN--
SHUSH!
YOU SAID A *TRADE.* WHAT WOULD WE GET?

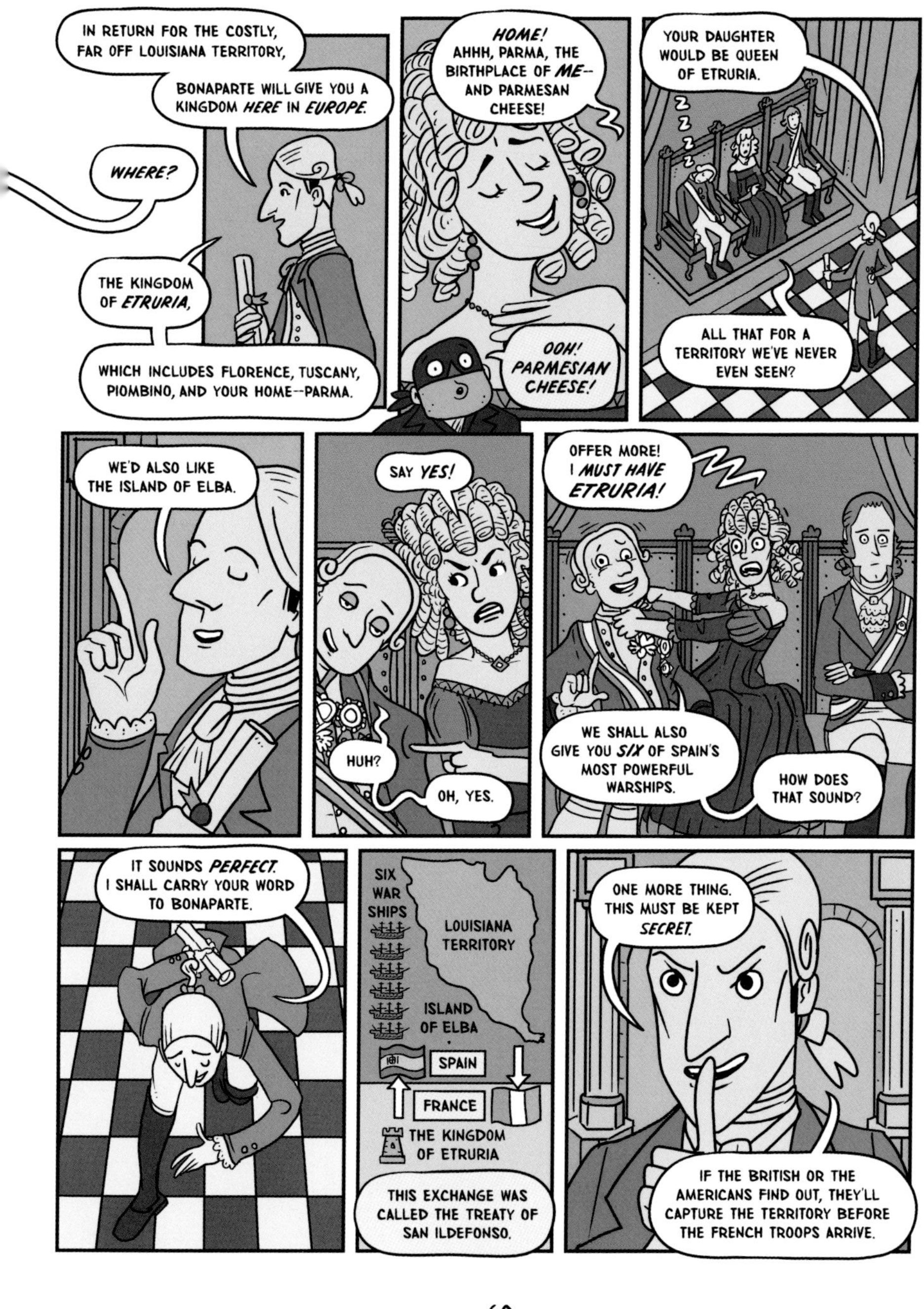
IN RETURN FOR THE COSTLY, FAR OFF LOUISIANA TERRITORY,
BONAPARTE WILL GIVE YOU A KINGDOM *HERE* IN *EUROPE*.
WHERE?
THE KINGDOM OF *ETRURIA*,
WHICH INCLUDES FLORENCE, TUSCANY, PIOMBINO, AND YOUR HOME--PARMA.
HOME! AHHH, PARMA, THE BIRTHPLACE OF *ME*-- AND PARMESAN CHEESE!
OOH! PARMESIAN CHEESE!
YOUR DAUGHTER WOULD BE QUEEN OF ETRURIA.
Z Z Z Z
ALL THAT FOR A TERRITORY WE'VE NEVER EVEN SEEN?
WE'D ALSO LIKE THE ISLAND OF ELBA.
SAY *YES!*
HUH?
OH, YES.
OFFER MORE! I *MUST HAVE ETRURIA!*
WE SHALL ALSO GIVE YOU *SIX* OF SPAIN'S MOST POWERFUL WARSHIPS.
HOW DOES THAT SOUND?
IT SOUNDS *PERFECT*. I SHALL CARRY YOUR WORD TO BONAPARTE.
SIX WAR SHIPS
LOUISIANA TERRITORY
ISLAND OF ELBA
SPAIN
FRANCE
THE KINGDOM OF ETRURIA
THIS EXCHANGE WAS CALLED THE TREATY OF SAN ILDEFONSO.
ONE MORE THING. THIS MUST BE KEPT *SECRET*.
IF THE BRITISH OR THE AMERICANS FIND OUT, THEY'LL CAPTURE THE TERRITORY BEFORE THE FRENCH TROOPS ARRIVE.

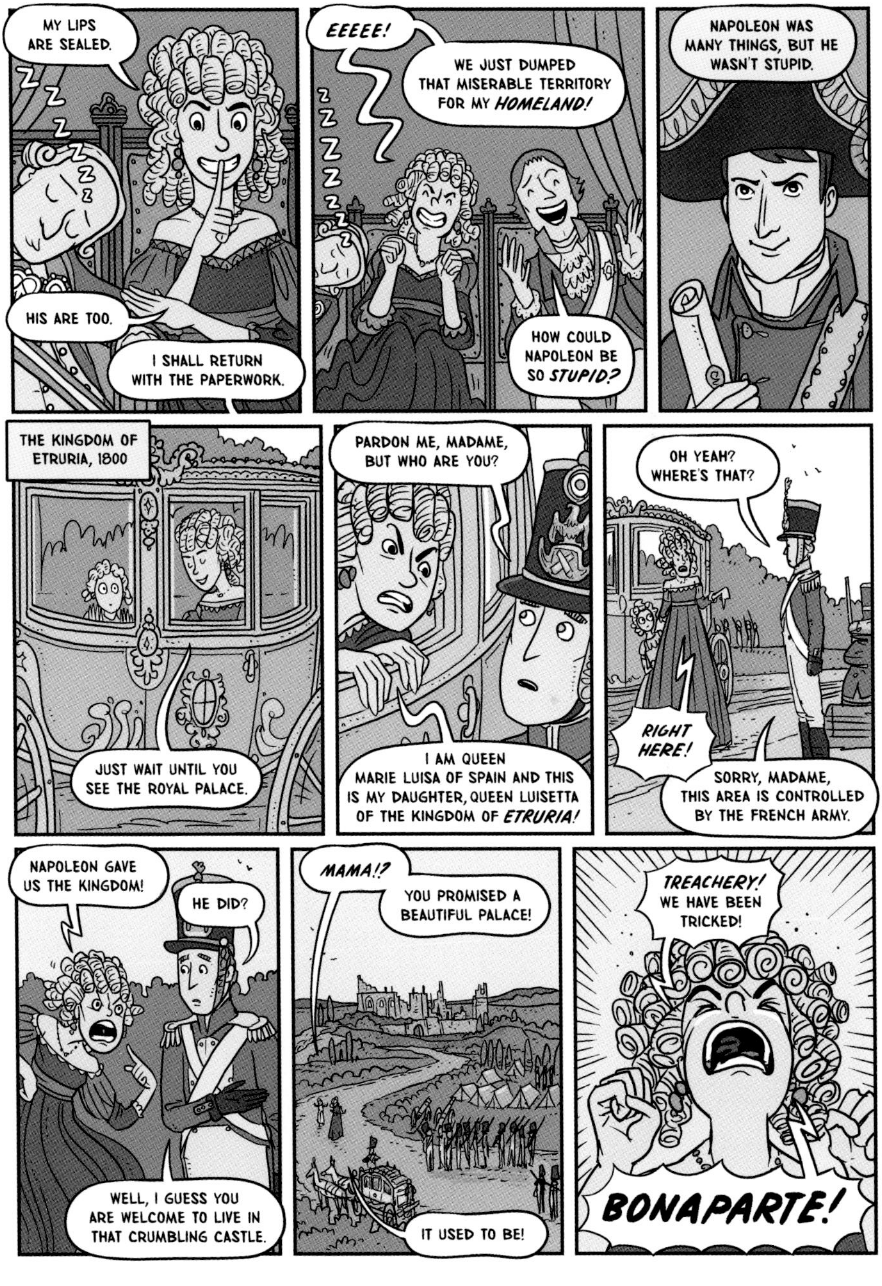

MY LIPS ARE SEALED.
HIS ARE TOO.
I SHALL RETURN WITH THE PAPERWORK.
EEEEE!
WE JUST DUMPED THAT MISERABLE TERRITORY FOR MY *HOMELAND!*
HOW COULD NAPOLEON BE SO *STUPID?*
NAPOLEON WAS MANY THINGS, BUT HE WASN'T STUPID.
THE KINGDOM OF ETRURIA, 1800
JUST WAIT UNTIL YOU SEE THE ROYAL PALACE.
PARDON ME, MADAME, BUT WHO ARE YOU?
I AM QUEEN MARIE LUISA OF SPAIN AND THIS IS MY DAUGHTER, QUEEN LUISETTA OF THE KINGDOM OF *ETRURIA!*
OH YEAH? WHERE'S THAT?
RIGHT HERE!
SORRY, MADAME, THIS AREA IS CONTROLLED BY THE FRENCH ARMY.
NAPOLEON GAVE US THE KINGDOM!
HE DID?
WELL, I GUESS YOU ARE WELCOME TO LIVE IN THAT CRUMBLING CASTLE.
MAMA!?
YOU PROMISED A BEAUTIFUL PALACE!
IT USED TO BE!
TREACHERY! WE HAVE BEEN TRICKED!
BONAPARTE!

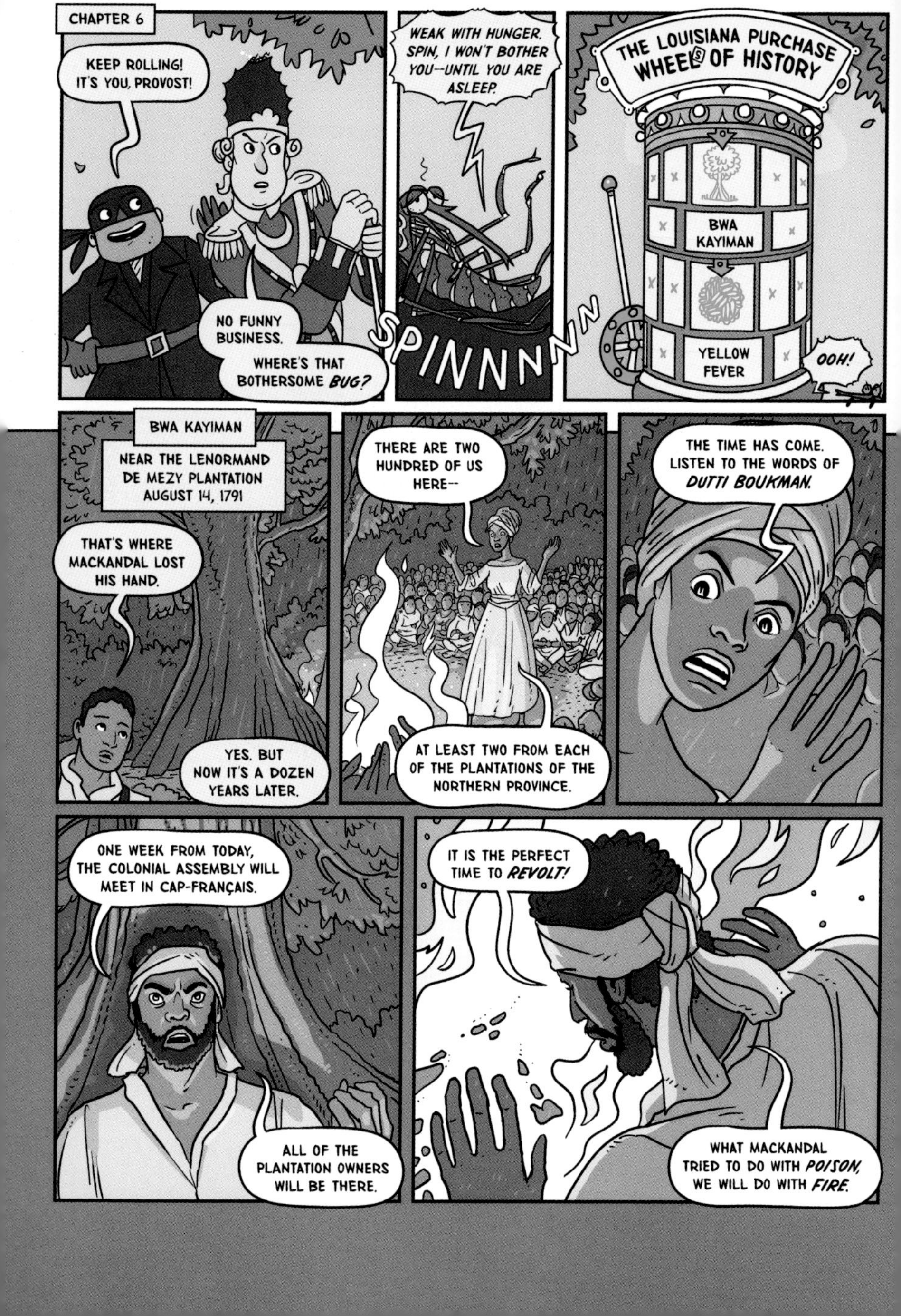
CHAPTER 6
KEEP ROLLING! IT'S YOU, PROVOST!
NO FUNNY BUSINESS.
WHERE'S THAT BOTHERSOME *BUG?*
WEAK WITH HUNGER. SPIN, I WON'T BOTHER YOU--UNTIL YOU ARE ASLEEP.
SPINNNNNNN
THE LOUISIANA PURCHASE WHEEL(S) OF HISTORY
BWA KAYIMAN
YELLOW FEVER
OOH!
BWA KAYIMAN
NEAR THE LENORMAND DE MEZY PLANTATION AUGUST 14, 1791
THAT'S WHERE MACKANDAL LOST HIS HAND.
YES. BUT NOW IT'S A DOZEN YEARS LATER.
THERE ARE TWO HUNDRED OF US HERE--
AT LEAST TWO FROM EACH OF THE PLANTATIONS OF THE NORTHERN PROVINCE.
THE TIME HAS COME. LISTEN TO THE WORDS OF *DUTTI BOUKMAN.*
ONE WEEK FROM TODAY, THE COLONIAL ASSEMBLY WILL MEET IN CAP-FRANÇAIS.
ALL OF THE PLANTATION OWNERS WILL BE THERE.
IT IS THE PERFECT TIME TO *REVOLT!*
WHAT MACKANDAL TRIED TO DO WITH *POISON,* WE WILL DO WITH *FIRE.*

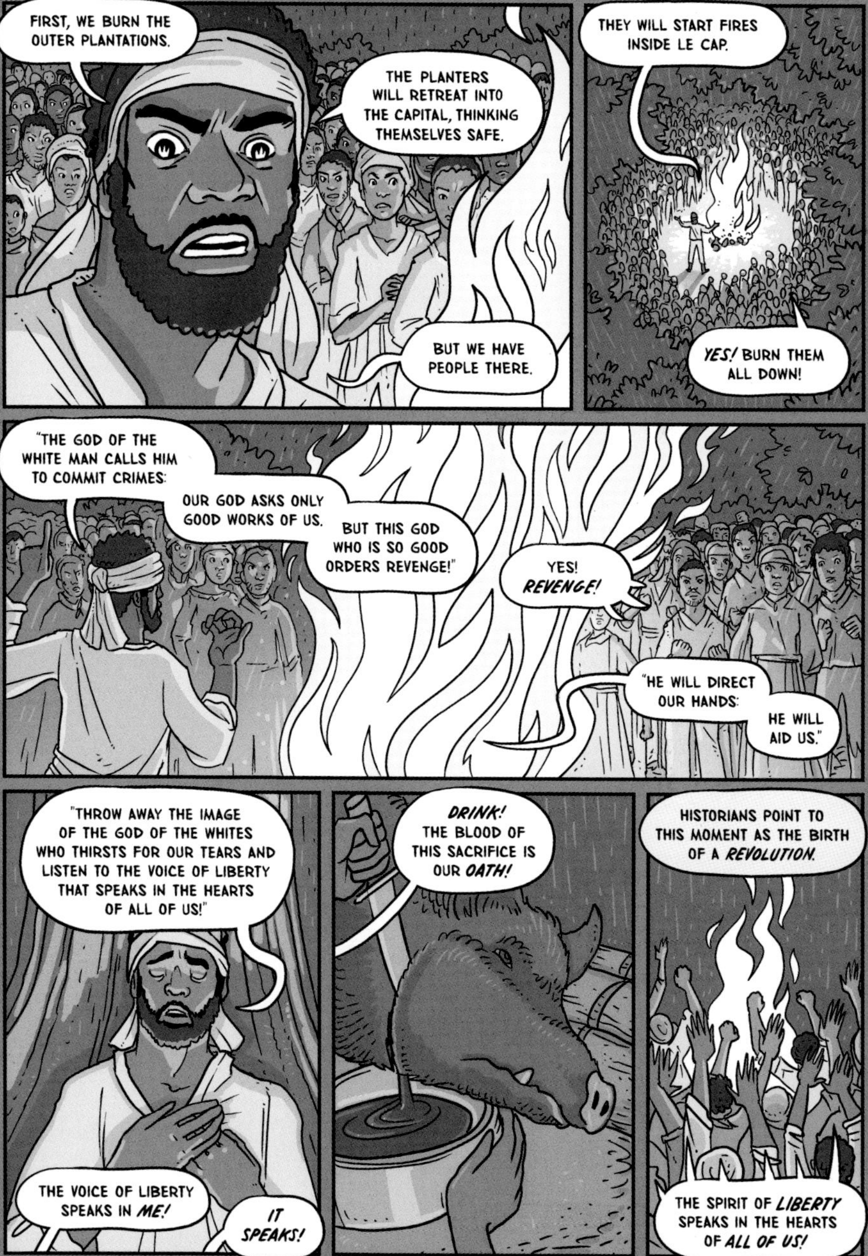
FIRST, WE BURN THE OUTER PLANTATIONS.
THE PLANTERS WILL RETREAT INTO THE CAPITAL, THINKING THEMSELVES SAFE.
BUT WE HAVE PEOPLE THERE.
THEY WILL START FIRES INSIDE LE CAP.
YES! BURN THEM ALL DOWN!
"THE GOD OF THE WHITE MAN CALLS HIM TO COMMIT CRIMES:
OUR GOD ASKS ONLY GOOD WORKS OF US.
BUT THIS GOD WHO IS SO GOOD ORDERS REVENGE!"
YES! REVENGE!
"HE WILL DIRECT OUR HANDS:
HE WILL AID US."
"THROW AWAY THE IMAGE OF THE GOD OF THE WHITES WHO THIRSTS FOR OUR TEARS AND LISTEN TO THE VOICE OF LIBERTY THAT SPEAKS IN THE HEARTS OF ALL OF US!"
THE VOICE OF LIBERTY SPEAKS IN ME!
IT SPEAKS!
DRINK! THE BLOOD OF THIS SACRIFICE IS OUR OATH!
HISTORIANS POINT TO THIS MOMENT AS THE BIRTH OF A REVOLUTION.
THE SPIRIT OF LIBERTY SPEAKS IN THE HEARTS OF ALL OF US!

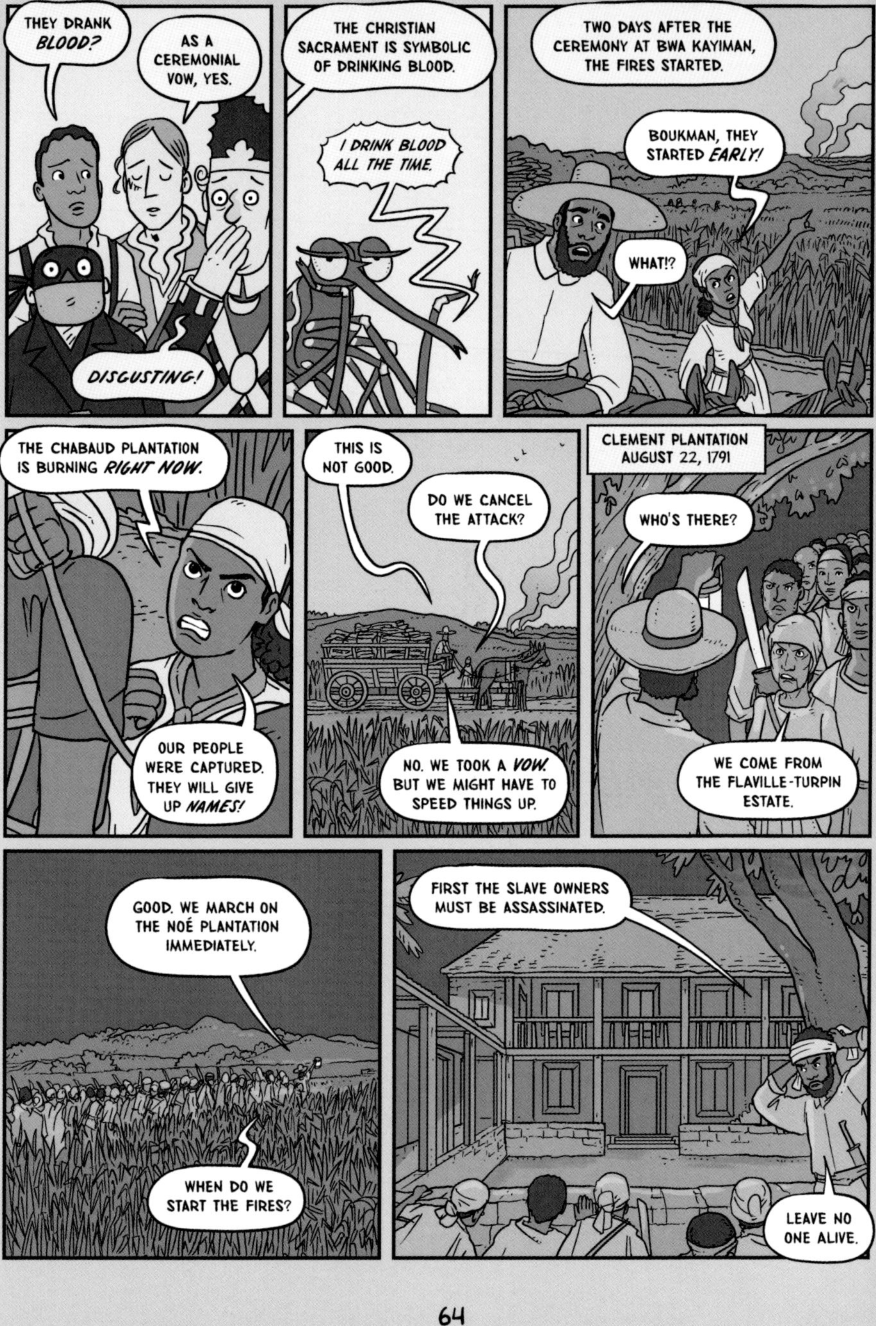
THEY DRANK BLOOD?
AS A CEREMONIAL VOW, YES.
DISGUSTING!
THE CHRISTIAN SACRAMENT IS SYMBOLIC OF DRINKING BLOOD.
I DRINK BLOOD ALL THE TIME.
TWO DAYS AFTER THE CEREMONY AT BWA KAYIMAN, THE FIRES STARTED.
BOUKMAN, THEY STARTED EARLY!
WHAT!?
THE CHABAUD PLANTATION IS BURNING RIGHT NOW.
OUR PEOPLE WERE CAPTURED. THEY WILL GIVE UP NAMES!
THIS IS NOT GOOD.
DO WE CANCEL THE ATTACK?
NO. WE TOOK A VOW. BUT WE MIGHT HAVE TO SPEED THINGS UP.
CLEMENT PLANTATION AUGUST 22, 1791
WHO'S THERE?
WE COME FROM THE FLAVILLE-TURPIN ESTATE.
GOOD. WE MARCH ON THE NOÉ PLANTATION IMMEDIATELY.
WHEN DO WE START THE FIRES?
FIRST THE SLAVE OWNERS MUST BE ASSASSINATED.
LEAVE NO ONE ALIVE.

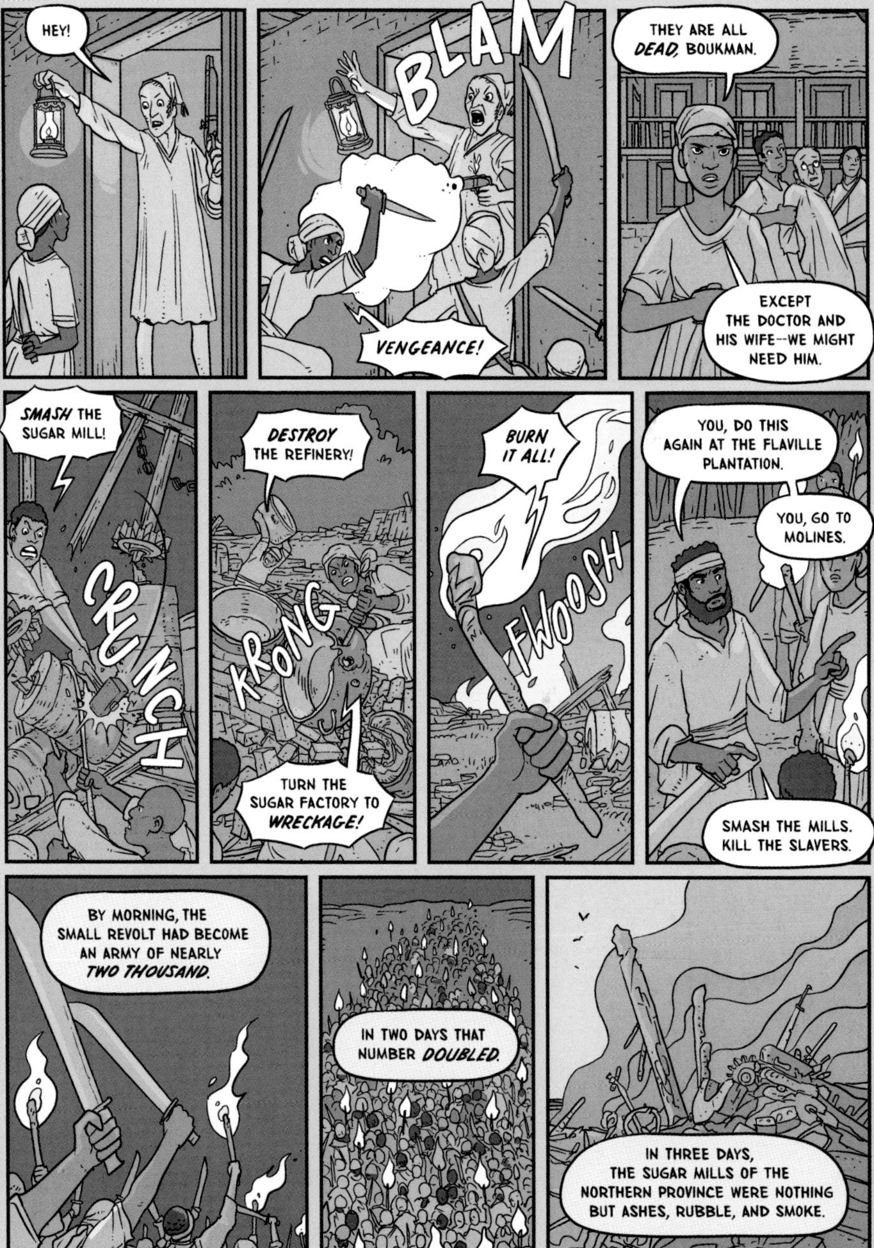
HEY!
BLAM
VENGEANCE!
THEY ARE ALL DEAD, BOUKMAN.
EXCEPT THE DOCTOR AND HIS WIFE--WE MIGHT NEED HIM.
SMASH THE SUGAR MILL!
CRUNCH
DESTROY THE REFINERY!
KRONG
TURN THE SUGAR FACTORY TO WRECKAGE!
BURN IT ALL!
FWOOSH
YOU, DO THIS AGAIN AT THE FLAVILLE PLANTATION.
YOU, GO TO MOLINES.
SMASH THE MILLS. KILL THE SLAVERS.
BY MORNING, THE SMALL REVOLT HAD BECOME AN ARMY OF NEARLY TWO THOUSAND.
IN TWO DAYS THAT NUMBER DOUBLED.
IN THREE DAYS, THE SUGAR MILLS OF THE NORTHERN PROVINCE WERE NOTHING BUT ASHES, RUBBLE, AND SMOKE.

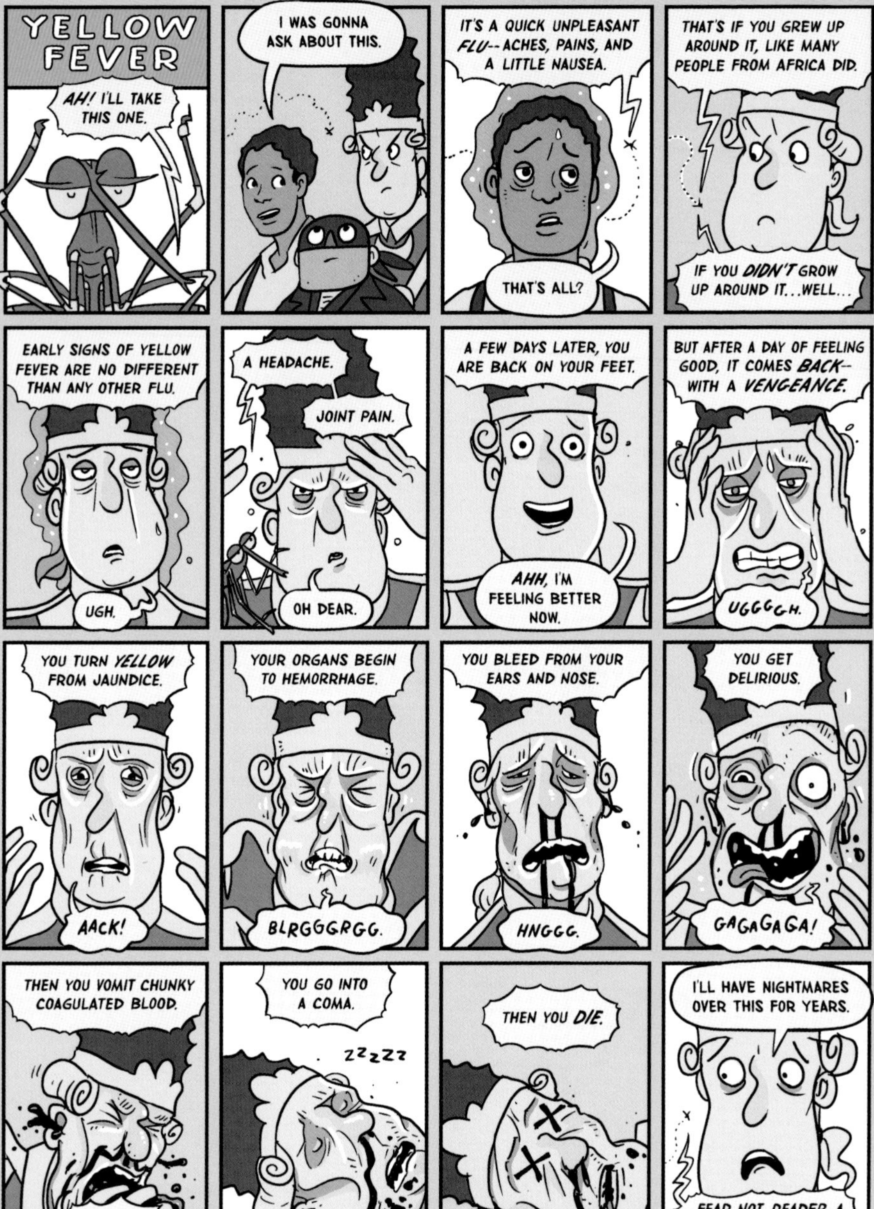
YELLOW FEVER
AH! I'LL TAKE THIS ONE.
I WAS GONNA ASK ABOUT THIS.
IT'S A QUICK UNPLEASANT FLU-- ACHES, PAINS, AND A LITTLE NAUSEA.
THAT'S ALL?
THAT'S IF YOU GREW UP AROUND IT, LIKE MANY PEOPLE FROM AFRICA DID.
IF YOU DIDN'T GROW UP AROUND IT...WELL...
EARLY SIGNS OF YELLOW FEVER ARE NO DIFFERENT THAN ANY OTHER FLU.
UGH.
A HEADACHE.
JOINT PAIN.
OH DEAR.
A FEW DAYS LATER, YOU ARE BACK ON YOUR FEET.
AHH, I'M FEELING BETTER NOW.
BUT AFTER A DAY OF FEELING GOOD, IT COMES BACK-- WITH A VENGEANCE.
UGGGGH.
YOU TURN YELLOW FROM JAUNDICE.
AACK!
YOUR ORGANS BEGIN TO HEMORRHAGE.
BLRGGGRGG.
YOU BLEED FROM YOUR EARS AND NOSE.
HNGGG.
YOU GET DELIRIOUS.
GAGAGAGA!
THEN YOU VOMIT CHUNKY COAGULATED BLOOD.
GROWLF
YOU GO INTO A COMA.
ZZZZZ
THEN YOU DIE.
I'LL HAVE NIGHTMARES OVER THIS FOR YEARS.
FEAR NOT, READER, A YELLOW FEVER VACCINE HAS BEEN AVAILABLE SINCE 1951.

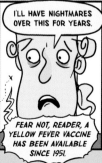

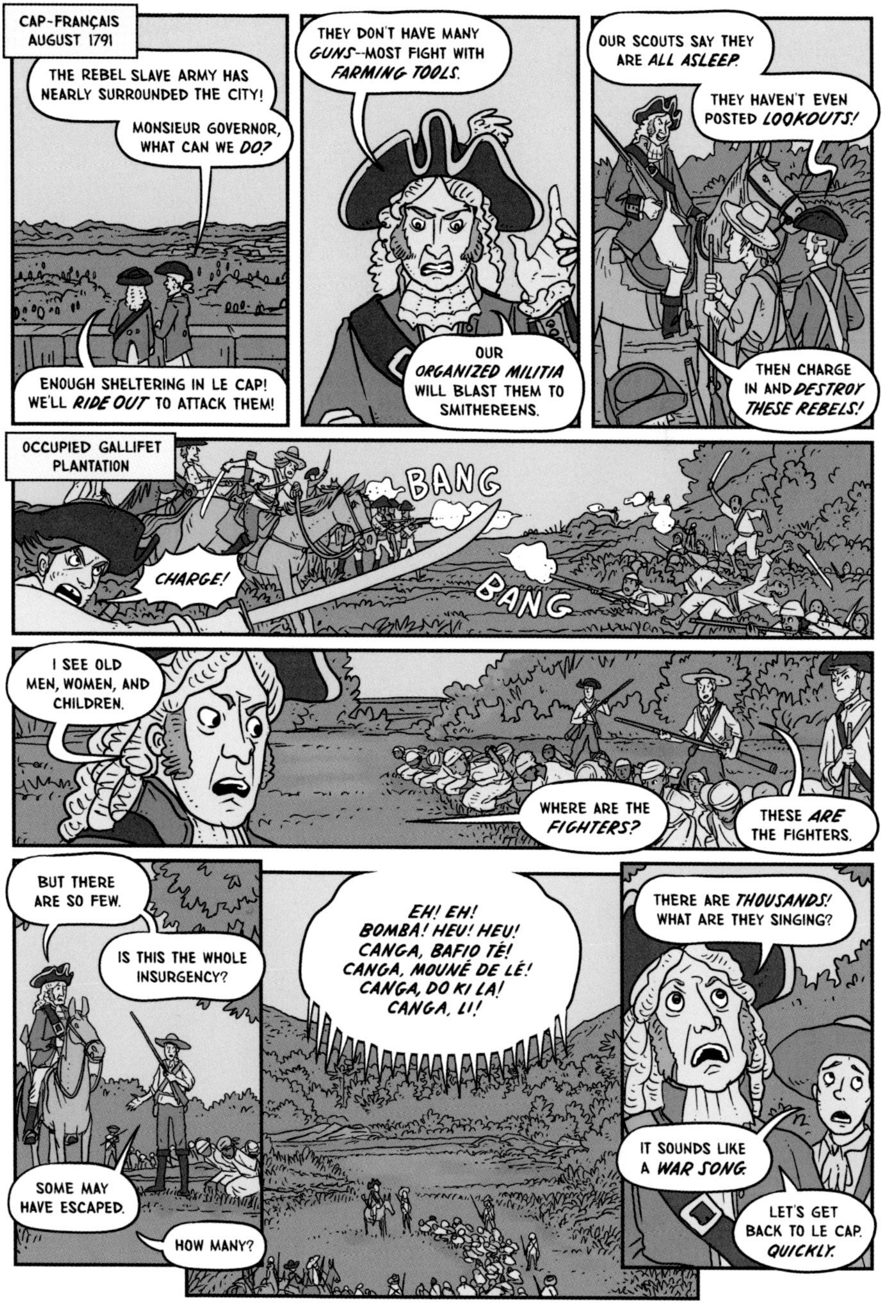
CAP-FRANÇAIS
AUGUST 1791
THE REBEL SLAVE ARMY HAS NEARLY SURROUNDED THE CITY!
MONSIEUR GOVERNOR, WHAT CAN WE DO?
ENOUGH SHELTERING IN LE CAP! WE'LL RIDE OUT TO ATTACK THEM!
THEY DON'T HAVE MANY GUNS--MOST FIGHT WITH FARMING TOOLS.
OUR ORGANIZED MILITIA WILL BLAST THEM TO SMITHEREENS.
OUR SCOUTS SAY THEY ARE ALL ASLEEP.
THEY HAVEN'T EVEN POSTED LOOKOUTS!
THEN CHARGE IN AND DESTROY THESE REBELS!
OCCUPIED GALLIFET PLANTATION
BANG
CHARGE!
BANG
I SEE OLD MEN, WOMEN, AND CHILDREN.
WHERE ARE THE FIGHTERS?
THESE ARE THE FIGHTERS.
BUT THERE ARE SO FEW.
IS THIS THE WHOLE INSURGENCY?
SOME MAY HAVE ESCAPED.
HOW MANY?
EH! EH!
BOMBA! HEU! HEU!
CANGA, BAFIO TÉ!
CANGA, MOUNÉ DE LÉ!
CANGA, DO KI LA!
CANGA, LI!
THERE ARE THOUSANDS! WHAT ARE THEY SINGING?
IT SOUNDS LIKE A WAR SONG.
LET'S GET BACK TO LE CAP. QUICKLY.

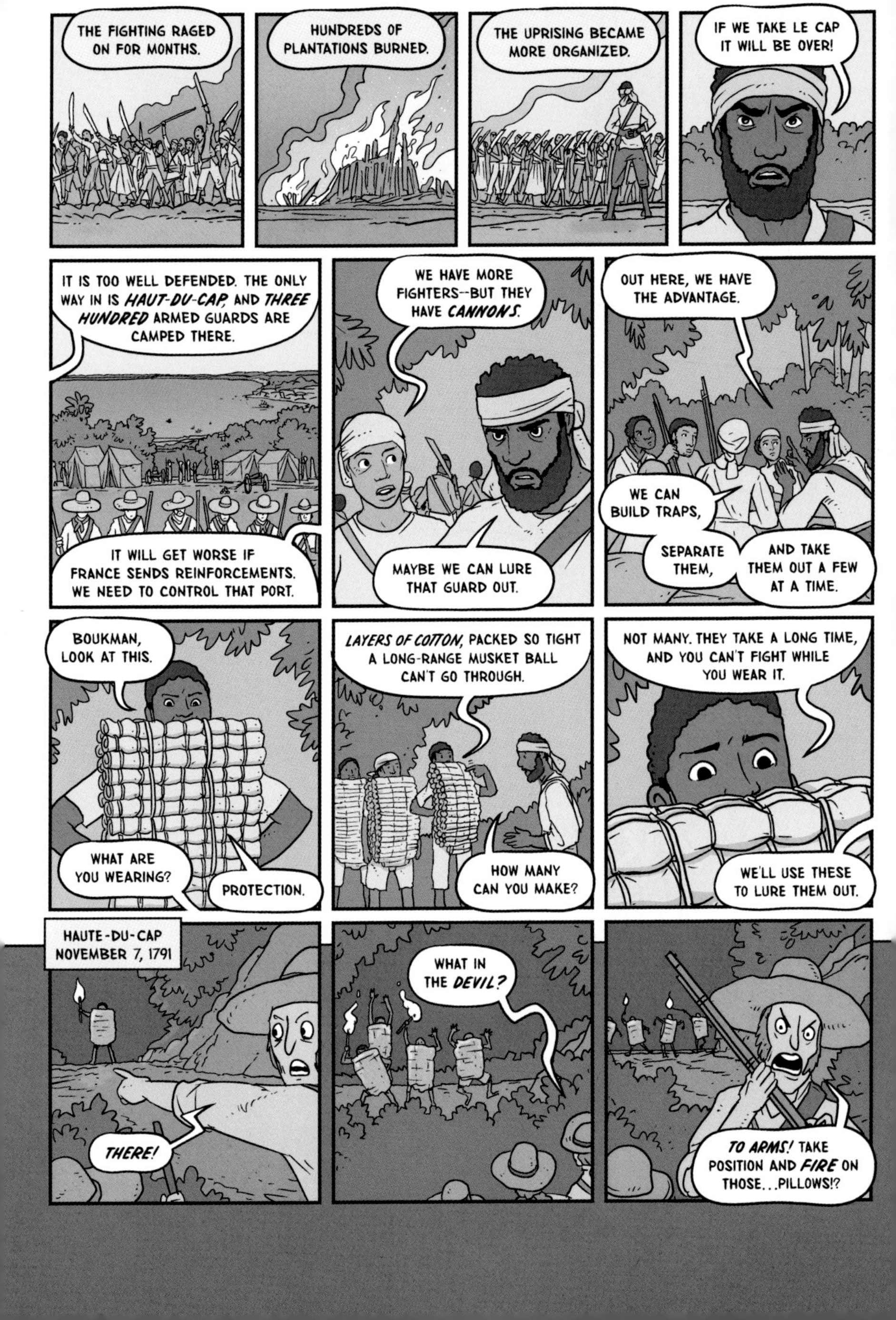
THE FIGHTING RAGED ON FOR MONTHS.
HUNDREDS OF PLANTATIONS BURNED.
THE UPRISING BECAME MORE ORGANIZED.
IF WE TAKE LE CAP IT WILL BE OVER!
IT IS TOO WELL DEFENDED. THE ONLY WAY IN IS *HAUT-DU-CAP,* AND *THREE HUNDRED* ARMED GUARDS ARE CAMPED THERE.
IT WILL GET WORSE IF FRANCE SENDS REINFORCEMENTS. WE NEED TO CONTROL THAT PORT.
WE HAVE MORE FIGHTERS--BUT THEY HAVE *CANNONS.*
MAYBE WE CAN LURE THAT GUARD OUT.
OUT HERE, WE HAVE THE ADVANTAGE.
WE CAN BUILD TRAPS,
SEPARATE THEM,
AND TAKE THEM OUT A FEW AT A TIME.
BOUKMAN, LOOK AT THIS.
WHAT ARE YOU WEARING?
PROTECTION.
LAYERS OF COTTON, PACKED SO TIGHT A LONG-RANGE MUSKET BALL CAN'T GO THROUGH.
HOW MANY CAN YOU MAKE?
NOT MANY. THEY TAKE A LONG TIME, AND YOU CAN'T FIGHT WHILE YOU WEAR IT.
WE'LL USE THESE TO LURE THEM OUT.
HAUTE-DU-CAP NOVEMBER 7, 1791
THERE!
WHAT IN THE *DEVIL?*
TO ARMS! TAKE POSITION AND *FIRE* ON THOSE. . .PILLOWS!?

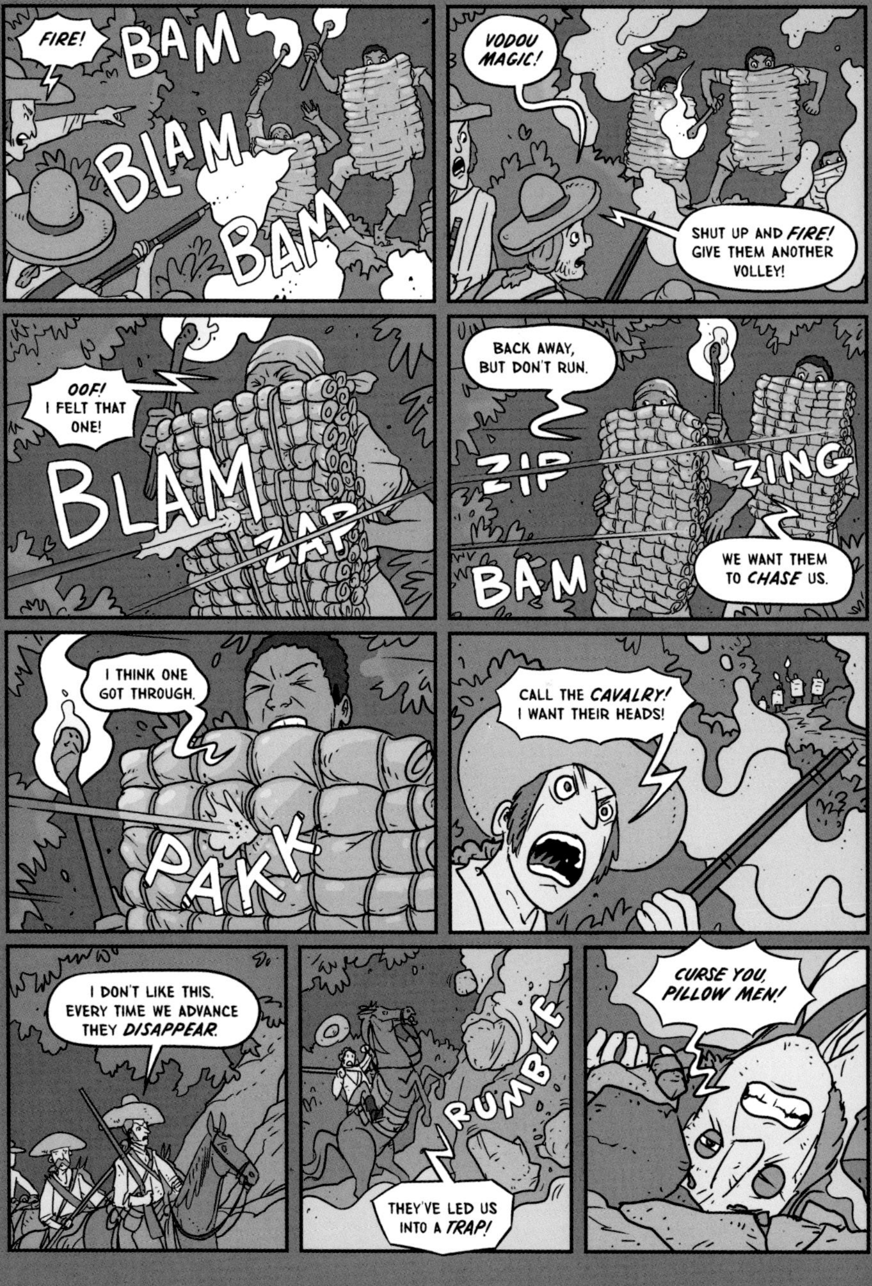
FIRE!
BAM
BLAM
BAM
VODOU MAGIC!
SHUT UP AND FIRE! GIVE THEM ANOTHER VOLLEY!
OOF! I FELT THAT ONE!
BLAM
ZAP
BACK AWAY, BUT DON'T RUN.
ZIP
ZING
BAM
WE WANT THEM TO CHASE US.
I THINK ONE GOT THROUGH.
PAKK
CALL THE CAVALRY! I WANT THEIR HEADS!
I DON'T LIKE THIS. EVERY TIME WE ADVANCE THEY DISAPPEAR.
RUMBLE
THEY'VE LED US INTO A TRAP!
CURSE YOU, PILLOW MEN!

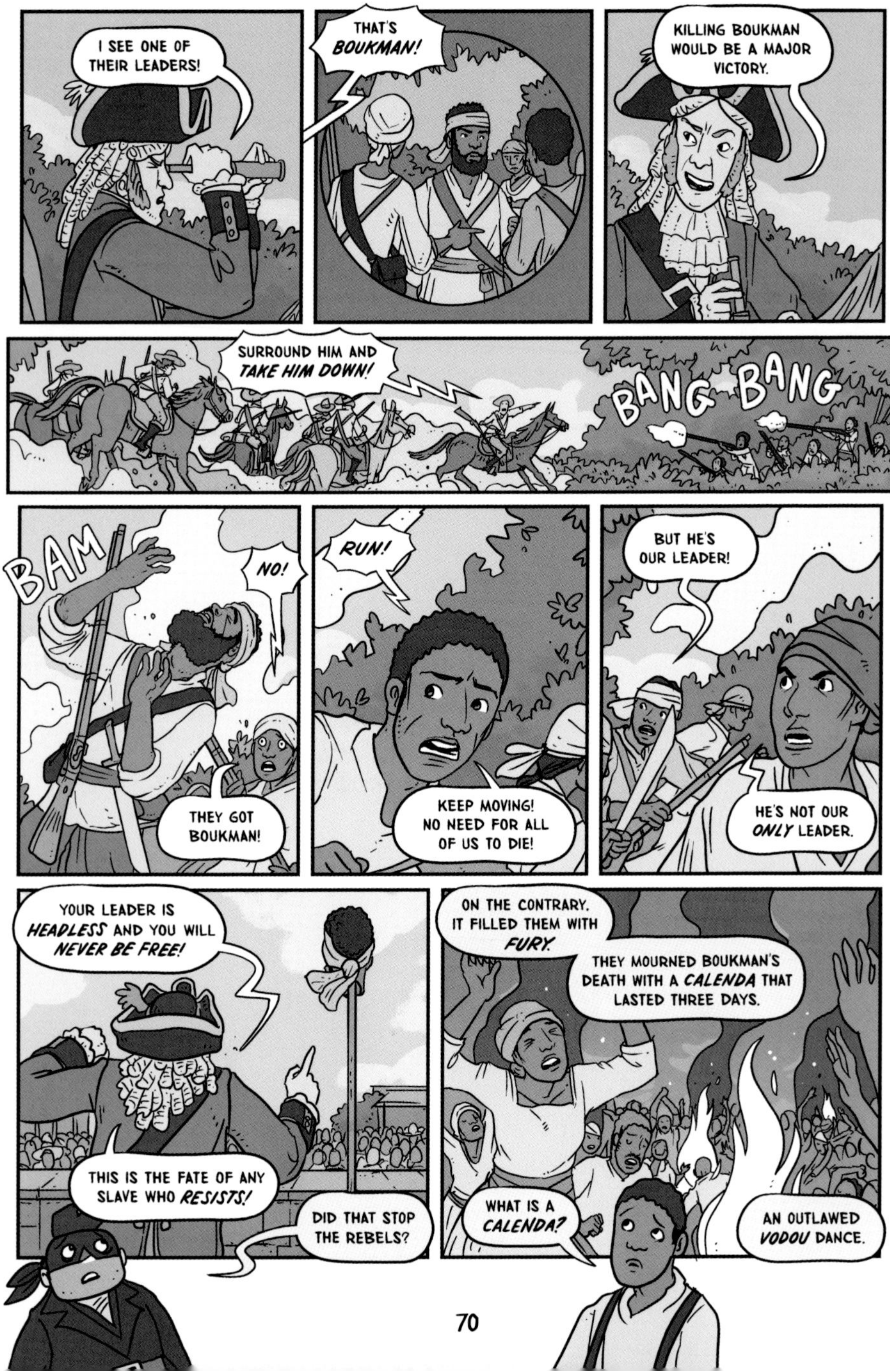
I SEE ONE OF THEIR LEADERS!
THAT'S *BOUKMAN!*
KILLING BOUKMAN WOULD BE A MAJOR VICTORY.
SURROUND HIM AND *TAKE HIM DOWN!*
BANG BANG
BAM
NO!
THEY GOT BOUKMAN!
RUN!
KEEP MOVING! NO NEED FOR ALL OF US TO DIE!
BUT HE'S OUR LEADER!
HE'S NOT OUR *ONLY* LEADER.
YOUR LEADER IS *HEADLESS* AND YOU WILL *NEVER BE FREE!*
THIS IS THE FATE OF ANY SLAVE WHO *RESISTS!*
DID THAT STOP THE REBELS?
ON THE CONTRARY. IT FILLED THEM WITH *FURY.*
THEY MOURNED BOUKMAN'S DEATH WITH A *CALENDA* THAT LASTED THREE DAYS.
WHAT IS A *CALENDA?*
AN OUTLAWED *VODOU* DANCE.

CHAPTER 7

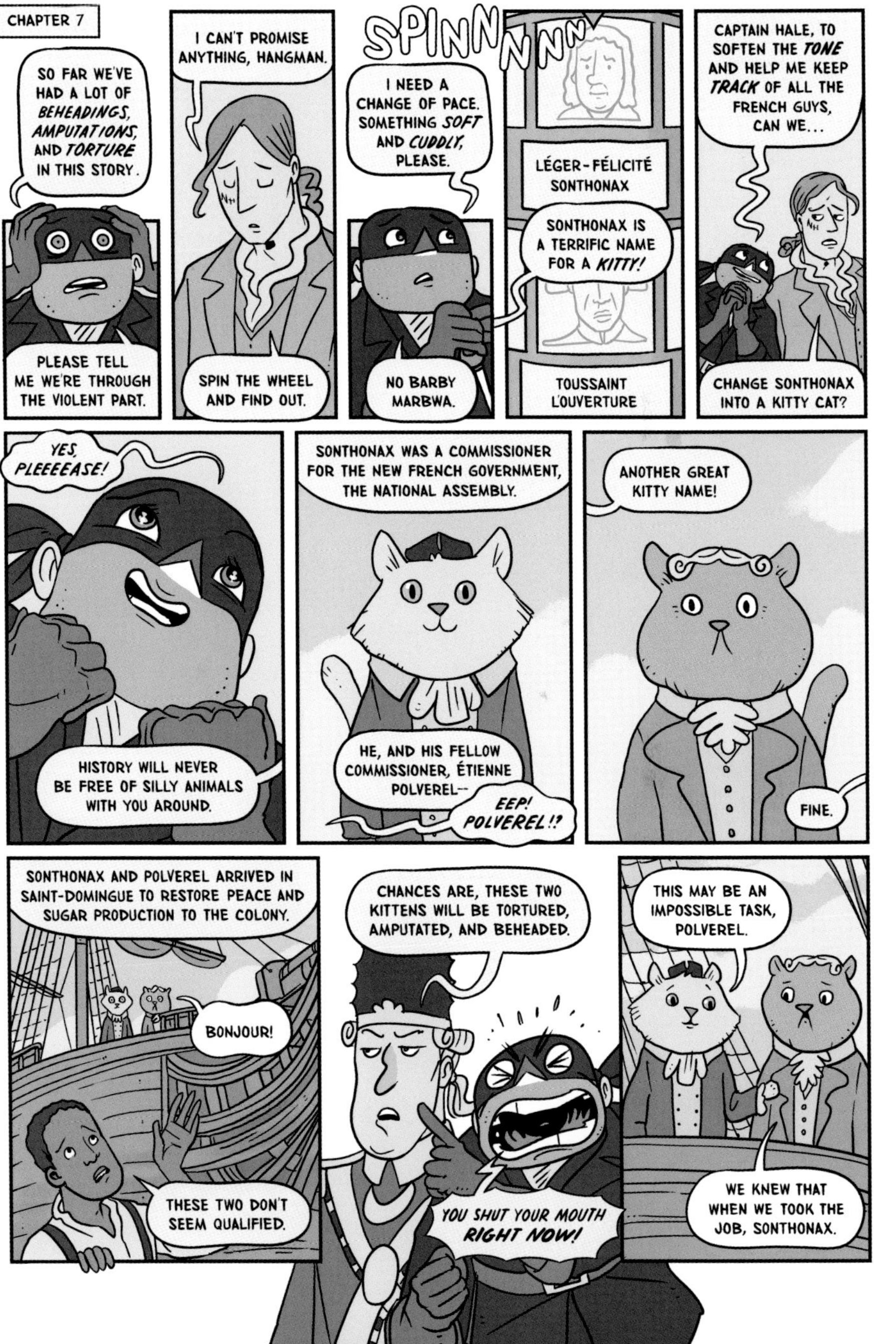
SO FAR WE'VE HAD A LOT OF BEHEADINGS, AMPUTATIONS, AND TORTURE IN THIS STORY.
PLEASE TELL ME WE'RE THROUGH THE VIOLENT PART.
I CAN'T PROMISE ANYTHING, HANGMAN.
SPIN THE WHEEL AND FIND OUT.
SPINNNNNN
I NEED A CHANGE OF PACE. SOMETHING SOFT AND CUDDLY, PLEASE.
NO BARBY MARBWA.
LÉGER-FÉLICITÉ SONTHONAX
SONTHONAX IS A TERRIFIC NAME FOR A KITTY!
TOUSSAINT L'OUVERTURE
CAPTAIN HALE, TO SOFTEN THE TONE AND HELP ME KEEP TRACK OF ALL THE FRENCH GUYS, CAN WE...
CHANGE SONTHONAX INTO A KITTY CAT?
YES, PLEEEEASE!
HISTORY WILL NEVER BE FREE OF SILLY ANIMALS WITH YOU AROUND.
SONTHONAX WAS A COMMISSIONER FOR THE NEW FRENCH GOVERNMENT, THE NATIONAL ASSEMBLY.
HE, AND HIS FELLOW COMMISSIONER, ÉTIENNE POLVEREL--
EEP! POLVEREL!?
ANOTHER GREAT KITTY NAME!
FINE.
SONTHONAX AND POLVEREL ARRIVED IN SAINT-DOMINGUE TO RESTORE PEACE AND SUGAR PRODUCTION TO THE COLONY.
BONJOUR!
THESE TWO DON'T SEEM QUALIFIED.
CHANCES ARE, THESE TWO KITTENS WILL BE TORTURED, AMPUTATED, AND BEHEADED.
YOU SHUT YOUR MOUTH RIGHT NOW!
THIS MAY BE AN IMPOSSIBLE TASK, POLVEREL.
WE KNEW THAT WHEN WE TOOK THE JOB, SONTHONAX.

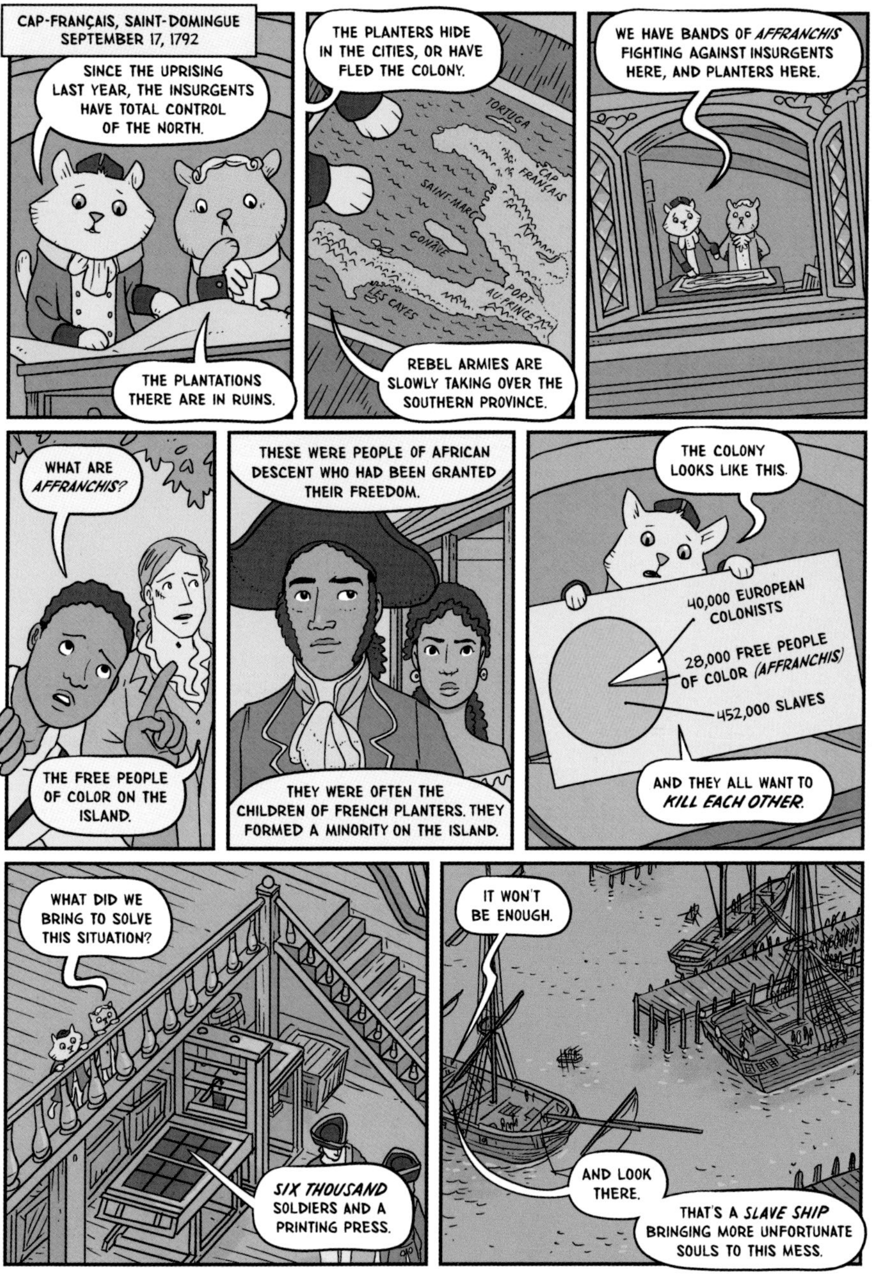
CAP-FRANÇAIS, SAINT-DOMINGUE
SEPTEMBER 17, 1792
SINCE THE UPRISING LAST YEAR, THE INSURGENTS HAVE TOTAL CONTROL OF THE NORTH.
THE PLANTATIONS THERE ARE IN RUINS.
THE PLANTERS HIDE IN THE CITIES, OR HAVE FLED THE COLONY.
TORTUGA
CAP FRANÇAIS
SAINT-MARC
GONÂVE
PORT AU PRINCE
LES CAYES
REBEL ARMIES ARE SLOWLY TAKING OVER THE SOUTHERN PROVINCE.
WE HAVE BANDS OF *AFFRANCHIS* FIGHTING AGAINST INSURGENTS HERE, AND PLANTERS HERE.
WHAT ARE *AFFRANCHIS*?
THE FREE PEOPLE OF COLOR ON THE ISLAND.
THESE WERE PEOPLE OF AFRICAN DESCENT WHO HAD BEEN GRANTED THEIR FREEDOM.
THEY WERE OFTEN THE CHILDREN OF FRENCH PLANTERS. THEY FORMED A MINORITY ON THE ISLAND.
THE COLONY LOOKS LIKE THIS.
40,000 EUROPEAN COLONISTS
28,000 FREE PEOPLE OF COLOR *(AFFRANCHIS)*
452,000 SLAVES
AND THEY ALL WANT TO ***KILL EACH OTHER***.
WHAT DID WE BRING TO SOLVE THIS SITUATION?
SIX THOUSAND SOLDIERS AND A PRINTING PRESS.
IT WON'T BE ENOUGH.
AND LOOK THERE.
THAT'S A ***SLAVE SHIP*** BRINGING MORE UNFORTUNATE SOULS TO THIS MESS.

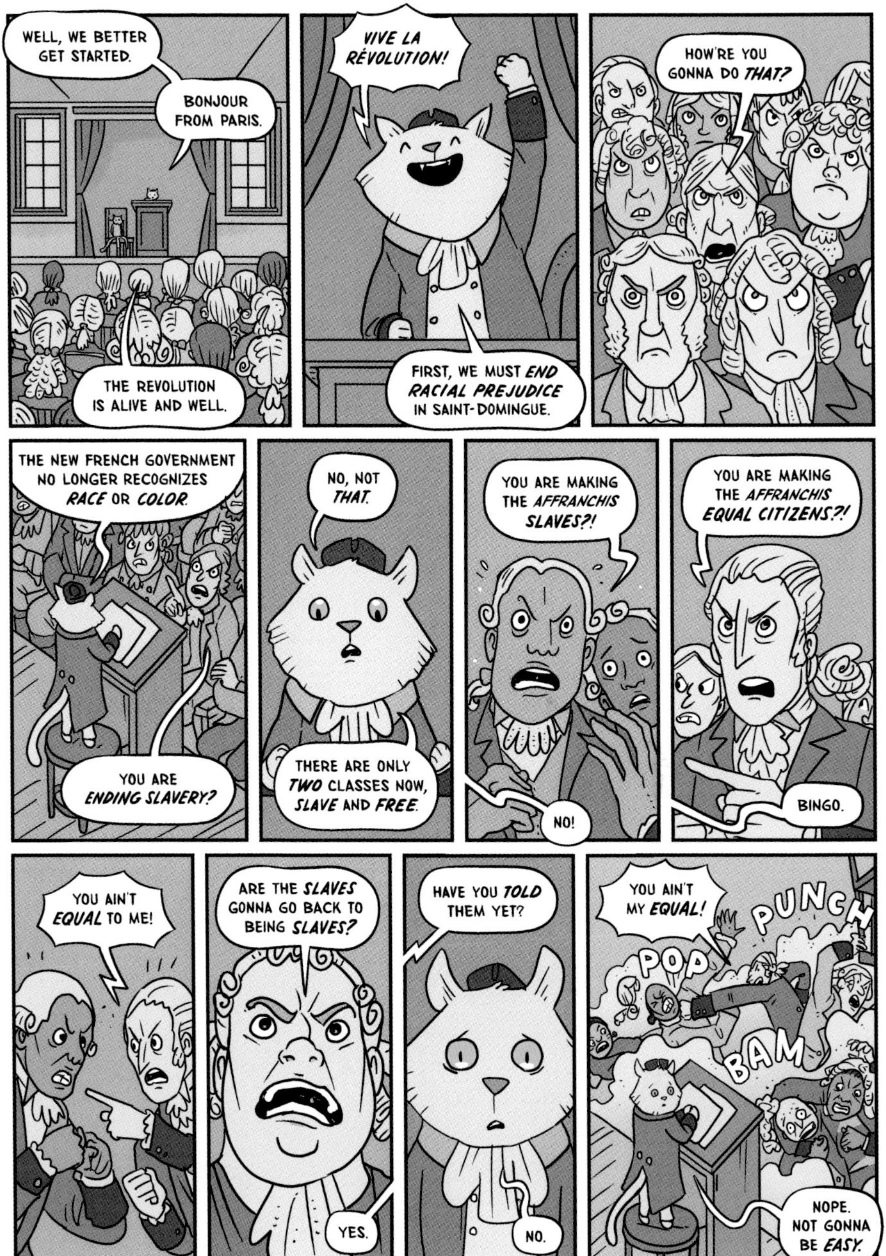
WELL, WE BETTER GET STARTED.
BONJOUR FROM PARIS.
THE REVOLUTION IS ALIVE AND WELL.
VIVE LA RÉVOLUTION!
FIRST, WE MUST END RACIAL PREJUDICE IN SAINT-DOMINGUE.
HOW'RE YOU GONNA DO THAT?
THE NEW FRENCH GOVERNMENT NO LONGER RECOGNIZES RACE OR COLOR.
YOU ARE ENDING SLAVERY?
NO, NOT THAT.
THERE ARE ONLY TWO CLASSES NOW, SLAVE AND FREE.
YOU ARE MAKING THE AFFRANCHIS SLAVES?!
NO!
YOU ARE MAKING THE AFFRANCHIS EQUAL CITIZENS?!
BINGO.
YOU AIN'T EQUAL TO ME!
ARE THE SLAVES GONNA GO BACK TO BEING SLAVES?
YES.
HAVE YOU TOLD THEM YET?
NO.
YOU AIN'T MY EQUAL!
PUNCH
POP
BAM
NOPE. NOT GONNA BE EASY.

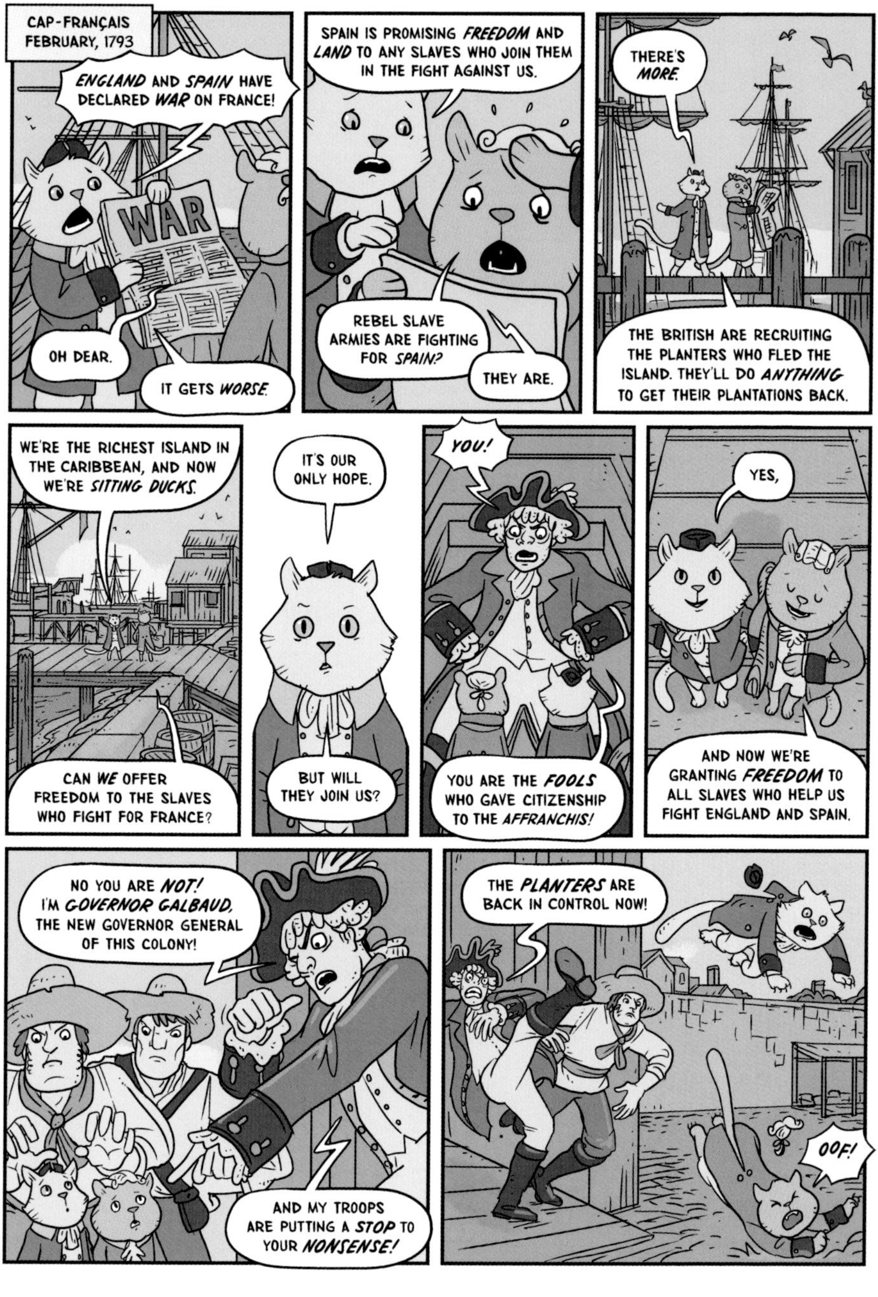
CAP-FRANÇAIS
FEBRUARY, 1793
ENGLAND AND SPAIN HAVE DECLARED WAR ON FRANCE!
WAR
OH DEAR.
IT GETS WORSE.
SPAIN IS PROMISING FREEDOM AND LAND TO ANY SLAVES WHO JOIN THEM IN THE FIGHT AGAINST US.
REBEL SLAVE ARMIES ARE FIGHTING FOR SPAIN?
THEY ARE.
THERE'S MORE.
THE BRITISH ARE RECRUITING THE PLANTERS WHO FLED THE ISLAND. THEY'LL DO ANYTHING TO GET THEIR PLANTATIONS BACK.
WE'RE THE RICHEST ISLAND IN THE CARIBBEAN, AND NOW WE'RE SITTING DUCKS.
CAN WE OFFER FREEDOM TO THE SLAVES WHO FIGHT FOR FRANCE?
IT'S OUR ONLY HOPE.
BUT WILL THEY JOIN US?
YOU!
YOU ARE THE FOOLS WHO GAVE CITIZENSHIP TO THE AFFRANCHIS!
YES,
AND NOW WE'RE GRANTING FREEDOM TO ALL SLAVES WHO HELP US FIGHT ENGLAND AND SPAIN.
NO YOU ARE NOT! I'M GOVERNOR GALBAUD, THE NEW GOVERNOR GENERAL OF THIS COLONY!
AND MY TROOPS ARE PUTTING A STOP TO YOUR NONSENSE!
THE PLANTERS ARE BACK IN CONTROL NOW!
OOF!

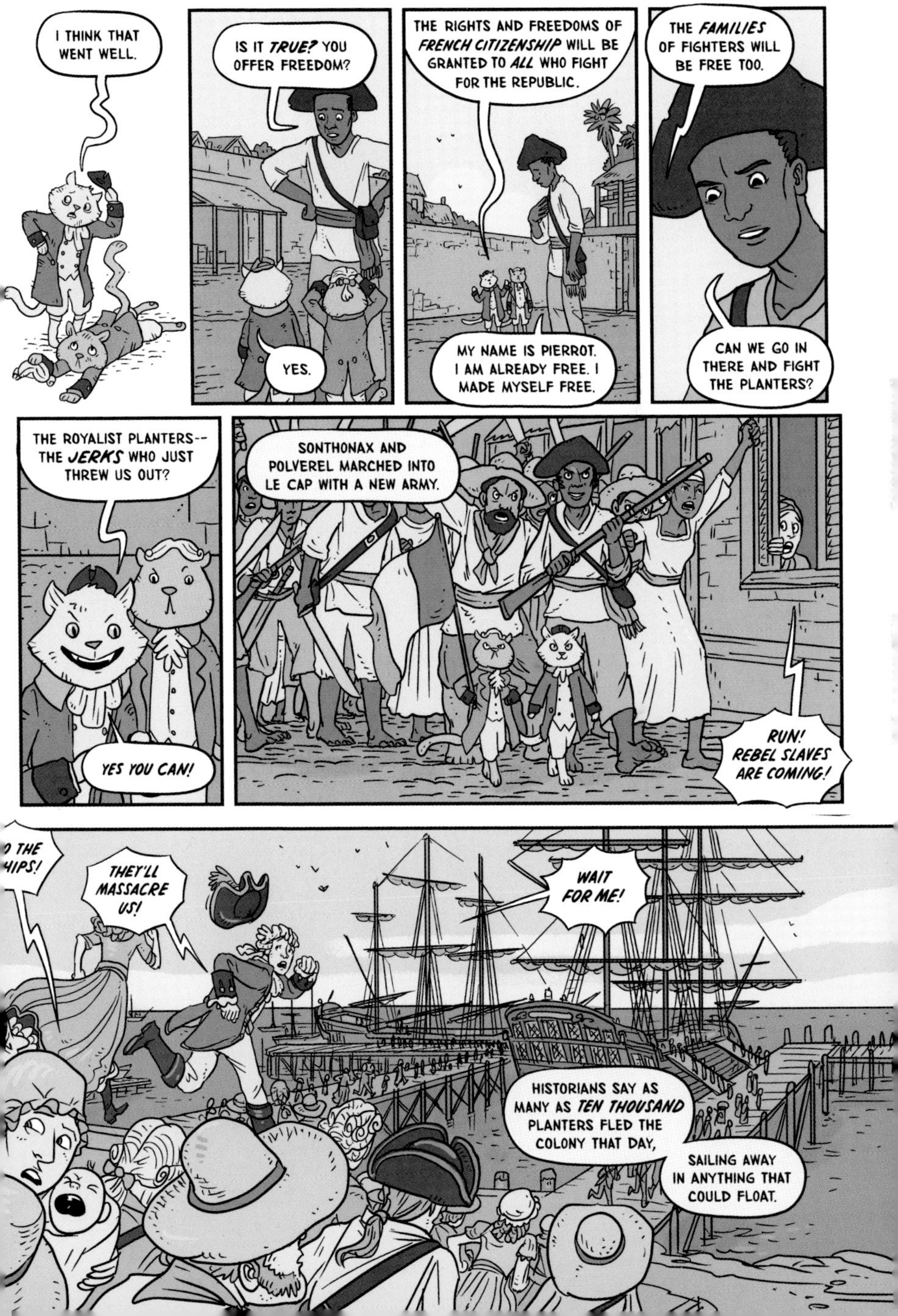
I THINK THAT WENT WELL.
IS IT TRUE? YOU OFFER FREEDOM?
YES.
THE RIGHTS AND FREEDOMS OF FRENCH CITIZENSHIP WILL BE GRANTED TO ALL WHO FIGHT FOR THE REPUBLIC.
MY NAME IS PIERROT. I AM ALREADY FREE. I MADE MYSELF FREE.
THE FAMILIES OF FIGHTERS WILL BE FREE TOO.
CAN WE GO IN THERE AND FIGHT THE PLANTERS?
THE ROYALIST PLANTERS-- THE JERKS WHO JUST THREW US OUT?
YES YOU CAN!
SONTHONAX AND POLVEREL MARCHED INTO LE CAP WITH A NEW ARMY.
RUN! REBEL SLAVES ARE COMING!
THEY'LL MASSACRE US!
WAIT FOR ME!
HISTORIANS SAY AS MANY AS TEN THOUSAND PLANTERS FLED THE COLONY THAT DAY,
SAILING AWAY IN ANYTHING THAT COULD FLOAT.

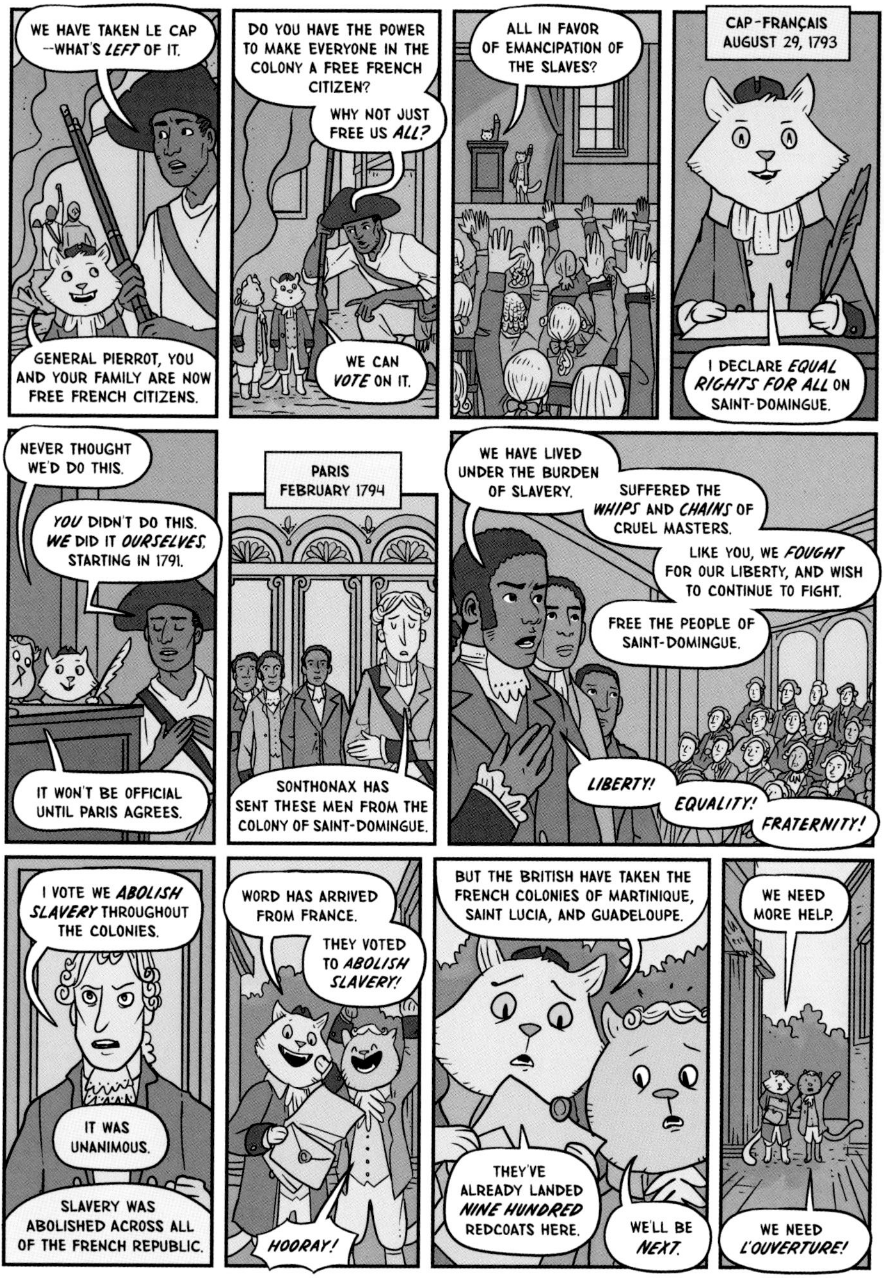
WE HAVE TAKEN LE CAP --WHAT'S *LEFT* OF IT.
GENERAL PIERROT, YOU AND YOUR FAMILY ARE NOW FREE FRENCH CITIZENS.
DO YOU HAVE THE POWER TO MAKE EVERYONE IN THE COLONY A FREE FRENCH CITIZEN?
WHY NOT JUST FREE US *ALL?*
WE CAN *VOTE* ON IT.
ALL IN FAVOR OF EMANCIPATION OF THE SLAVES?
CAP-FRANÇAIS AUGUST 29, 1793
I DECLARE *EQUAL RIGHTS FOR ALL* ON SAINT-DOMINGUE.
NEVER THOUGHT WE'D DO THIS.
YOU DIDN'T DO THIS. *WE* DID IT *OURSELVES,* STARTING IN 1791.
IT WON'T BE OFFICIAL UNTIL PARIS AGREES.
PARIS FEBRUARY 1794
SONTHONAX HAS SENT THESE MEN FROM THE COLONY OF SAINT-DOMINGUE.
WE HAVE LIVED UNDER THE BURDEN OF SLAVERY.
SUFFERED THE *WHIPS* AND *CHAINS* OF CRUEL MASTERS.
LIKE YOU, WE *FOUGHT* FOR OUR LIBERTY, AND WISH TO CONTINUE TO FIGHT.
FREE THE PEOPLE OF SAINT-DOMINGUE.
LIBERTY!
EQUALITY!
FRATERNITY!
I VOTE WE *ABOLISH SLAVERY* THROUGHOUT THE COLONIES.
IT WAS UNANIMOUS.
SLAVERY WAS ABOLISHED ACROSS ALL OF THE FRENCH REPUBLIC.
WORD HAS ARRIVED FROM FRANCE.
THEY VOTED TO *ABOLISH SLAVERY!*
HOORAY!
BUT THE BRITISH HAVE TAKEN THE FRENCH COLONIES OF MARTINIQUE, SAINT LUCIA, AND GUADELOUPE.
THEY'VE ALREADY LANDED *NINE HUNDRED* REDCOATS HERE.
WE'LL BE *NEXT.*
WE NEED MORE HELP.
WE NEED *L'OUVERTURE!*

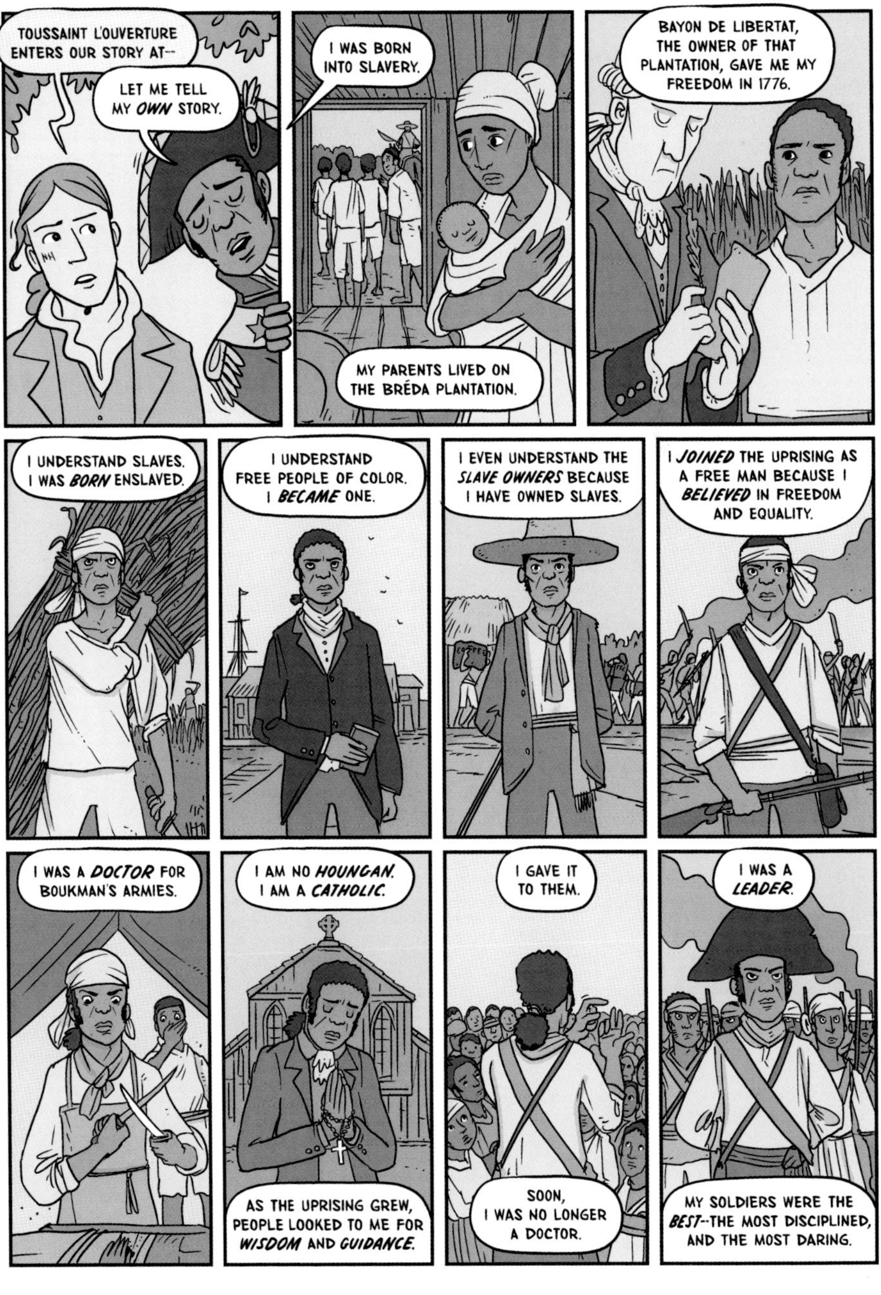
TOUSSAINT L'OUVERTURE ENTERS OUR STORY AT--
LET ME TELL MY *OWN* STORY.
I WAS BORN INTO SLAVERY.
MY PARENTS LIVED ON THE BRÉDA PLANTATION.
BAYON DE LIBERTAT, THE OWNER OF THAT PLANTATION, GAVE ME MY FREEDOM IN 1776.
I UNDERSTAND SLAVES. I WAS *BORN* ENSLAVED.
I UNDERSTAND FREE PEOPLE OF COLOR. I *BECAME* ONE.
I EVEN UNDERSTAND THE *SLAVE OWNERS* BECAUSE I HAVE OWNED SLAVES.
I *JOINED* THE UPRISING AS A FREE MAN BECAUSE I *BELIEVED* IN FREEDOM AND EQUALITY.
I WAS A *DOCTOR* FOR BOUKMAN'S ARMIES.
I AM NO *HOUNGAN*. I AM A *CATHOLIC*.
AS THE UPRISING GREW, PEOPLE LOOKED TO ME FOR *WISDOM* AND *GUIDANCE*.
I GAVE IT TO THEM.
SOON, I WAS NO LONGER A DOCTOR.
I WAS A *LEADER*.
MY SOLDIERS WERE THE *BEST*--THE MOST DISCIPLINED, AND THE MOST DARING.

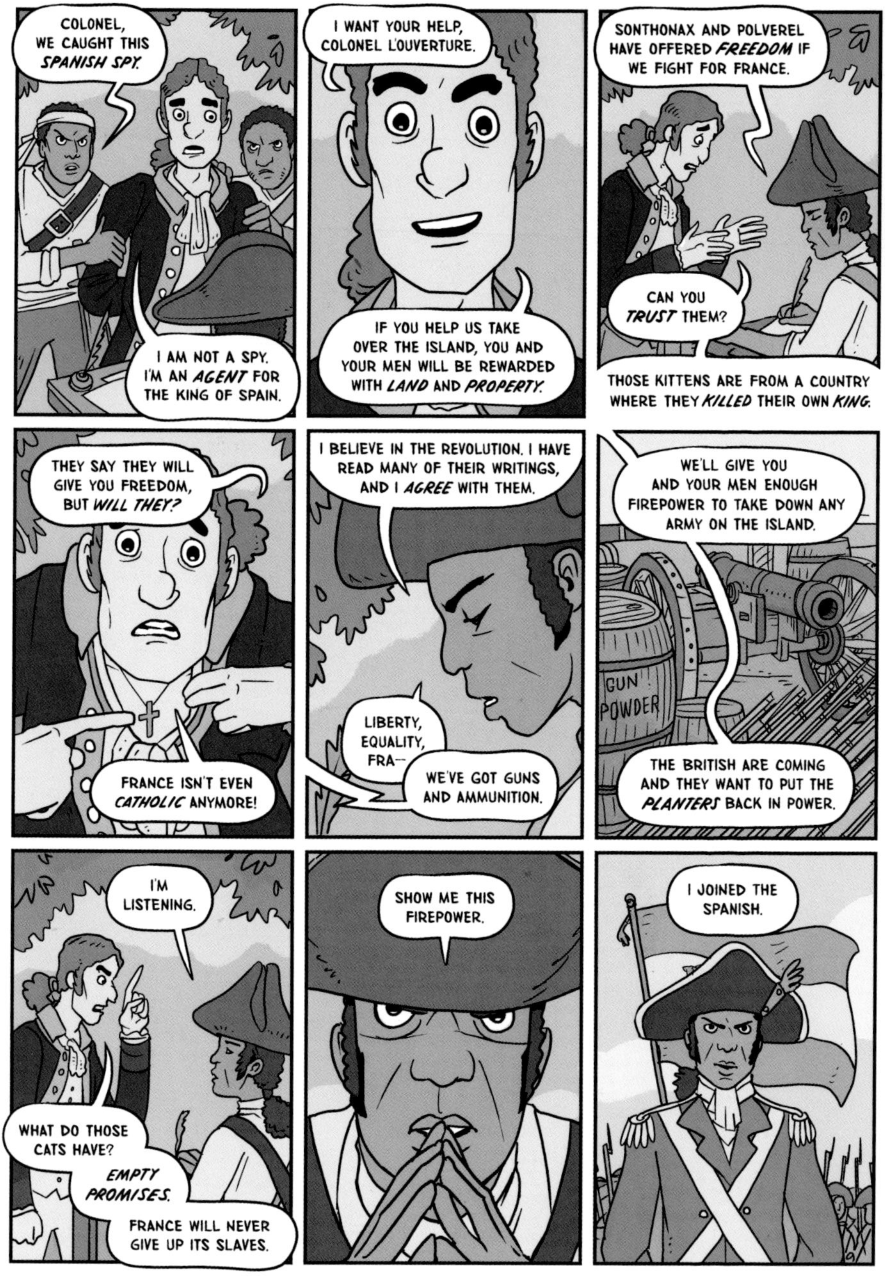
COLONEL, WE CAUGHT THIS SPANISH SPY.
I AM NOT A SPY. I'M AN AGENT FOR THE KING OF SPAIN.
I WANT YOUR HELP, COLONEL L'OUVERTURE.
IF YOU HELP US TAKE OVER THE ISLAND, YOU AND YOUR MEN WILL BE REWARDED WITH LAND AND PROPERTY.
SONTHONAX AND POLVEREL HAVE OFFERED FREEDOM IF WE FIGHT FOR FRANCE.
CAN YOU TRUST THEM?
THOSE KITTENS ARE FROM A COUNTRY WHERE THEY KILLED THEIR OWN KING.
THEY SAY THEY WILL GIVE YOU FREEDOM, BUT WILL THEY?
FRANCE ISN'T EVEN CATHOLIC ANYMORE!
I BELIEVE IN THE REVOLUTION. I HAVE READ MANY OF THEIR WRITINGS, AND I AGREE WITH THEM.
LIBERTY, EQUALITY, FRA--
WE'VE GOT GUNS AND AMMUNITION.
WE'LL GIVE YOU AND YOUR MEN ENOUGH FIREPOWER TO TAKE DOWN ANY ARMY ON THE ISLAND.
GUN POWDER
THE BRITISH ARE COMING AND THEY WANT TO PUT THE PLANTERS BACK IN POWER.
I'M LISTENING.
WHAT DO THOSE CATS HAVE?
EMPTY PROMISES.
FRANCE WILL NEVER GIVE UP ITS SLAVES.
SHOW ME THIS FIREPOWER.
I JOINED THE SPANISH.

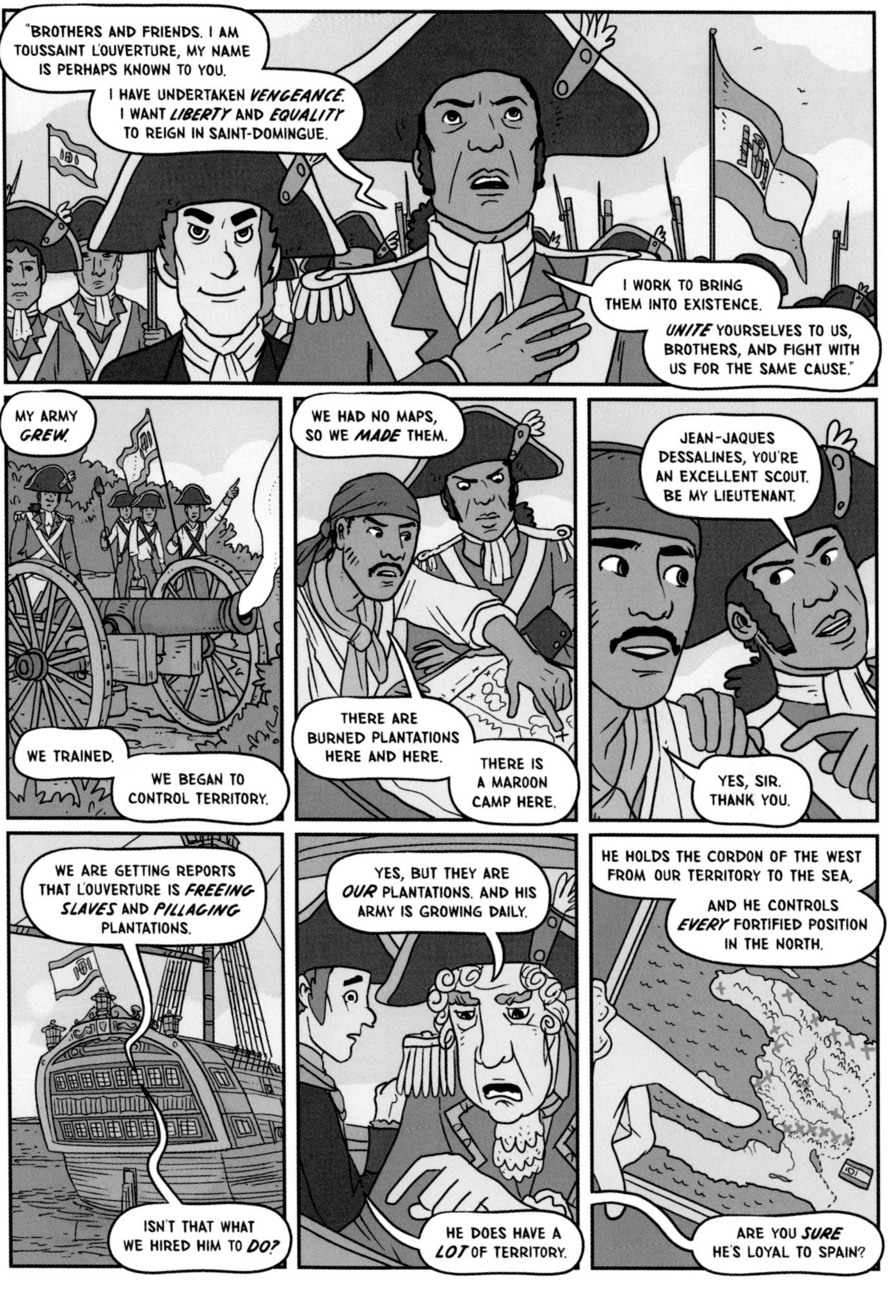
"BROTHERS AND FRIENDS. I AM TOUSSAINT L'OUVERTURE, MY NAME IS PERHAPS KNOWN TO YOU.
I HAVE UNDERTAKEN *VENGEANCE*. I WANT *LIBERTY* AND *EQUALITY* TO REIGN IN SAINT-DOMINGUE.
I WORK TO BRING THEM INTO EXISTENCE.
UNITE YOURSELVES TO US, BROTHERS, AND FIGHT WITH US FOR THE SAME CAUSE."
MY ARMY *GREW*.
WE TRAINED.
WE BEGAN TO CONTROL TERRITORY.
WE HAD NO MAPS, SO WE *MADE* THEM.
THERE ARE BURNED PLANTATIONS HERE AND HERE.
THERE IS A MAROON CAMP HERE.
JEAN-JAQUES DESSALINES, YOU'RE AN EXCELLENT SCOUT. BE MY LIEUTENANT.
YES, SIR. THANK YOU.
WE ARE GETTING REPORTS THAT L'OUVERTURE IS *FREEING SLAVES* AND *PILLAGING* PLANTATIONS.
ISN'T THAT WHAT WE HIRED HIM TO *DO*?
YES, BUT THEY ARE *OUR* PLANTATIONS. AND HIS ARMY IS GROWING DAILY.
HE DOES HAVE A *LOT* OF TERRITORY.
HE HOLDS THE CORDON OF THE WEST FROM OUR TERRITORY TO THE SEA,
AND HE CONTROLS *EVERY* FORTIFIED POSITION IN THE NORTH.
ARE YOU *SURE* HE'S LOYAL TO SPAIN?

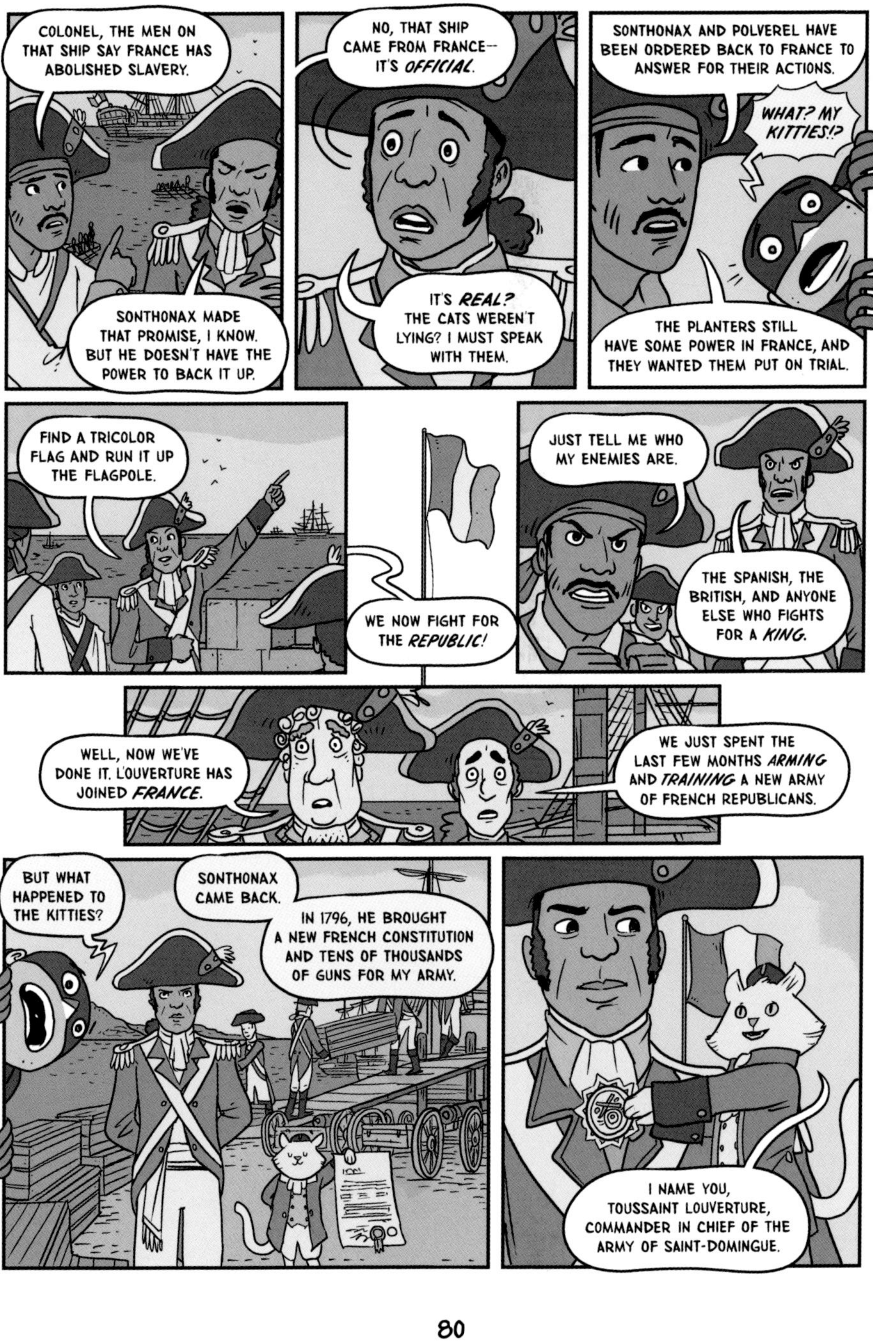
COLONEL, THE MEN ON THAT SHIP SAY FRANCE HAS ABOLISHED SLAVERY.
SONTHONAX MADE THAT PROMISE, I KNOW. BUT HE DOESN'T HAVE THE POWER TO BACK IT UP.
NO, THAT SHIP CAME FROM FRANCE-- IT'S *OFFICIAL*.
IT'S *REAL?* THE CATS WEREN'T LYING? I MUST SPEAK WITH THEM.
SONTHONAX AND POLVEREL HAVE BEEN ORDERED BACK TO FRANCE TO ANSWER FOR THEIR ACTIONS.
WHAT? MY KITTIES!?
THE PLANTERS STILL HAVE SOME POWER IN FRANCE, AND THEY WANTED THEM PUT ON TRIAL.
FIND A TRICOLOR FLAG AND RUN IT UP THE FLAGPOLE.
WE NOW FIGHT FOR THE *REPUBLIC!*
JUST TELL ME WHO MY ENEMIES ARE.
THE SPANISH, THE BRITISH, AND ANYONE ELSE WHO FIGHTS FOR A *KING*.
WELL, NOW WE'VE DONE IT. L'OUVERTURE HAS JOINED *FRANCE*.
WE JUST SPENT THE LAST FEW MONTHS *ARMING* AND *TRAINING* A NEW ARMY OF FRENCH REPUBLICANS.
BUT WHAT HAPPENED TO THE KITTIES?
SONTHONAX CAME BACK.
IN 1796, HE BROUGHT A NEW FRENCH CONSTITUTION AND TENS OF THOUSANDS OF GUNS FOR MY ARMY.
I NAME YOU, TOUSSAINT LOUVERTURE, COMMANDER IN CHIEF OF THE ARMY OF SAINT-DOMINGUE.

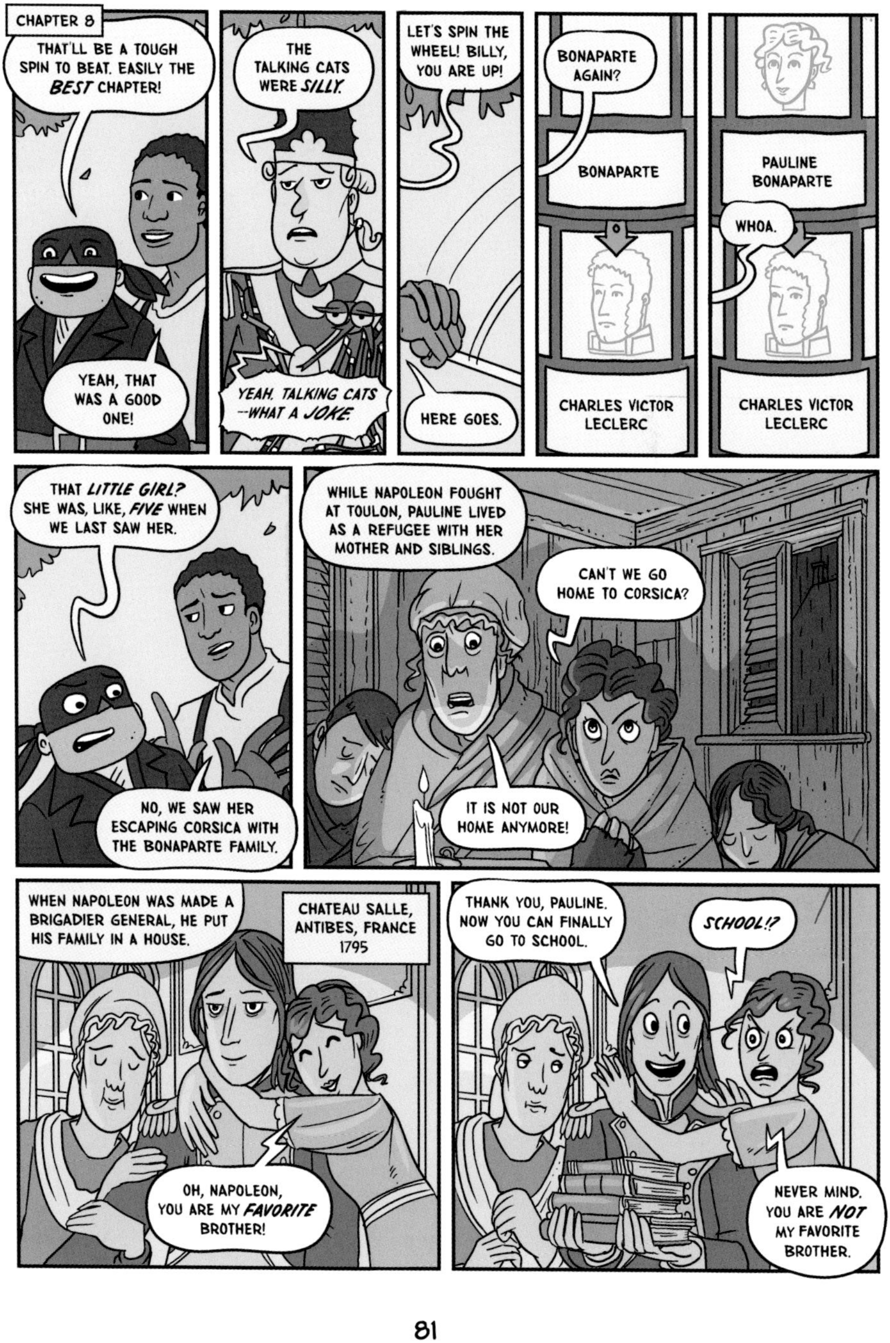
CHAPTER 8
THAT'LL BE A TOUGH SPIN TO BEAT. EASILY THE *BEST* CHAPTER!
YEAH, THAT WAS A GOOD ONE!
THE TALKING CATS WERE *SILLY.*
YEAH. TALKING CATS --WHAT A JOKE.
LET'S SPIN THE WHEEL! BILLY, YOU ARE UP!
HERE GOES.
BONAPARTE AGAIN?
BONAPARTE
CHARLES VICTOR LECLERC
PAULINE BONAPARTE
WHOA.
CHARLES VICTOR LECLERC
THAT *LITTLE GIRL?* SHE WAS, LIKE, *FIVE* WHEN WE LAST SAW HER.
NO, WE SAW HER ESCAPING CORSICA WITH THE BONAPARTE FAMILY.
WHILE NAPOLEON FOUGHT AT TOULON, PAULINE LIVED AS A REFUGEE WITH HER MOTHER AND SIBLINGS.
CAN'T WE GO HOME TO CORSICA?
IT IS NOT OUR HOME ANYMORE!
WHEN NAPOLEON WAS MADE A BRIGADIER GENERAL, HE PUT HIS FAMILY IN A HOUSE.
CHATEAU SALLE, ANTIBES, FRANCE 1795
OH, NAPOLEON, YOU ARE MY *FAVORITE* BROTHER!
THANK YOU, PAULINE. NOW YOU CAN FINALLY GO TO SCHOOL.
SCHOOL!?
NEVER MIND. YOU ARE *NOT* MY FAVORITE BROTHER.

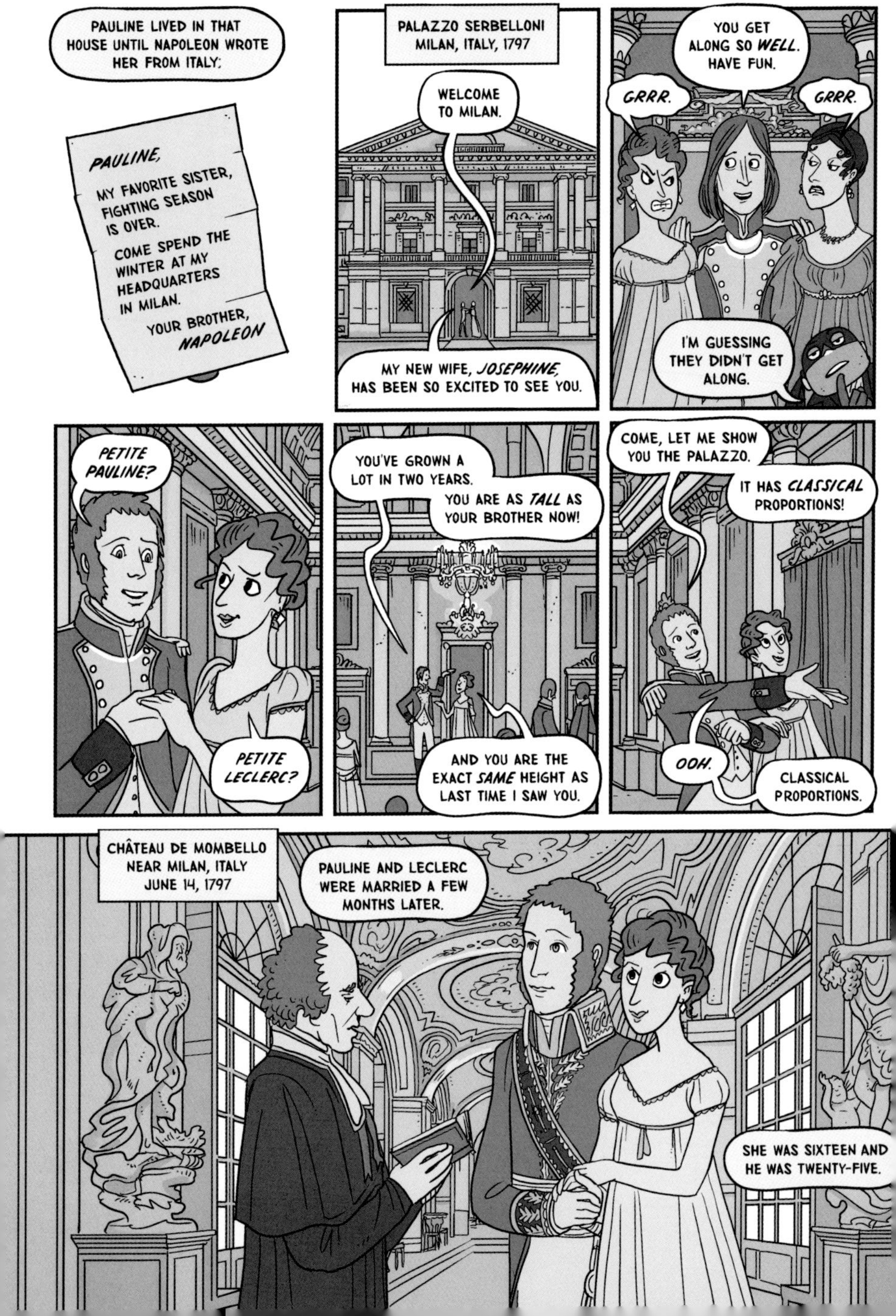
PAULINE LIVED IN THAT HOUSE UNTIL NAPOLEON WROTE HER FROM ITALY:
PAULINE,
MY FAVORITE SISTER, FIGHTING SEASON IS OVER.
COME SPEND THE WINTER AT MY HEADQUARTERS IN MILAN.
YOUR BROTHER, NAPOLEON
PALAZZO SERBELLONI MILAN, ITALY, 1797
WELCOME TO MILAN.
MY NEW WIFE, JOSEPHINE, HAS BEEN SO EXCITED TO SEE YOU.
GRRR.
YOU GET ALONG SO WELL. HAVE FUN.
GRRR.
I'M GUESSING THEY DIDN'T GET ALONG.
PETITE PAULINE?
PETITE LECLERC?
YOU'VE GROWN A LOT IN TWO YEARS.
YOU ARE AS TALL AS YOUR BROTHER NOW!
AND YOU ARE THE EXACT SAME HEIGHT AS LAST TIME I SAW YOU.
COME, LET ME SHOW YOU THE PALAZZO.
IT HAS CLASSICAL PROPORTIONS!
OOH.
CLASSICAL PROPORTIONS.
CHÂTEAU DE MOMBELLO NEAR MILAN, ITALY JUNE 14, 1797
PAULINE AND LECLERC WERE MARRIED A FEW MONTHS LATER.
SHE WAS SIXTEEN AND HE WAS TWENTY-FIVE.

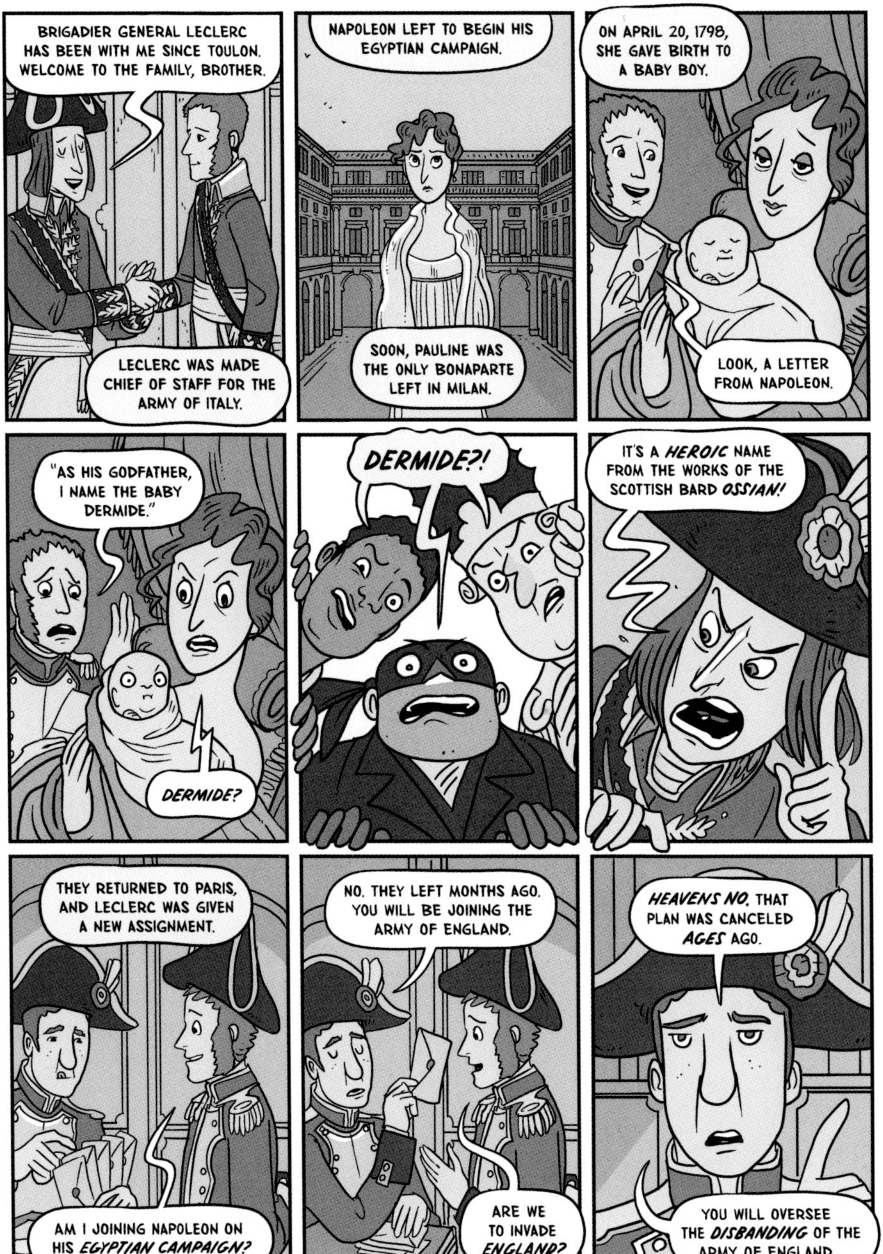
BRIGADIER GENERAL LECLERC HAS BEEN WITH ME SINCE TOULON. WELCOME TO THE FAMILY, BROTHER.
LECLERC WAS MADE CHIEF OF STAFF FOR THE ARMY OF ITALY.
NAPOLEON LEFT TO BEGIN HIS EGYPTIAN CAMPAIGN.
SOON, PAULINE WAS THE ONLY BONAPARTE LEFT IN MILAN.
ON APRIL 20, 1798, SHE GAVE BIRTH TO A BABY BOY.
LOOK, A LETTER FROM NAPOLEON.
"AS HIS GODFATHER, I NAME THE BABY DERMIDE."
DERMIDE?
DERMIDE?!
IT'S A *HEROIC* NAME FROM THE WORKS OF THE SCOTTISH BARD *OSSIAN!*
THEY RETURNED TO PARIS, AND LECLERC WAS GIVEN A NEW ASSIGNMENT.
AM I JOINING NAPOLEON ON HIS *EGYPTIAN CAMPAIGN?*
NO. THEY LEFT MONTHS AGO. YOU WILL BE JOINING THE ARMY OF ENGLAND.
ARE WE TO INVADE *ENGLAND?*
HEAVENS NO. THAT PLAN WAS CANCELED *AGES* AGO.
YOU WILL OVERSEE THE *DISBANDING* OF THE ARMY OF ENGLAND.

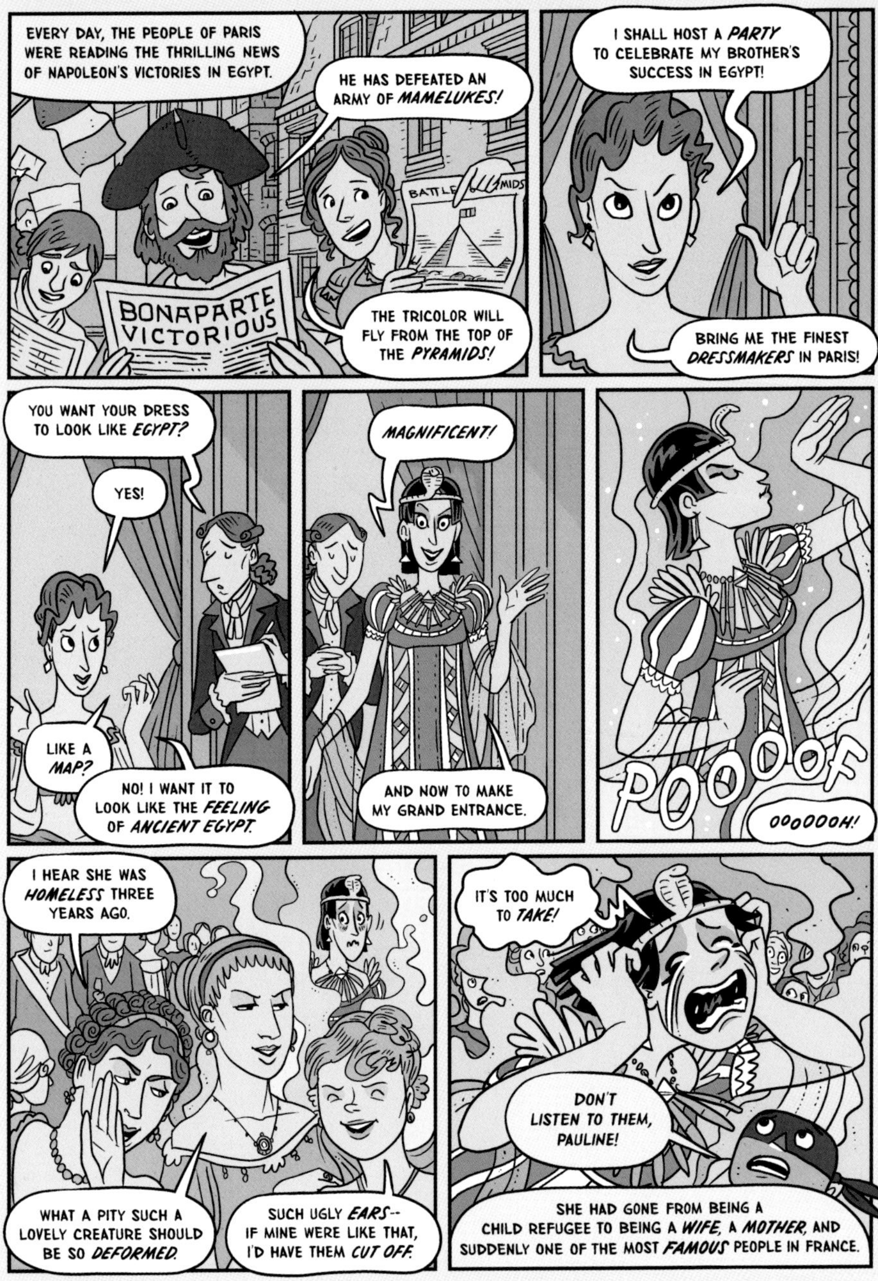
EVERY DAY, THE PEOPLE OF PARIS WERE READING THE THRILLING NEWS OF NAPOLEON'S VICTORIES IN EGYPT.
HE HAS DEFEATED AN ARMY OF *MAMELUKES!*
BONAPARTE VICTORIOUS
THE TRICOLOR WILL FLY FROM THE TOP OF THE *PYRAMIDS!*
I SHALL HOST A *PARTY* TO CELEBRATE MY BROTHER'S SUCCESS IN EGYPT!
BRING ME THE FINEST *DRESSMAKERS* IN PARIS!
YOU WANT YOUR DRESS TO LOOK LIKE *EGYPT?*
YES!
LIKE A *MAP?*
NO! I WANT IT TO LOOK LIKE THE *FEELING* OF *ANCIENT EGYPT.*
MAGNIFICENT!
AND NOW TO MAKE MY GRAND ENTRANCE.
POOOOF
OOOOOOH!
I HEAR SHE WAS *HOMELESS* THREE YEARS AGO.
WHAT A PITY SUCH A LOVELY CREATURE SHOULD BE SO *DEFORMED.*
SUCH UGLY *EARS*-- IF MINE WERE LIKE THAT, I'D HAVE THEM *CUT OFF.*
IT'S TOO MUCH TO *TAKE!*
DON'T LISTEN TO THEM, PAULINE!
SHE HAD GONE FROM BEING A CHILD REFUGEE TO BEING A *WIFE*, A *MOTHER*, AND SUDDENLY ONE OF THE MOST *FAMOUS* PEOPLE IN FRANCE.

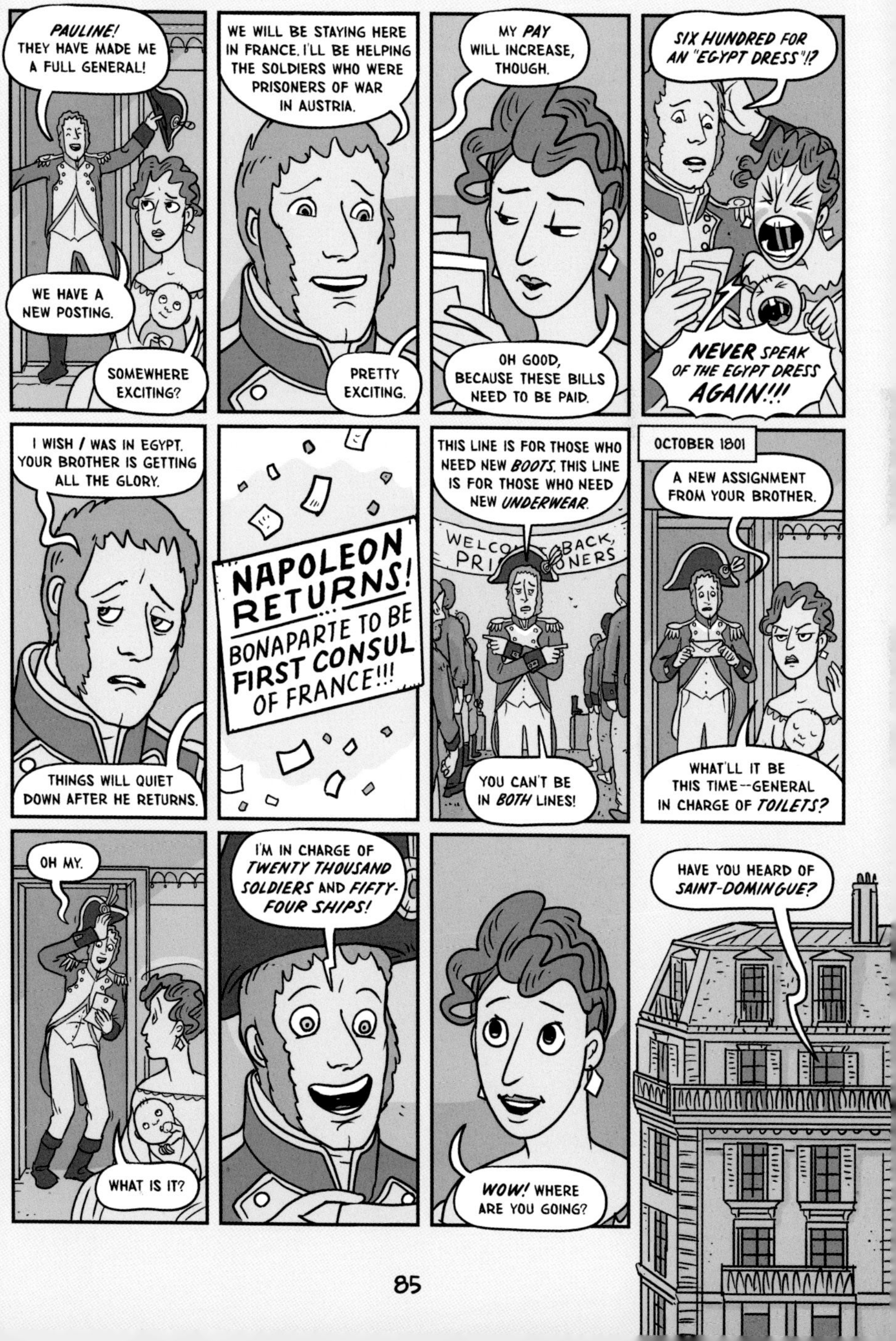
PAULINE! THEY HAVE MADE ME A FULL GENERAL!
WE HAVE A NEW POSTING.
SOMEWHERE EXCITING?
WE WILL BE STAYING HERE IN FRANCE. I'LL BE HELPING THE SOLDIERS WHO WERE PRISONERS OF WAR IN AUSTRIA.
PRETTY EXCITING.
MY PAY WILL INCREASE, THOUGH.
OH GOOD, BECAUSE THESE BILLS NEED TO BE PAID.
SIX HUNDRED FOR AN "EGYPT DRESS"!?
NEVER SPEAK OF THE EGYPT DRESS AGAIN!!!
I WISH I WAS IN EGYPT. YOUR BROTHER IS GETTING ALL THE GLORY.
THINGS WILL QUIET DOWN AFTER HE RETURNS.
NAPOLEON RETURNS!
BONAPARTE TO BE FIRST CONSUL OF FRANCE!!!
THIS LINE IS FOR THOSE WHO NEED NEW BOOTS. THIS LINE IS FOR THOSE WHO NEED NEW UNDERWEAR.
WELCOME BACK, PRISONERS
YOU CAN'T BE IN BOTH LINES!
OCTOBER 1801
A NEW ASSIGNMENT FROM YOUR BROTHER.
WHAT'LL IT BE THIS TIME--GENERAL IN CHARGE OF TOILETS?
OH MY.
WHAT IS IT?
I'M IN CHARGE OF TWENTY THOUSAND SOLDIERS AND FIFTY-FOUR SHIPS!
WOW! WHERE ARE YOU GOING?
HAVE YOU HEARD OF SAINT-DOMINGUE?

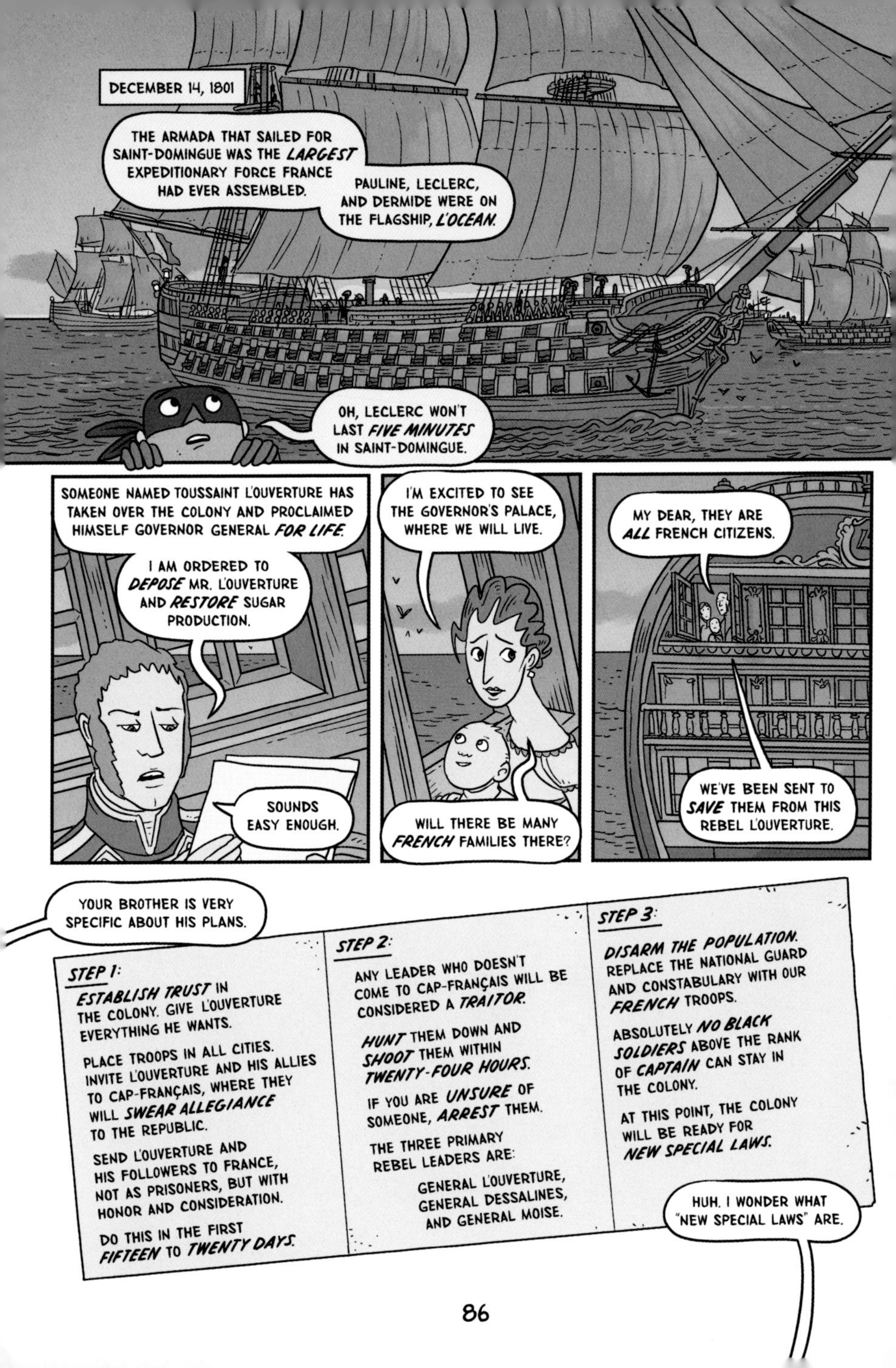

DECEMBER 14, 1801
THE ARMADA THAT SAILED FOR SAINT-DOMINGUE WAS THE LARGEST EXPEDITIONARY FORCE FRANCE HAD EVER ASSEMBLED.
PAULINE, LECLERC, AND DERMIDE WERE ON THE FLAGSHIP, L'OCEAN.
OH, LECLERC WON'T LAST FIVE MINUTES IN SAINT-DOMINGUE.
SOMEONE NAMED TOUSSAINT L'OUVERTURE HAS TAKEN OVER THE COLONY AND PROCLAIMED HIMSELF GOVERNOR GENERAL FOR LIFE.
I AM ORDERED TO DEPOSE MR. L'OUVERTURE AND RESTORE SUGAR PRODUCTION.
SOUNDS EASY ENOUGH.
I'M EXCITED TO SEE THE GOVERNOR'S PALACE, WHERE WE WILL LIVE.
WILL THERE BE MANY FRENCH FAMILIES THERE?
MY DEAR, THEY ARE ALL FRENCH CITIZENS.
WE'VE BEEN SENT TO SAVE THEM FROM THIS REBEL L'OUVERTURE.
YOUR BROTHER IS VERY SPECIFIC ABOUT HIS PLANS.
STEP 1:
ESTABLISH TRUST IN THE COLONY. GIVE L'OUVERTURE EVERYTHING HE WANTS.
PLACE TROOPS IN ALL CITIES. INVITE L'OUVERTURE AND HIS ALLIES TO CAP-FRANÇAIS, WHERE THEY WILL SWEAR ALLEGIANCE TO THE REPUBLIC.
SEND L'OUVERTURE AND HIS FOLLOWERS TO FRANCE, NOT AS PRISONERS, BUT WITH HONOR AND CONSIDERATION.
DO THIS IN THE FIRST FIFTEEN TO TWENTY DAYS.
STEP 2:
ANY LEADER WHO DOESN'T COME TO CAP-FRANÇAIS WILL BE CONSIDERED A TRAITOR.
HUNT THEM DOWN AND SHOOT THEM WITHIN TWENTY-FOUR HOURS.
IF YOU ARE UNSURE OF SOMEONE, ARREST THEM.
THE THREE PRIMARY REBEL LEADERS ARE:
GENERAL L'OUVERTURE, GENERAL DESSALINES, AND GENERAL MOISE.
STEP 3:
DISARM THE POPULATION. REPLACE THE NATIONAL GUARD AND CONSTABULARY WITH OUR FRENCH TROOPS.
ABSOLUTELY NO BLACK SOLDIERS ABOVE THE RANK OF CAPTAIN CAN STAY IN THE COLONY.
AT THIS POINT, THE COLONY WILL BE READY FOR NEW SPECIAL LAWS.
HUH. I WONDER WHAT "NEW SPECIAL LAWS" ARE.

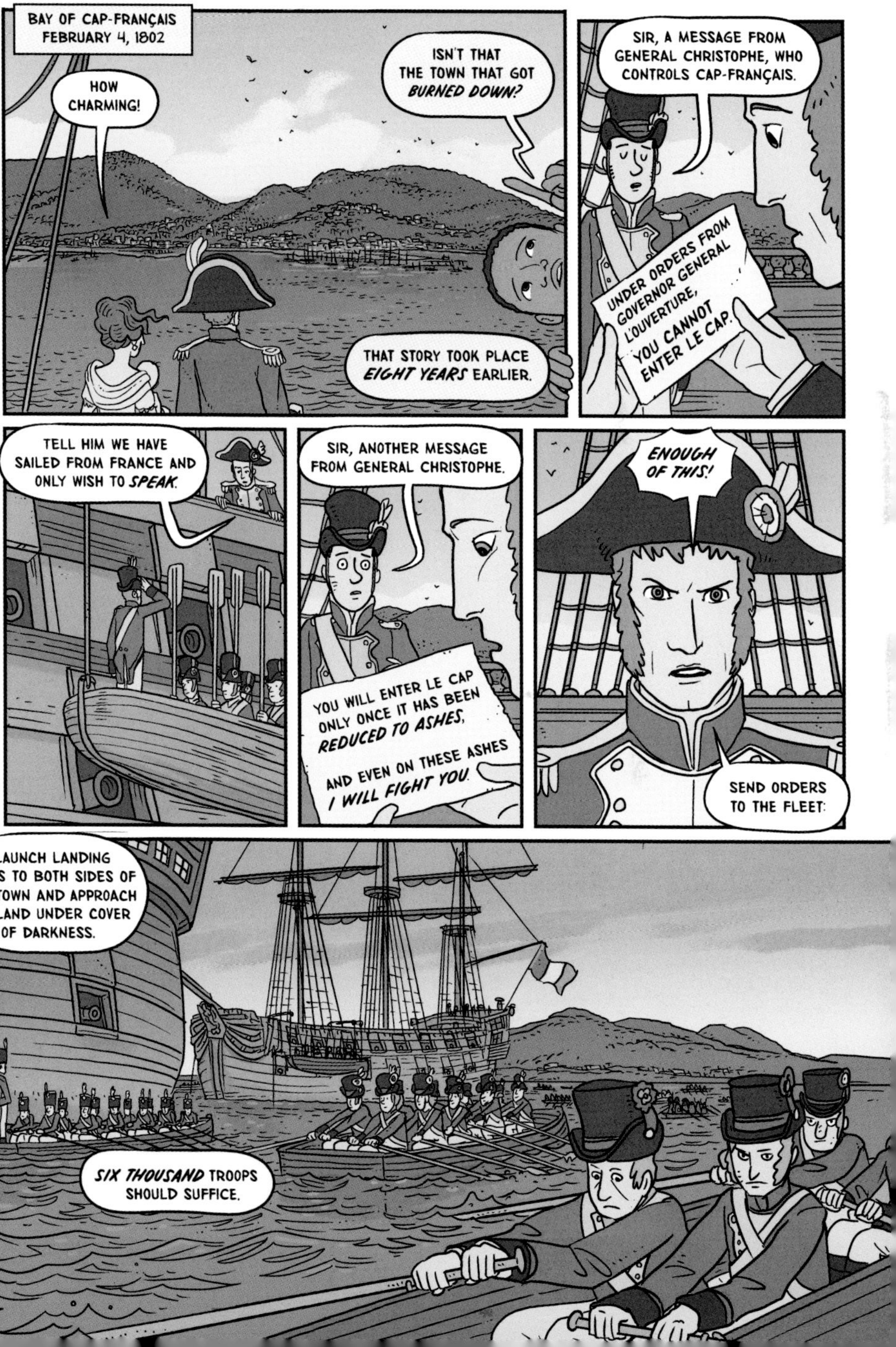

BAY OF CAP-FRANÇAIS
FEBRUARY 4, 1802
HOW CHARMING!
ISN'T THAT THE TOWN THAT GOT *BURNED DOWN?*
THAT STORY TOOK PLACE *EIGHT YEARS* EARLIER.
SIR, A MESSAGE FROM GENERAL CHRISTOPHE, WHO CONTROLS CAP-FRANÇAIS.
UNDER ORDERS FROM GOVERNOR GENERAL L'OUVERTURE, YOU CANNOT ENTER LE CAP.
TELL HIM WE HAVE SAILED FROM FRANCE AND ONLY WISH TO *SPEAK*.
SIR, ANOTHER MESSAGE FROM GENERAL CHRISTOPHE.
YOU WILL ENTER LE CAP ONLY ONCE IT HAS BEEN *REDUCED TO ASHES*,
AND EVEN ON THESE ASHES *I WILL FIGHT YOU*.
ENOUGH OF THIS!
SEND ORDERS TO THE FLEET:
LAUNCH LANDING ATS TO BOTH SIDES OF E TOWN AND APPROACH N LAND UNDER COVER OF DARKNESS.
SIX THOUSAND TROOPS SHOULD SUFFICE.

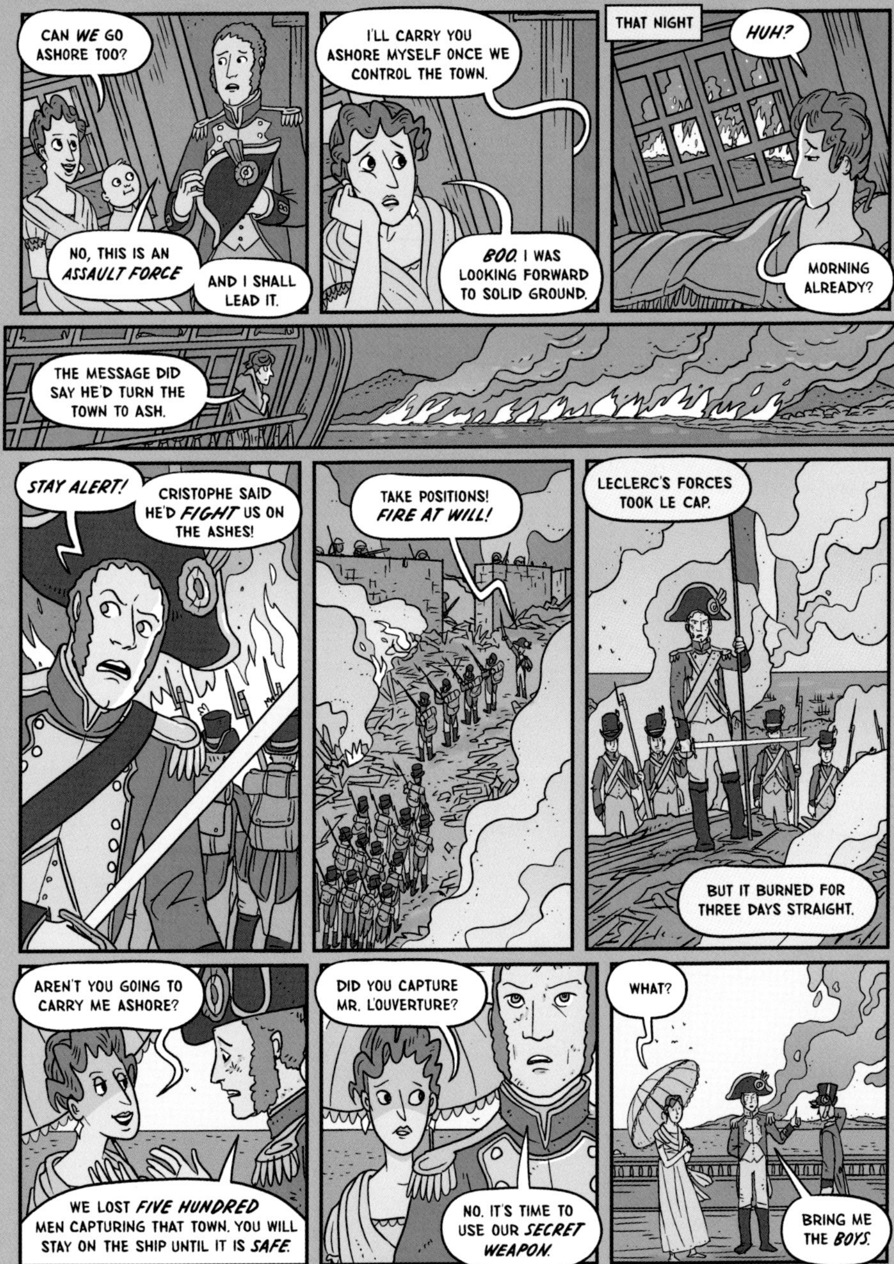
CAN *WE* GO ASHORE TOO?
NO, THIS IS AN *ASSAULT FORCE*
AND I SHALL LEAD IT.
I'LL CARRY YOU ASHORE MYSELF ONCE WE CONTROL THE TOWN.
BOO. I WAS LOOKING FORWARD TO SOLID GROUND.
THAT NIGHT
HUH?
MORNING ALREADY?
THE MESSAGE DID SAY HE'D TURN THE TOWN TO ASH.
STAY ALERT!
CRISTOPHE SAID HE'D *FIGHT* US ON THE ASHES!
TAKE POSITIONS! *FIRE AT WILL!*
LECLERC'S FORCES TOOK LE CAP.
BUT IT BURNED FOR THREE DAYS STRAIGHT.
AREN'T YOU GOING TO CARRY ME ASHORE?
WE LOST *FIVE HUNDRED* MEN CAPTURING THAT TOWN. YOU WILL STAY ON THE SHIP UNTIL IT IS *SAFE.*
DID YOU CAPTURE MR. L'OUVERTURE?
NO. IT'S TIME TO USE OUR *SECRET WEAPON.*
WHAT?
BRING ME THE *BOYS.*

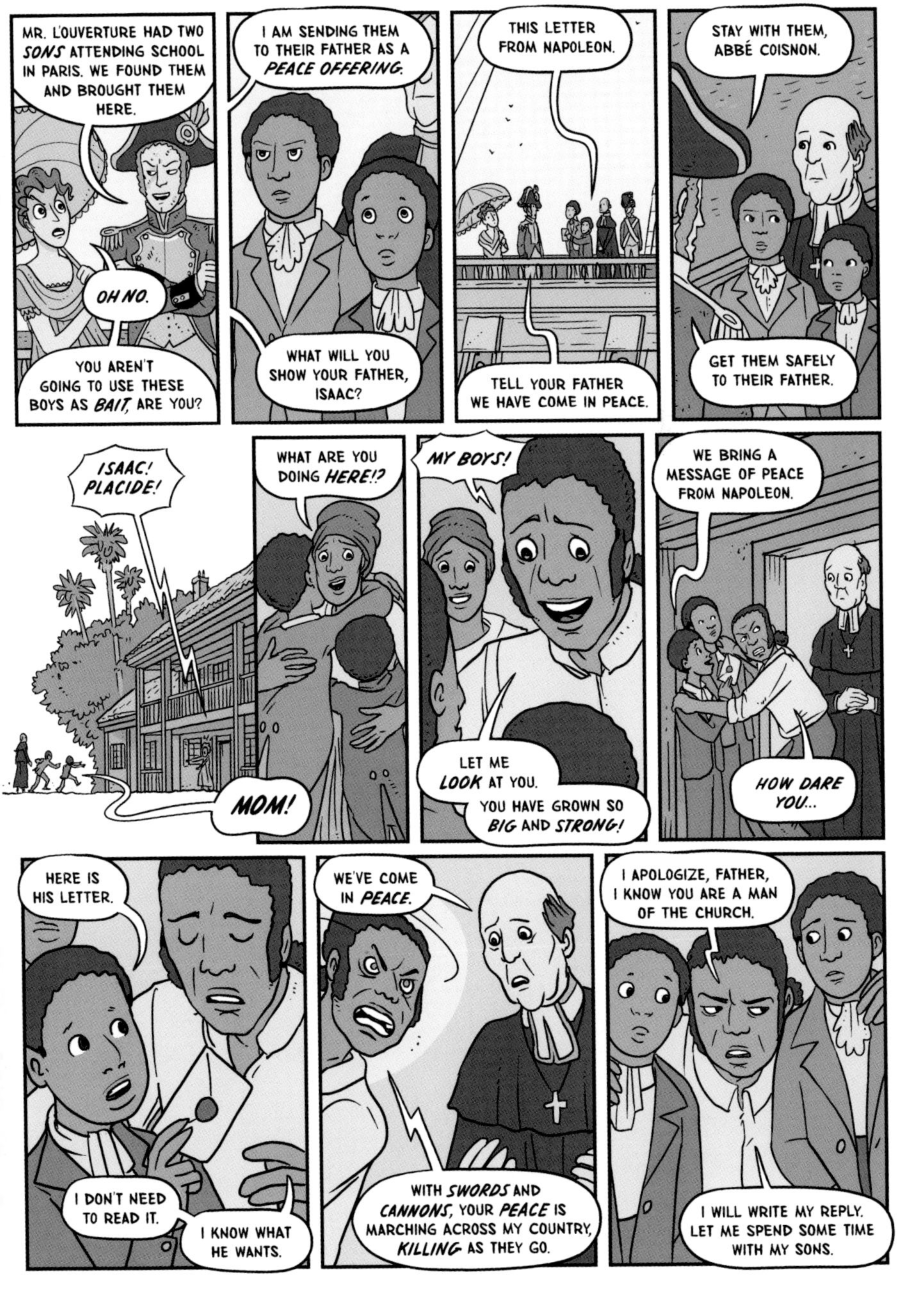
MR. L'OUVERTURE HAD TWO SONS ATTENDING SCHOOL IN PARIS. WE FOUND THEM AND BROUGHT THEM HERE.
OH NO.
YOU AREN'T GOING TO USE THESE BOYS AS BAIT, ARE YOU?
I AM SENDING THEM TO THEIR FATHER AS A PEACE OFFERING.
WHAT WILL YOU SHOW YOUR FATHER, ISAAC?
THIS LETTER FROM NAPOLEON.
TELL YOUR FATHER WE HAVE COME IN PEACE.
STAY WITH THEM, ABBÉ COISNON.
GET THEM SAFELY TO THEIR FATHER.
ISAAC! PLACIDE!
MOM!
WHAT ARE YOU DOING HERE!?
MY BOYS!
LET ME LOOK AT YOU.
YOU HAVE GROWN SO BIG AND STRONG!
WE BRING A MESSAGE OF PEACE FROM NAPOLEON.
HOW DARE YOU...
HERE IS HIS LETTER.
I DON'T NEED TO READ IT.
I KNOW WHAT HE WANTS.
WE'VE COME IN PEACE.
WITH SWORDS AND CANNONS, YOUR PEACE IS MARCHING ACROSS MY COUNTRY, KILLING AS THEY GO.
I APOLOGIZE, FATHER, I KNOW YOU ARE A MAN OF THE CHURCH.
I WILL WRITE MY REPLY. LET ME SPEND SOME TIME WITH MY SONS.

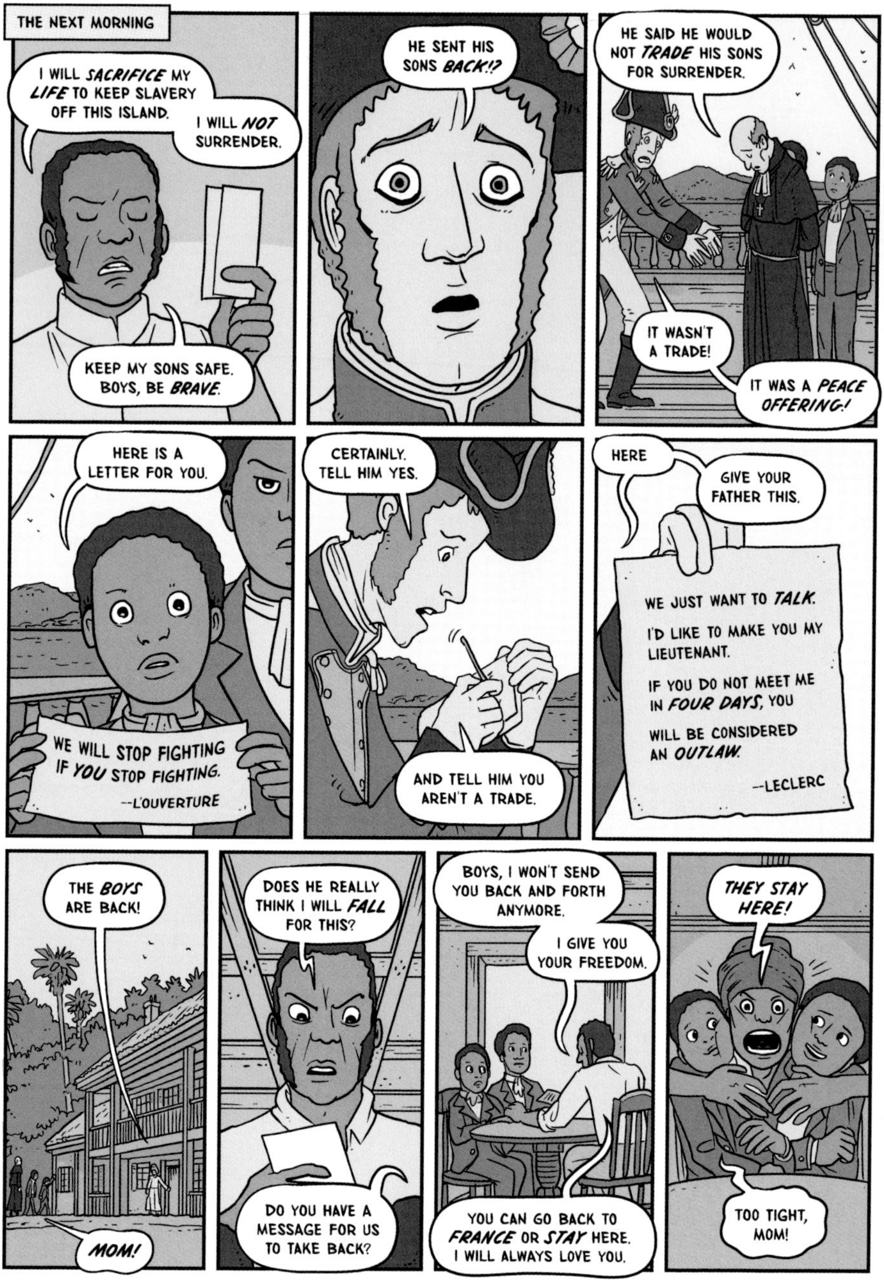
THE NEXT MORNING
I WILL SACRIFICE MY LIFE TO KEEP SLAVERY OFF THIS ISLAND.
I WILL NOT SURRENDER.
KEEP MY SONS SAFE. BOYS, BE BRAVE.
HE SENT HIS SONS BACK!?
HE SAID HE WOULD NOT TRADE HIS SONS FOR SURRENDER.
IT WASN'T A TRADE!
IT WAS A PEACE OFFERING!
HERE IS A LETTER FOR YOU.
WE WILL STOP FIGHTING IF YOU STOP FIGHTING.
--L'OUVERTURE
CERTAINLY. TELL HIM YES.
AND TELL HIM YOU AREN'T A TRADE.
HERE
GIVE YOUR FATHER THIS.
WE JUST WANT TO TALK.
I'D LIKE TO MAKE YOU MY LIEUTENANT.
IF YOU DO NOT MEET ME IN FOUR DAYS, YOU WILL BE CONSIDERED AN OUTLAW.
--LECLERC
THE BOYS ARE BACK!
MOM!
DOES HE REALLY THINK I WILL FALL FOR THIS?
DO YOU HAVE A MESSAGE FOR US TO TAKE BACK?
BOYS, I WON'T SEND YOU BACK AND FORTH ANYMORE.
I GIVE YOU YOUR FREEDOM.
YOU CAN GO BACK TO FRANCE OR STAY HERE. I WILL ALWAYS LOVE YOU.
THEY STAY HERE!
TOO TIGHT, MOM!

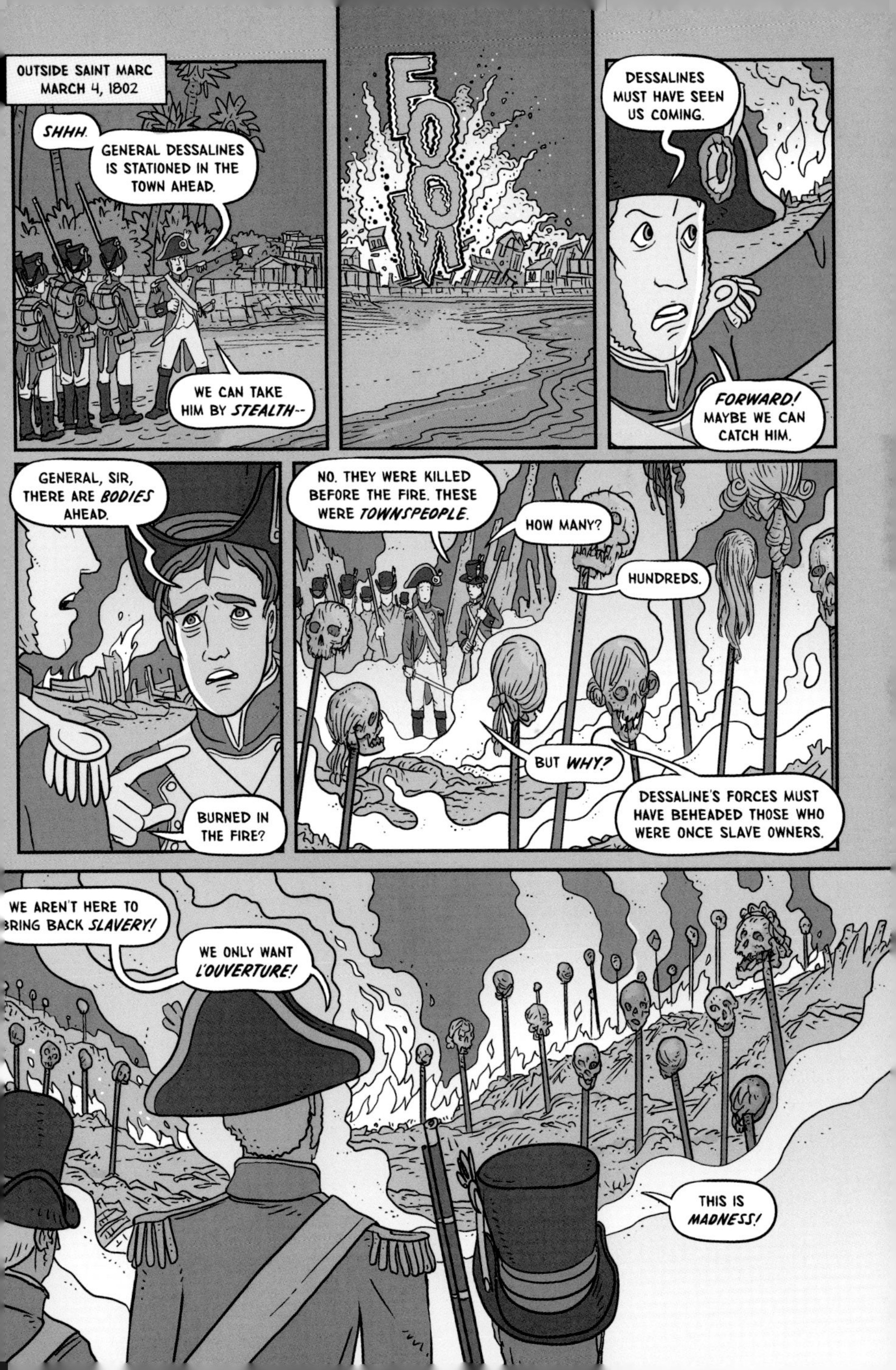
OUTSIDE SAINT MARC
MARCH 4, 1802
SHHH.
GENERAL DESSALINES IS STATIONED IN THE TOWN AHEAD.
WE CAN TAKE HIM BY STEALTH--
FOOM
DESSALINES MUST HAVE SEEN US COMING.
FORWARD! MAYBE WE CAN CATCH HIM.
GENERAL, SIR, THERE ARE BODIES AHEAD.
BURNED IN THE FIRE?
NO. THEY WERE KILLED BEFORE THE FIRE. THESE WERE TOWNSPEOPLE.
HOW MANY?
HUNDREDS.
BUT WHY?
DESSALINE'S FORCES MUST HAVE BEHEADED THOSE WHO WERE ONCE SLAVE OWNERS.
WE AREN'T HERE TO BRING BACK SLAVERY!
WE ONLY WANT L'OUVERTURE!
THIS IS MADNESS!

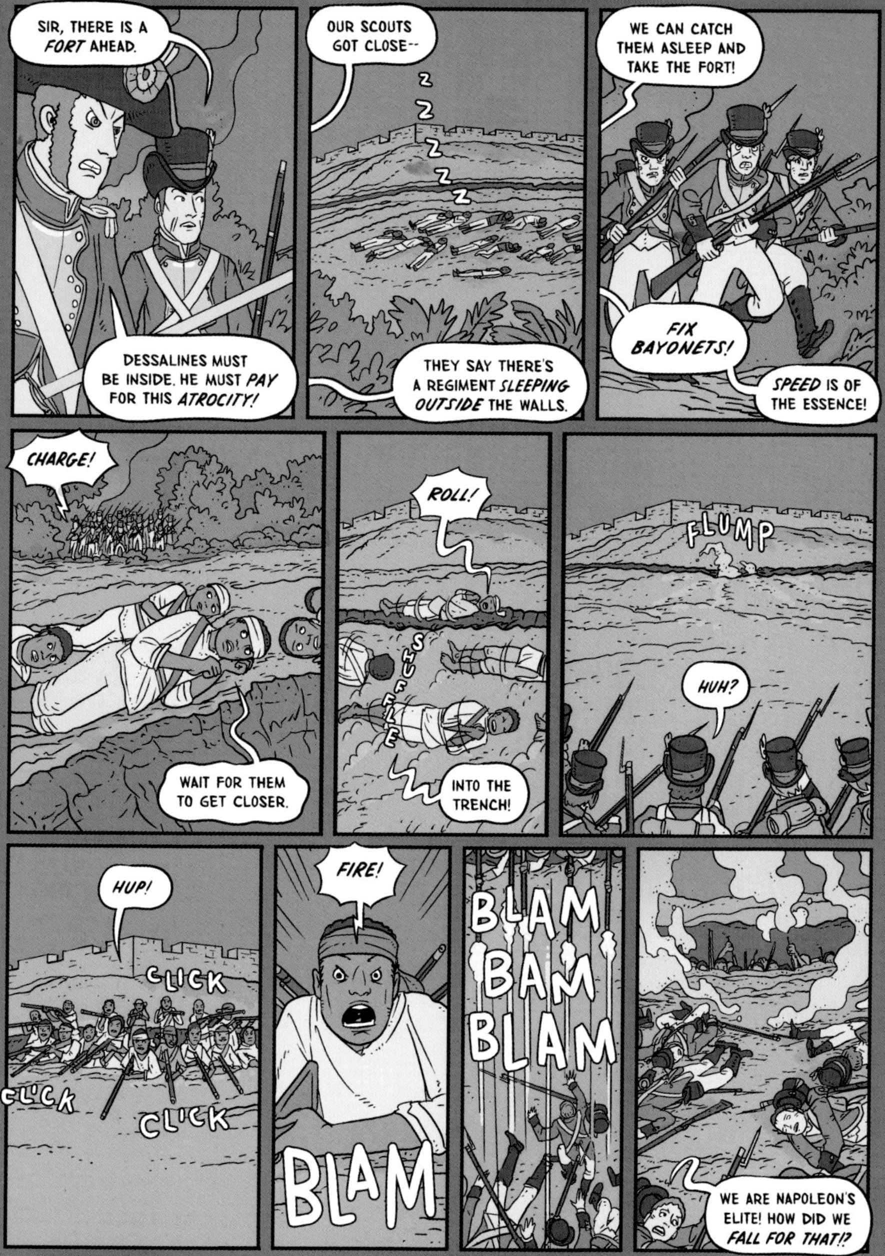
SIR, THERE IS A FORT AHEAD.
DESSALINES MUST BE INSIDE. HE MUST PAY FOR THIS ATROCITY!
OUR SCOUTS GOT CLOSE--
Z Z Z Z Z
THEY SAY THERE'S A REGIMENT SLEEPING OUTSIDE THE WALLS.
WE CAN CATCH THEM ASLEEP AND TAKE THE FORT!
FIX BAYONETS!
SPEED IS OF THE ESSENCE!
CHARGE!
WAIT FOR THEM TO GET CLOSER.
ROLL!
SHUFFLE
INTO THE TRENCH!
FLUMP
HUH?
HUP!
CLICK
CLICK
CLICK
FIRE!
BLAM
BLAM
BAM
BLAM
WE ARE NAPOLEON'S ELITE! HOW DID WE FALL FOR THAT!?

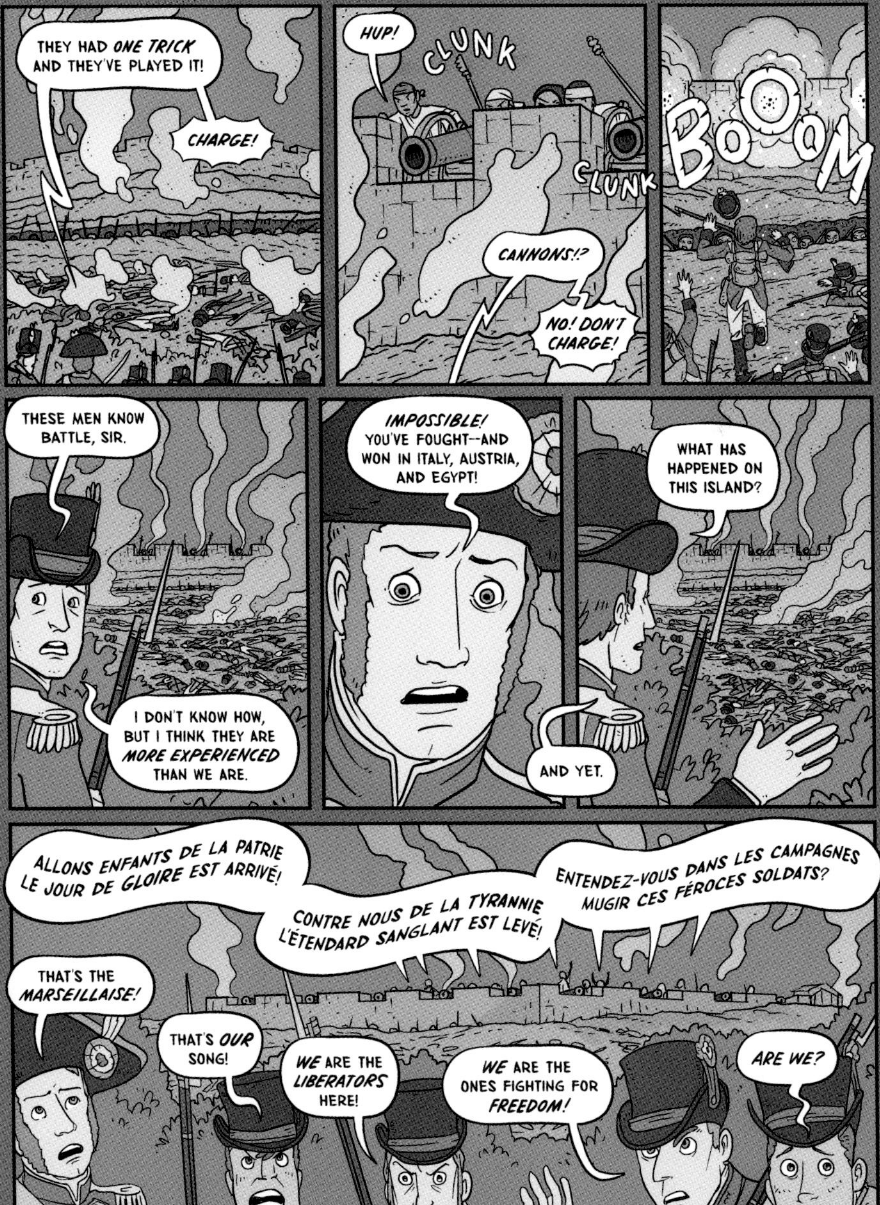
THEY HAD ONE TRICK AND THEY'VE PLAYED IT!
CHARGE!
HUP!
CLUNK
CLUNK
CANNONS!?
NO! DON'T CHARGE!
BOOOM
THESE MEN KNOW BATTLE, SIR.
I DON'T KNOW HOW, BUT I THINK THEY ARE MORE EXPERIENCED THAN WE ARE.
IMPOSSIBLE! YOU'VE FOUGHT--AND WON IN ITALY, AUSTRIA, AND EGYPT!
WHAT HAS HAPPENED ON THIS ISLAND?
AND YET.
ALLONS ENFANTS DE LA PATRIE LE JOUR DE GLOIRE EST ARRIVÉ!
CONTRE NOUS DE LA TYRANNIE L'ÉTENDARD SANGLANT EST LEVÉ!
ENTENDEZ-VOUS DANS LES CAMPAGNES MUGIR CES FÉROCES SOLDATS?
THAT'S THE MARSEILLAISE!
THAT'S OUR SONG!
WE ARE THE LIBERATORS HERE!
WE ARE THE ONES FIGHTING FOR FREEDOM!
ARE WE?

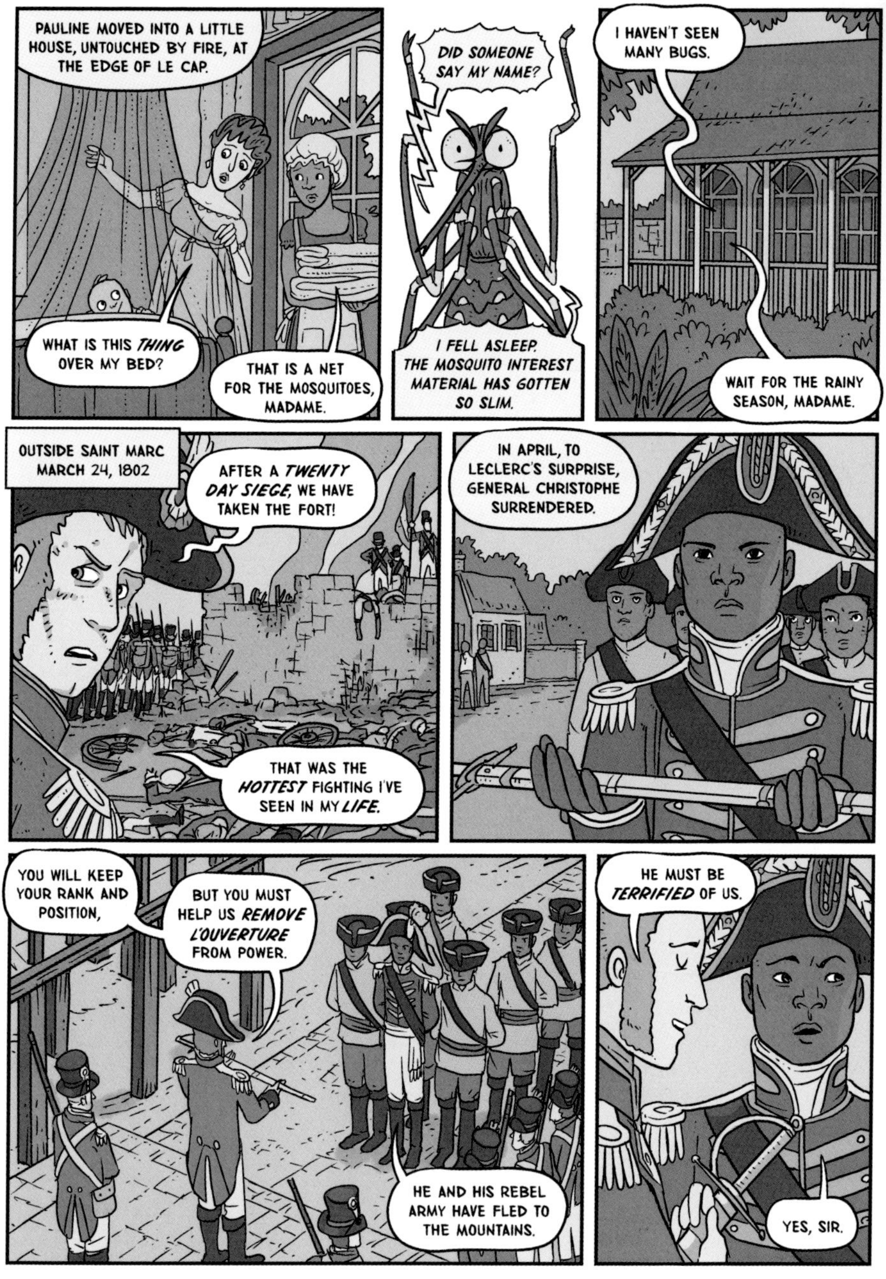
PAULINE MOVED INTO A LITTLE HOUSE, UNTOUCHED BY FIRE, AT THE EDGE OF LE CAP.
WHAT IS THIS *THING* OVER MY BED?
THAT IS A NET FOR THE MOSQUITOES, MADAME.
DID SOMEONE SAY MY NAME?
I FELL ASLEEP. THE MOSQUITO INTEREST MATERIAL HAS GOTTEN SO SLIM.
I HAVEN'T SEEN MANY BUGS.
WAIT FOR THE RAINY SEASON, MADAME.
OUTSIDE SAINT MARC MARCH 24, 1802
AFTER A *TWENTY DAY SIEGE*, WE HAVE TAKEN THE FORT!
THAT WAS THE *HOTTEST* FIGHTING I'VE SEEN IN MY *LIFE*.
IN APRIL, TO LECLERC'S SURPRISE, GENERAL CHRISTOPHE SURRENDERED.
YOU WILL KEEP YOUR RANK AND POSITION,
BUT YOU MUST HELP US *REMOVE L'OUVERTURE* FROM POWER.
HE AND HIS REBEL ARMY HAVE FLED TO THE MOUNTAINS.
HE MUST BE *TERRIFIED* OF US.
YES, SIR.

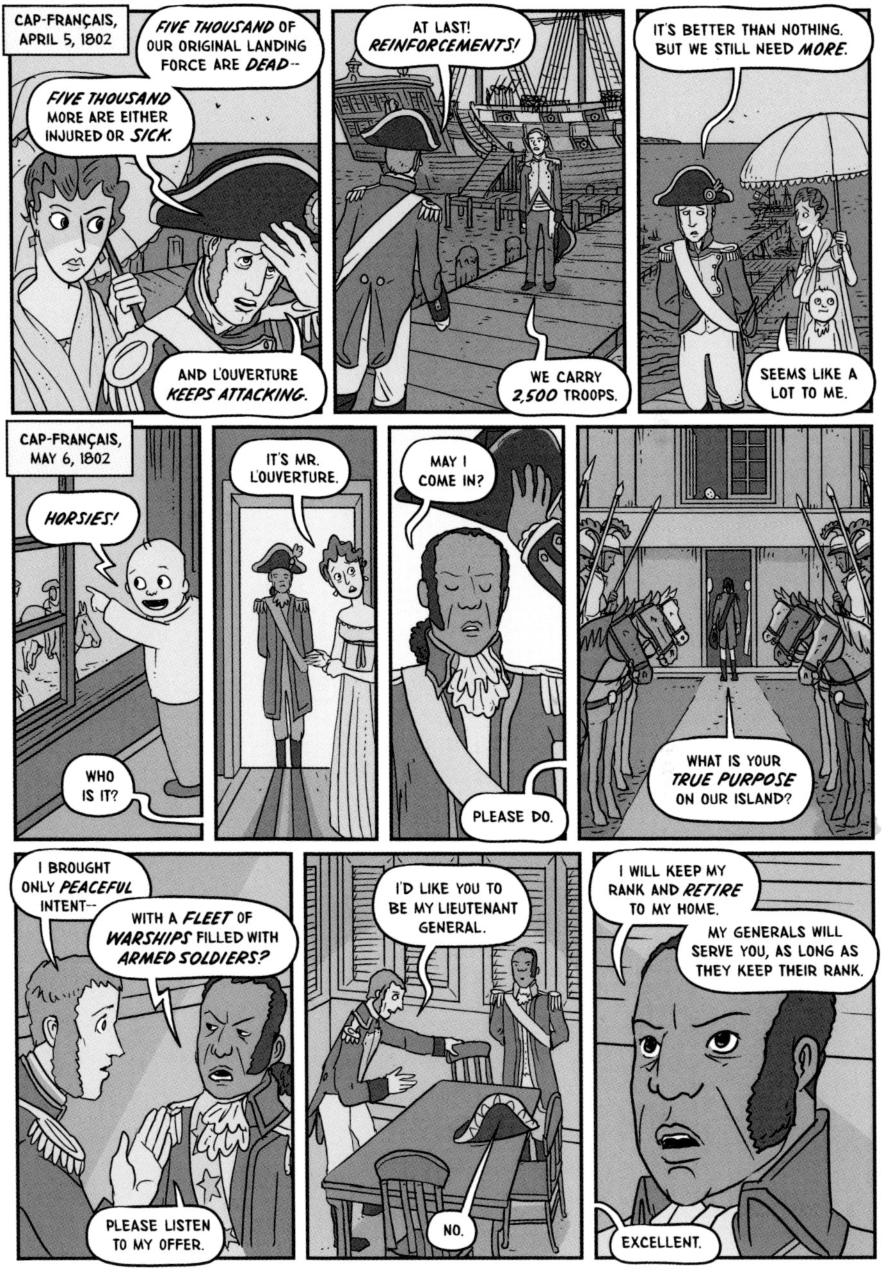
CAP-FRANÇAIS, APRIL 5, 1802
FIVE THOUSAND OF OUR ORIGINAL LANDING FORCE ARE DEAD--
FIVE THOUSAND MORE ARE EITHER INJURED OR SICK.
AND L'OUVERTURE KEEPS ATTACKING.
AT LAST! REINFORCEMENTS!
WE CARRY 2,500 TROOPS.
IT'S BETTER THAN NOTHING. BUT WE STILL NEED MORE.
SEEMS LIKE A LOT TO ME.
CAP-FRANÇAIS, MAY 6, 1802
HORSIES!
WHO IS IT?
IT'S MR. L'OUVERTURE.
MAY I COME IN?
PLEASE DO.
WHAT IS YOUR TRUE PURPOSE ON OUR ISLAND?
I BROUGHT ONLY PEACEFUL INTENT--
WITH A FLEET OF WARSHIPS FILLED WITH ARMED SOLDIERS?
PLEASE LISTEN TO MY OFFER.
I'D LIKE YOU TO BE MY LIEUTENANT GENERAL.
NO.
I WILL KEEP MY RANK AND RETIRE TO MY HOME.
MY GENERALS WILL SERVE YOU, AS LONG AS THEY KEEP THEIR RANK.
EXCELLENT.

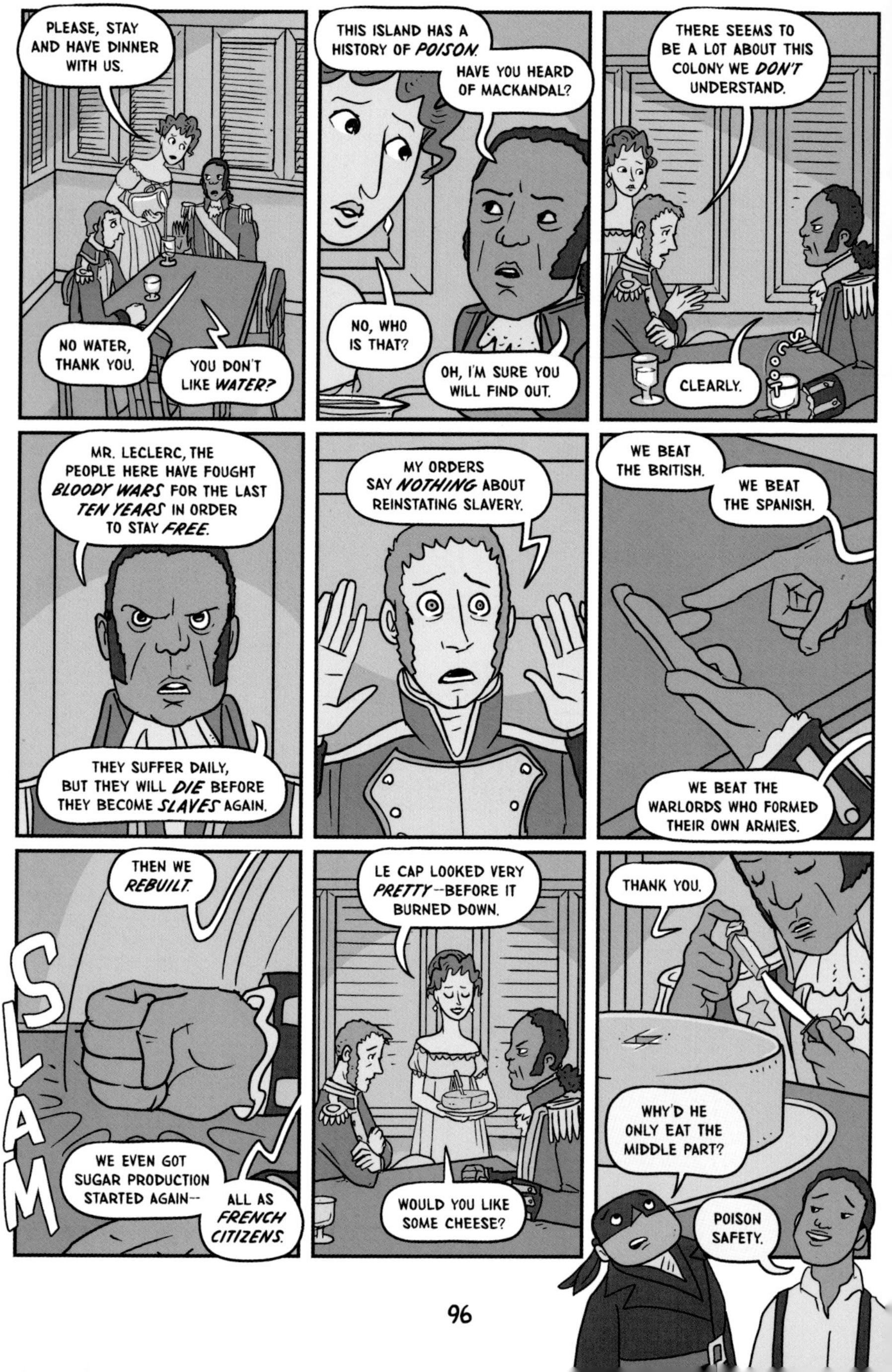

PLEASE, STAY AND HAVE DINNER WITH US.
NO WATER, THANK YOU.
YOU DON'T LIKE WATER?
THIS ISLAND HAS A HISTORY OF POISON.
HAVE YOU HEARD OF MACKANDAL?
NO, WHO IS THAT?
OH, I'M SURE YOU WILL FIND OUT.
THERE SEEMS TO BE A LOT ABOUT THIS COLONY WE DON'T UNDERSTAND.
CLEARLY.
MR. LECLERC, THE PEOPLE HERE HAVE FOUGHT BLOODY WARS FOR THE LAST TEN YEARS IN ORDER TO STAY FREE.
THEY SUFFER DAILY, BUT THEY WILL DIE BEFORE THEY BECOME SLAVES AGAIN.
MY ORDERS SAY NOTHING ABOUT REINSTATING SLAVERY.
WE BEAT THE BRITISH.
WE BEAT THE SPANISH.
WE BEAT THE WARLORDS WHO FORMED THEIR OWN ARMIES.
THEN WE REBUILT.
SLAM
WE EVEN GOT SUGAR PRODUCTION STARTED AGAIN--
ALL AS FRENCH CITIZENS.
LE CAP LOOKED VERY PRETTY--BEFORE IT BURNED DOWN.
WOULD YOU LIKE SOME CHEESE?
THANK YOU.
WHY'D HE ONLY EAT THE MIDDLE PART?
POISON SAFETY.

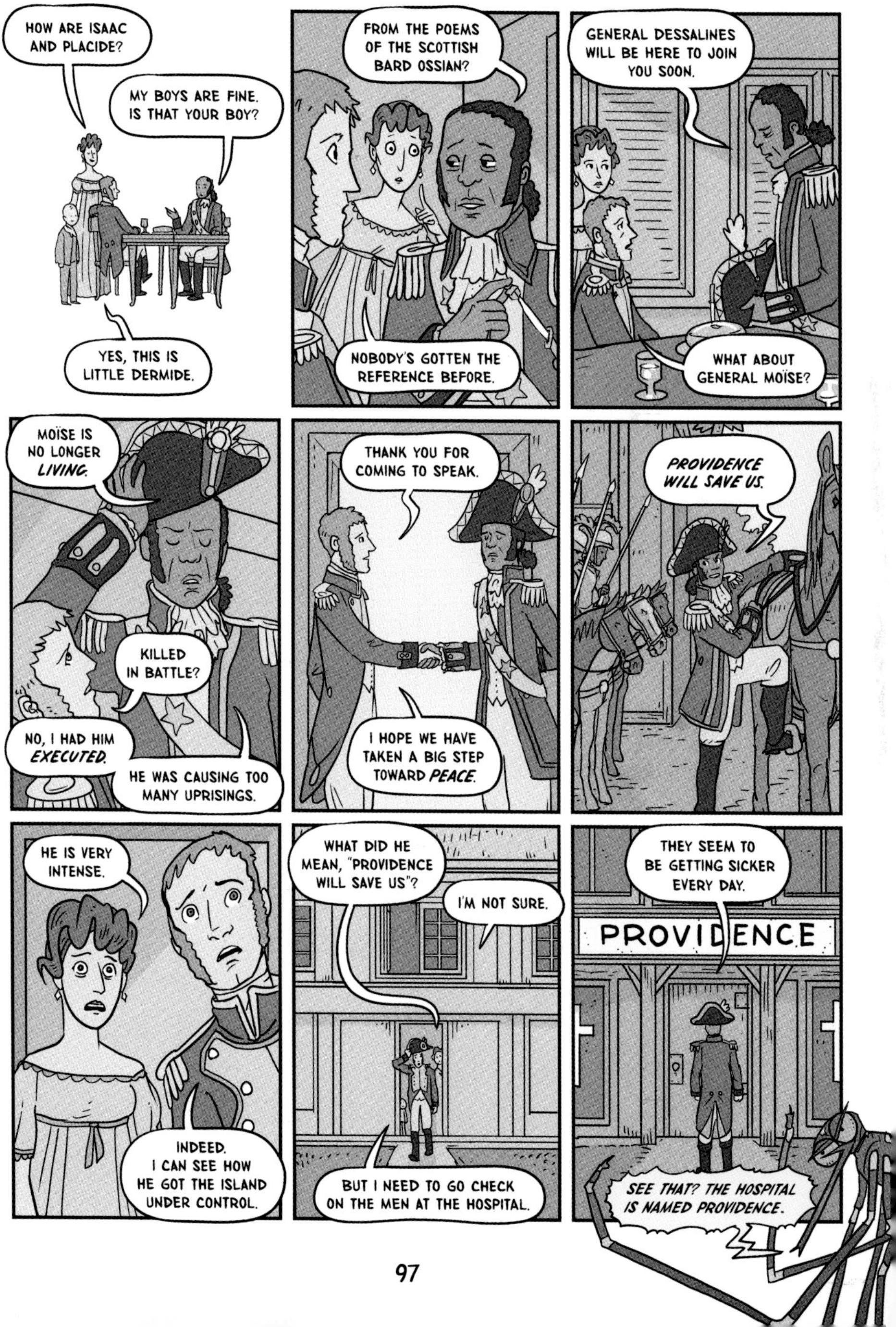
HOW ARE ISAAC AND PLACIDE?
MY BOYS ARE FINE. IS THAT YOUR BOY?
YES, THIS IS LITTLE DERMIDE.
FROM THE POEMS OF THE SCOTTISH BARD OSSIAN?
NOBODY'S GOTTEN THE REFERENCE BEFORE.
GENERAL DESSALINES WILL BE HERE TO JOIN YOU SOON.
WHAT ABOUT GENERAL MOÏSE?
MOÏSE IS NO LONGER *LIVING.*
KILLED IN BATTLE?
NO, I HAD HIM *EXECUTED.*
HE WAS CAUSING TOO MANY UPRISINGS.
THANK YOU FOR COMING TO SPEAK.
I HOPE WE HAVE TAKEN A BIG STEP TOWARD *PEACE.*
PROVIDENCE WILL SAVE US.
HE IS VERY INTENSE.
INDEED. I CAN SEE HOW HE GOT THE ISLAND UNDER CONTROL.
WHAT DID HE MEAN, "PROVIDENCE WILL SAVE US"?
I'M NOT SURE.
BUT I NEED TO GO CHECK ON THE MEN AT THE HOSPITAL.
THEY SEEM TO BE GETTING SICKER EVERY DAY.
PROVIDENCE
SEE THAT? THE HOSPITAL IS NAMED PROVIDENCE.

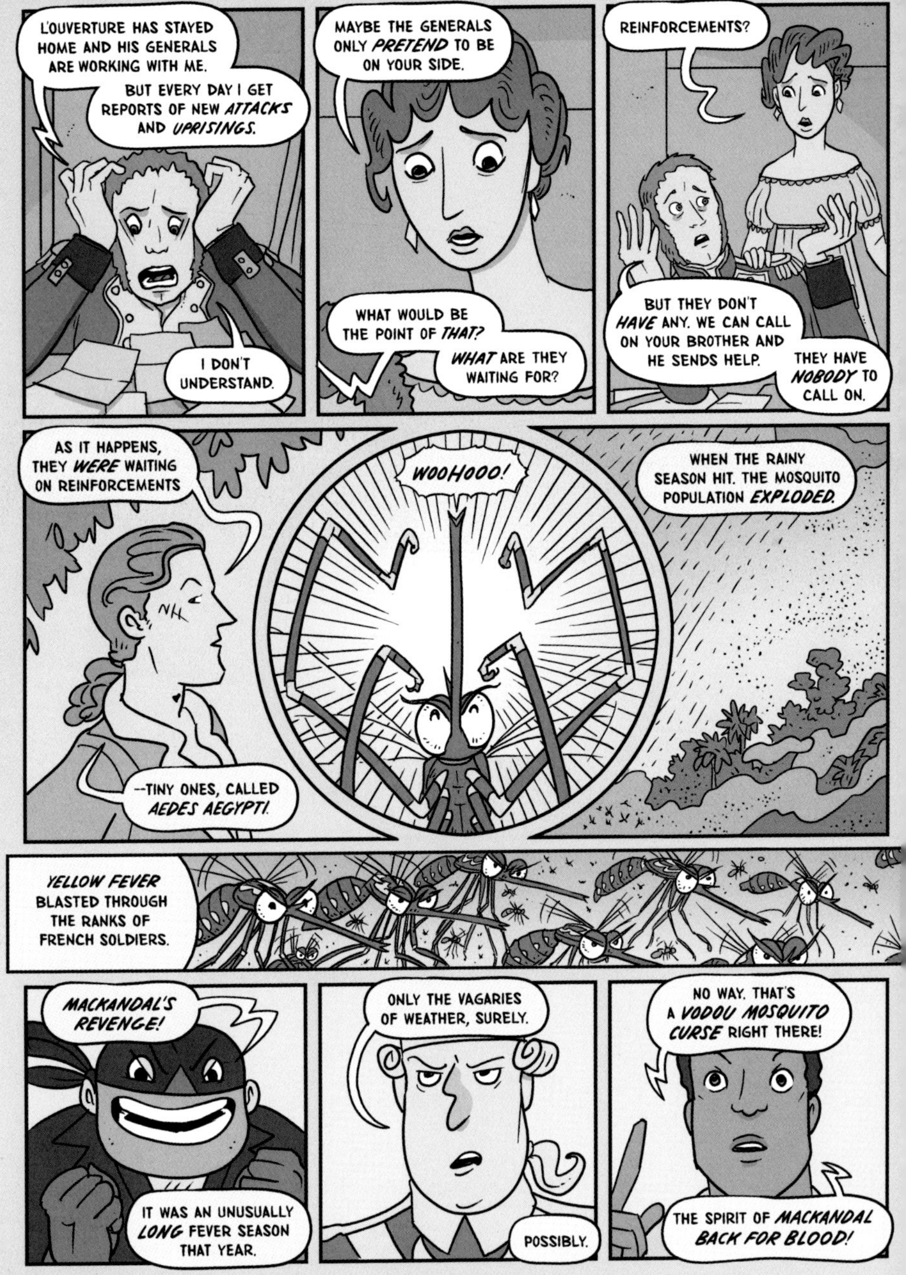

L'OUVERTURE HAS STAYED HOME AND HIS GENERALS ARE WORKING WITH ME.
BUT EVERY DAY I GET REPORTS OF NEW *ATTACKS* AND *UPRISINGS.*
I DON'T UNDERSTAND.
MAYBE THE GENERALS ONLY *PRETEND* TO BE ON YOUR SIDE.
WHAT WOULD BE THE POINT OF *THAT?*
WHAT ARE THEY WAITING FOR?
REINFORCEMENTS?
BUT THEY DON'T *HAVE* ANY. WE CAN CALL ON YOUR BROTHER AND HE SENDS HELP.
THEY HAVE *NOBODY* TO CALL ON.
AS IT HAPPENS, THEY *WERE* WAITING ON REINFORCEMENTS
--TINY ONES, CALLED *AEDES AEGYPTI.*
WOOHOOO!
WHEN THE RAINY SEASON HIT, THE MOSQUITO POPULATION *EXPLODED.*
YELLOW FEVER BLASTED THROUGH THE RANKS OF FRENCH SOLDIERS.
MACKANDAL'S REVENGE!
IT WAS AN UNUSUALLY *LONG* FEVER SEASON THAT YEAR.
ONLY THE VAGARIES OF WEATHER, SURELY.
POSSIBLY.
NO WAY. THAT'S A *VODOU MOSQUITO CURSE* RIGHT THERE!
THE SPIRIT OF *MACKANDAL BACK FOR BLOOD!*

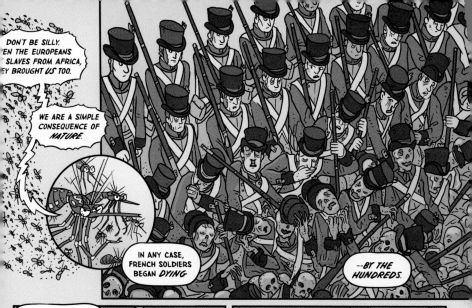

DON'T BE SILLY. 'EN THE EUROPEANS ' SLAVES FROM AFRICA, EY BROUGHT *US* TOO.

WE ARE A SIMPLE CONSEQUENCE OF *NATURE*.

IN ANY CASE, FRENCH SOLDIERS BEGAN *DYING*

--*BY THE HUNDREDS*.

PAULINE, GET DERMIDE. I'M TAKING YOU AWAY FROM HERE.

NO. I'M NOT A *COWARD!* MY BROTHER WANTS ME HERE.

JUST AWAY FROM LE CAP.

THEY MOVED INTO A HOUSE HIGH ABOVE CAP-FRANÇAIS.

YOU'LL BE SAFER FROM THE DISEASE IN THE HILLS.

I BELIEVE L'OUVERTURE IS SECRETLY ENCOURAGING THESE UPRISINGS.

AND WITH MY TROOPS GETTING SICK, WE ARE *LOSING CONTROL*.

WE NEED TO BE RID OF HIS INFLUENCE.

DON'T *KILL* HIM! THOSE SWEET BOYS OF HIS WOULD BE SO *SAD!*

NO. I WON'T KILL HIM. BUT I WILL *DEPORT* HIM.

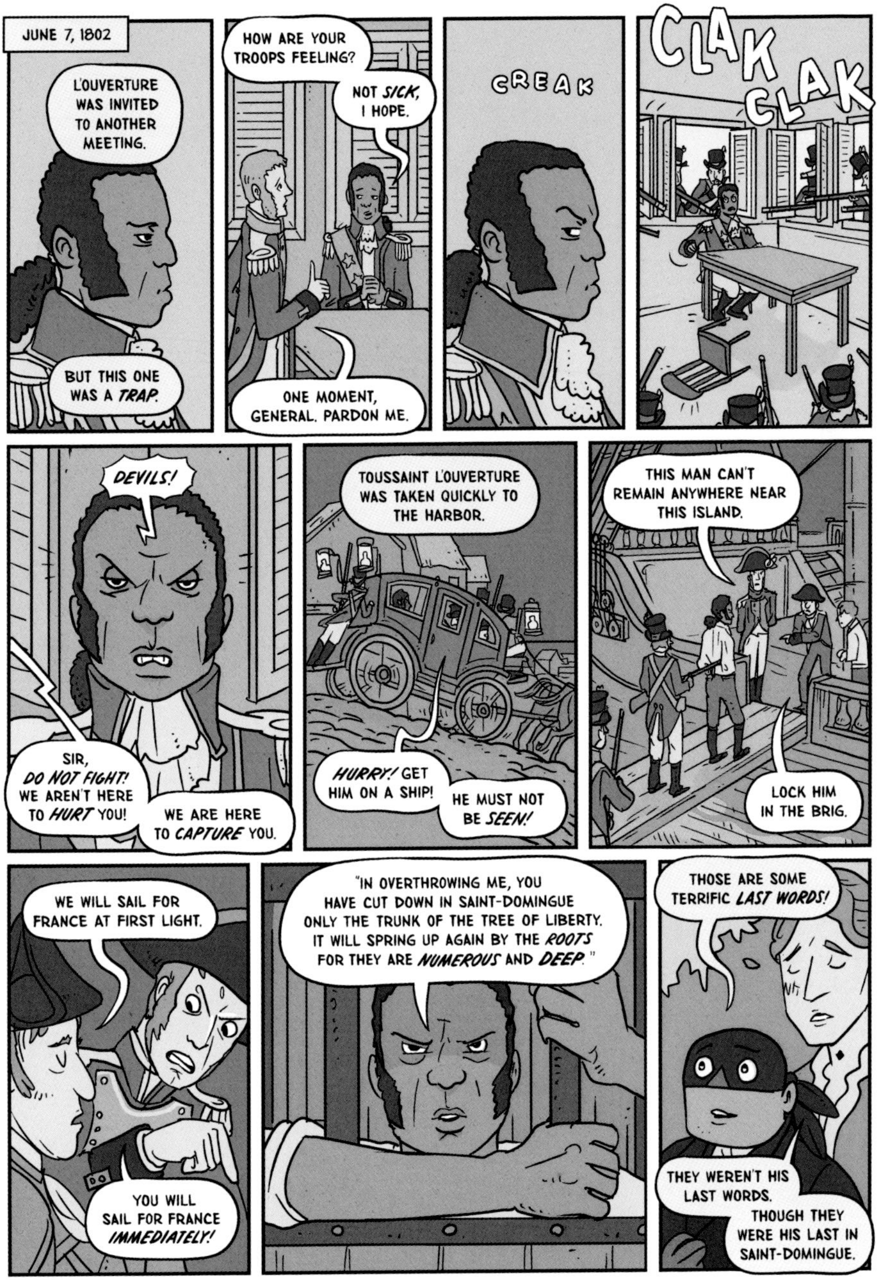
JUNE 7, 1802
L'OUVERTURE WAS INVITED TO ANOTHER MEETING.
BUT THIS ONE WAS A *TRAP*.
HOW ARE YOUR TROOPS FEELING?
NOT *SICK*, I HOPE.
ONE MOMENT, GENERAL. PARDON ME.
CREAK
CLAK CLAK
DEVILS!
SIR, *DO NOT FIGHT!* WE AREN'T HERE TO *HURT* YOU!
WE ARE HERE TO *CAPTURE* YOU.
TOUSSAINT L'OUVERTURE WAS TAKEN QUICKLY TO THE HARBOR.
HURRY! GET HIM ON A SHIP!
HE MUST NOT BE *SEEN!*
THIS MAN CAN'T REMAIN ANYWHERE NEAR THIS ISLAND.
LOCK HIM IN THE BRIG.
WE WILL SAIL FOR FRANCE AT FIRST LIGHT.
YOU WILL SAIL FOR FRANCE *IMMEDIATELY!*
"IN OVERTHROWING ME, YOU HAVE CUT DOWN IN SAINT-DOMINGUE ONLY THE TRUNK OF THE TREE OF LIBERTY. IT WILL SPRING UP AGAIN BY THE *ROOTS* FOR THEY ARE *NUMEROUS* AND *DEEP*."
THOSE ARE SOME TERRIFIC *LAST WORDS!*
THEY WEREN'T HIS LAST WORDS.
THOUGH THEY WERE HIS LAST IN SAINT-DOMINGUE.

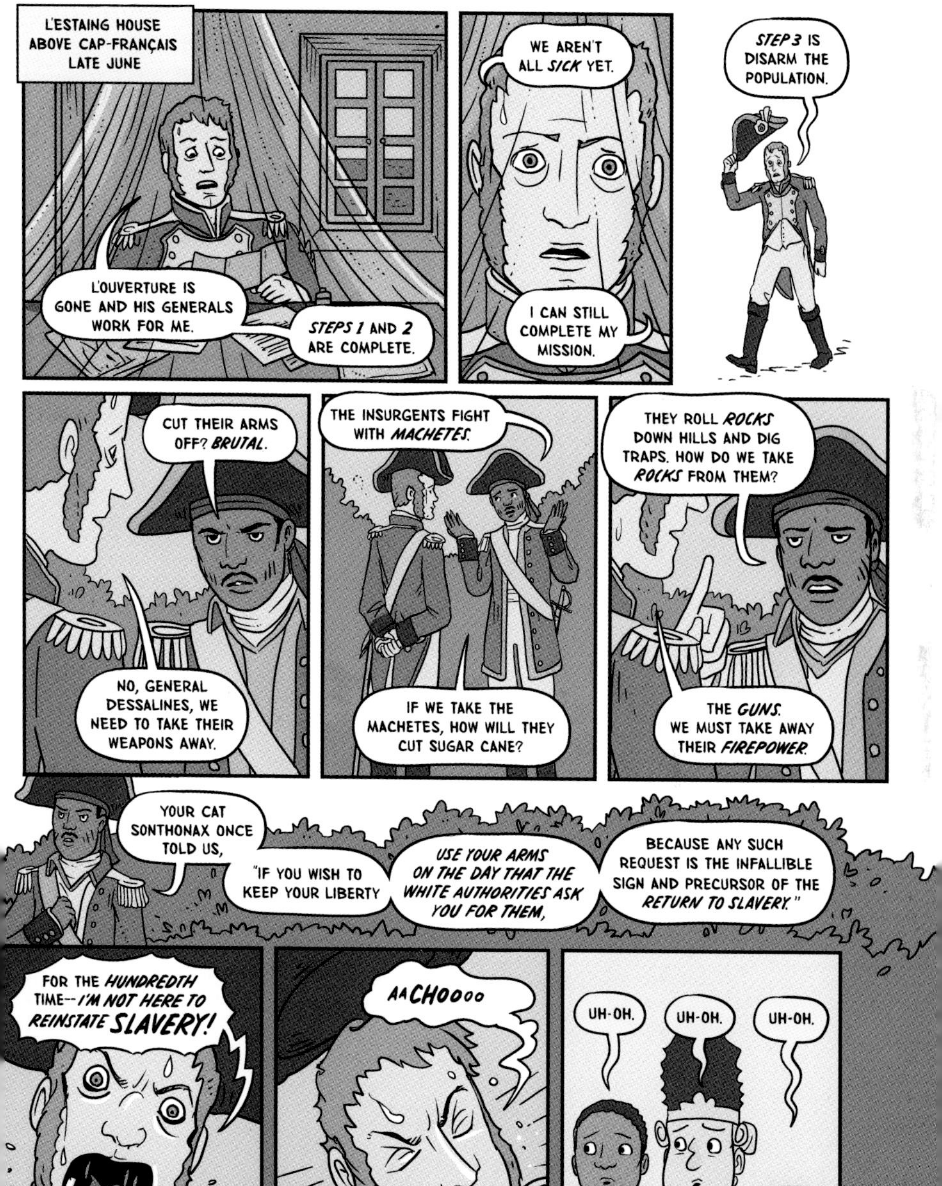
L'ESTAING HOUSE
ABOVE CAP-FRANÇAIS
LATE JUNE
L'OUVERTURE IS GONE AND HIS GENERALS WORK FOR ME.
STEPS 1 AND 2 ARE COMPLETE.
WE AREN'T ALL SICK YET.
I CAN STILL COMPLETE MY MISSION.
STEP 3 IS DISARM THE POPULATION.
CUT THEIR ARMS OFF? BRUTAL.
NO, GENERAL DESSALINES, WE NEED TO TAKE THEIR WEAPONS AWAY.
THE INSURGENTS FIGHT WITH MACHETES.
IF WE TAKE THE MACHETES, HOW WILL THEY CUT SUGAR CANE?
THEY ROLL ROCKS DOWN HILLS AND DIG TRAPS. HOW DO WE TAKE ROCKS FROM THEM?
THE GUNS. WE MUST TAKE AWAY THEIR FIREPOWER.
YOUR CAT SONTHONAX ONCE TOLD US,
"IF YOU WISH TO KEEP YOUR LIBERTY
USE YOUR ARMS ON THE DAY THAT THE WHITE AUTHORITIES ASK YOU FOR THEM,
BECAUSE ANY SUCH REQUEST IS THE INFALLIBLE SIGN AND PRECURSOR OF THE RETURN TO SLAVERY."
FOR THE HUNDREDTH TIME-- I'M NOT HERE TO REINSTATE SLAVERY!
AACHOOOO
UH-OH.
UH-OH.
UH-OH.

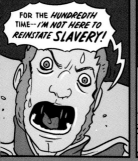

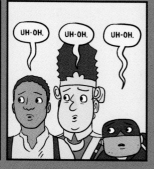

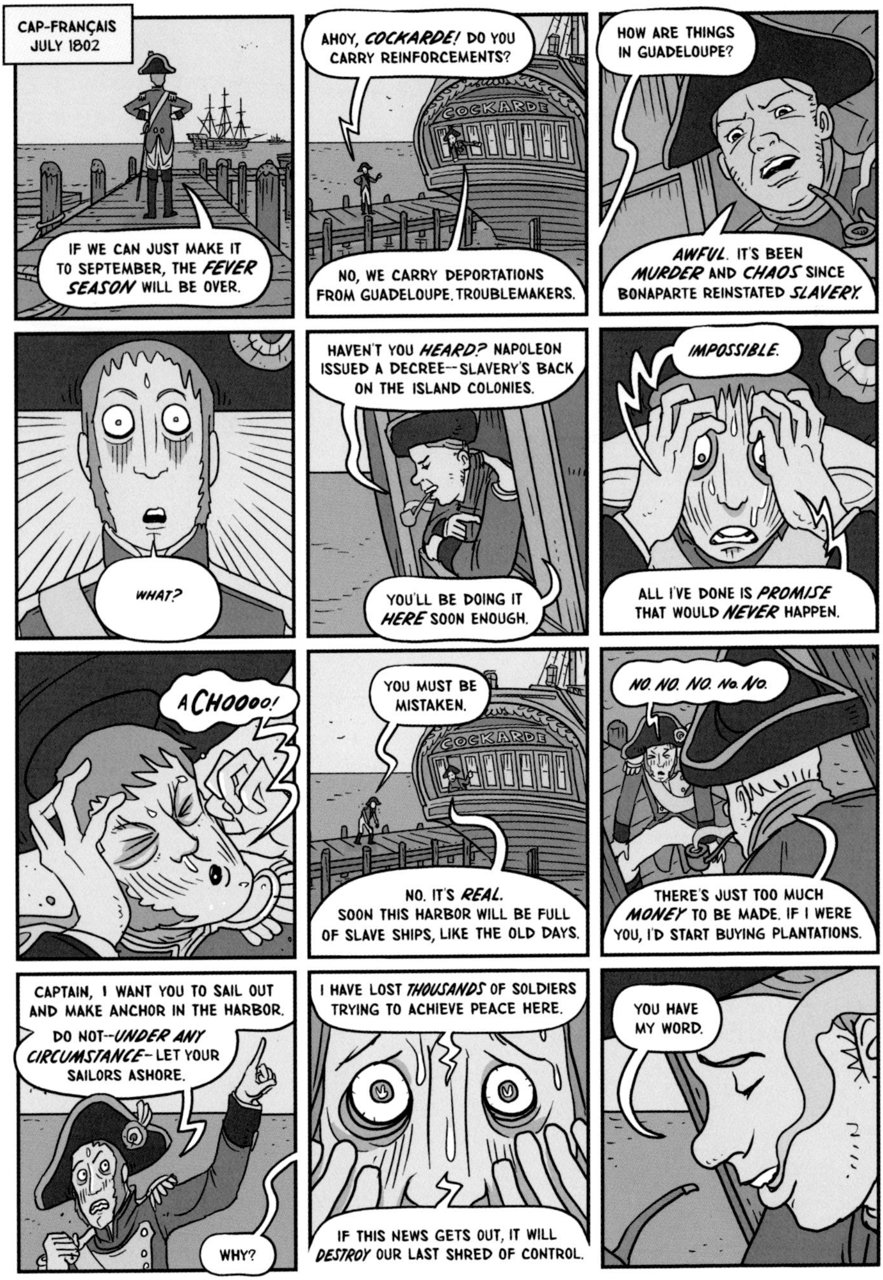
CAP-FRANÇAIS
JULY 1802
IF WE CAN JUST MAKE IT TO SEPTEMBER, THE FEVER SEASON WILL BE OVER.
AHOY, COCKARDE! DO YOU CARRY REINFORCEMENTS?
COCKARDE
NO, WE CARRY DEPORTATIONS FROM GUADELOUPE. TROUBLEMAKERS.
HOW ARE THINGS IN GUADELOUPE?
AWFUL. IT'S BEEN MURDER AND CHAOS SINCE BONAPARTE REINSTATED SLAVERY.
WHAT?
HAVEN'T YOU HEARD? NAPOLEON ISSUED A DECREE--SLAVERY'S BACK ON THE ISLAND COLONIES.
YOU'LL BE DOING IT HERE SOON ENOUGH.
IMPOSSIBLE.
ALL I'VE DONE IS PROMISE THAT WOULD NEVER HAPPEN.
A CHOOOO!
YOU MUST BE MISTAKEN.
COCKARDE
NO. IT'S REAL.
SOON THIS HARBOR WILL BE FULL OF SLAVE SHIPS, LIKE THE OLD DAYS.
NO. NO. NO. No. No.
THERE'S JUST TOO MUCH MONEY TO BE MADE. IF I WERE YOU, I'D START BUYING PLANTATIONS.
CAPTAIN, I WANT YOU TO SAIL OUT AND MAKE ANCHOR IN THE HARBOR.
DO NOT--UNDER ANY CIRCUMSTANCE-- LET YOUR SAILORS ASHORE.
WHY?
I HAVE LOST THOUSANDS OF SOLDIERS TRYING TO ACHIEVE PEACE HERE.
IF THIS NEWS GETS OUT, IT WILL DESTROY OUR LAST SHRED OF CONTROL.
YOU HAVE MY WORD.

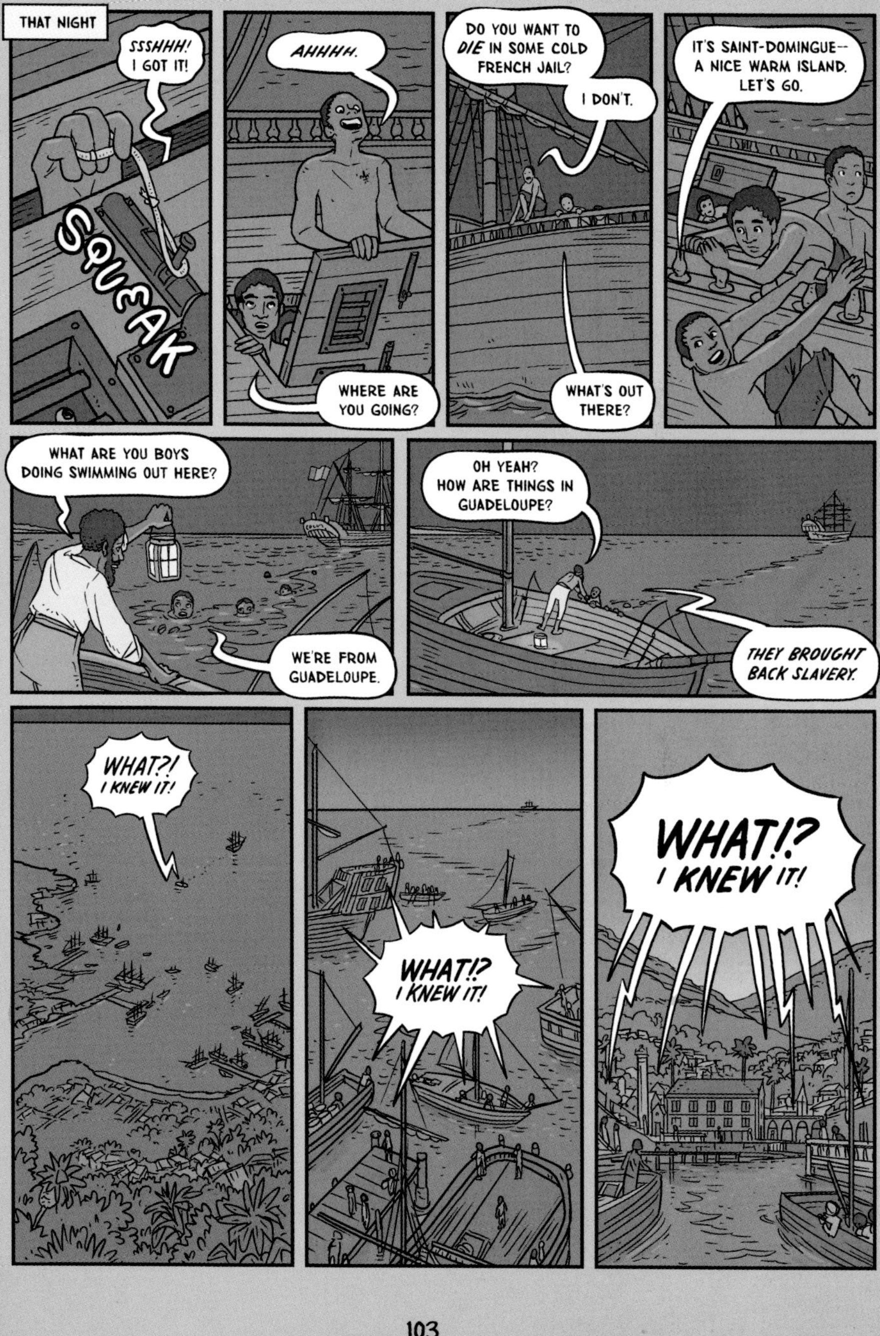
THAT NIGHT
SSSHHH! I GOT IT!
SQUEAK
AHHHH.
WHERE ARE YOU GOING?
DO YOU WANT TO DIE IN SOME COLD FRENCH JAIL?
I DON'T.
WHAT'S OUT THERE?
IT'S SAINT-DOMINGUE-- A NICE WARM ISLAND. LET'S GO.
WHAT ARE YOU BOYS DOING SWIMMING OUT HERE?
WE'RE FROM GUADELOUPE.
OH YEAH? HOW ARE THINGS IN GUADELOUPE?
THEY BROUGHT BACK SLAVERY.
WHAT?! I KNEW IT!
WHAT!? I KNEW IT!
WHAT!? I KNEW IT!

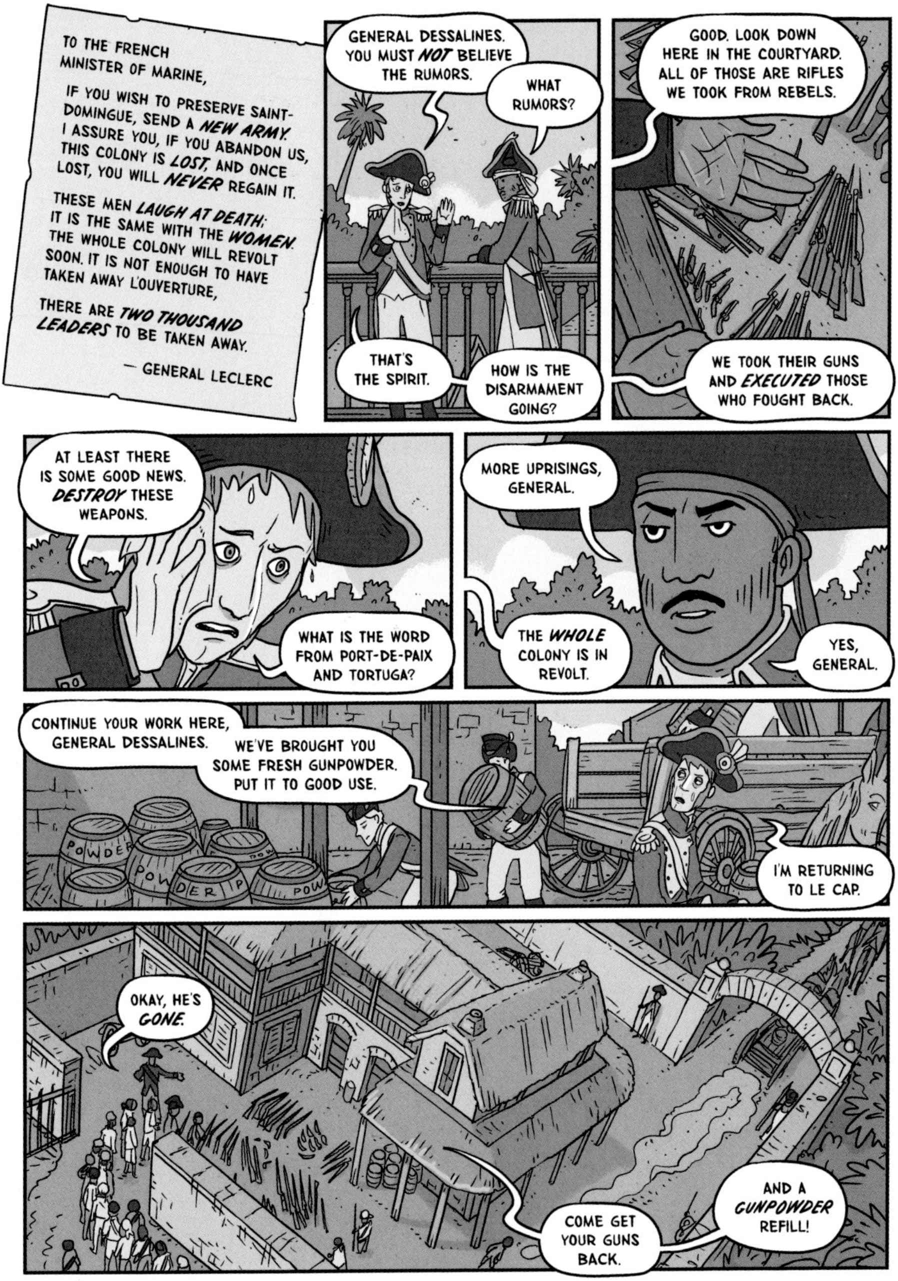
TO THE FRENCH MINISTER OF MARINE,
IF YOU WISH TO PRESERVE SAINT-DOMINGUE, SEND A NEW ARMY. I ASSURE YOU, IF YOU ABANDON US, THIS COLONY IS LOST, AND ONCE LOST, YOU WILL NEVER REGAIN IT.
THESE MEN LAUGH AT DEATH; IT IS THE SAME WITH THE WOMEN. THE WHOLE COLONY WILL REVOLT SOON. IT IS NOT ENOUGH TO HAVE TAKEN AWAY L'OUVERTURE,
THERE ARE TWO THOUSAND LEADERS TO BE TAKEN AWAY.
— GENERAL LECLERC
GENERAL DESSALINES. YOU MUST NOT BELIEVE THE RUMORS.
WHAT RUMORS?
THAT'S THE SPIRIT.
HOW IS THE DISARMAMENT GOING?
GOOD. LOOK DOWN HERE IN THE COURTYARD. ALL OF THOSE ARE RIFLES WE TOOK FROM REBELS.
WE TOOK THEIR GUNS AND EXECUTED THOSE WHO FOUGHT BACK.
AT LEAST THERE IS SOME GOOD NEWS. DESTROY THESE WEAPONS.
WHAT IS THE WORD FROM PORT-DE-PAIX AND TORTUGA?
MORE UPRISINGS, GENERAL.
THE WHOLE COLONY IS IN REVOLT.
YES, GENERAL.
CONTINUE YOUR WORK HERE, GENERAL DESSALINES.
WE'VE BROUGHT YOU SOME FRESH GUNPOWDER. PUT IT TO GOOD USE.
POWDER
POWDER
I'M RETURNING TO LE CAP.
OKAY, HE'S GONE.
COME GET YOUR GUNS BACK.
AND A GUNPOWDER REFILL!

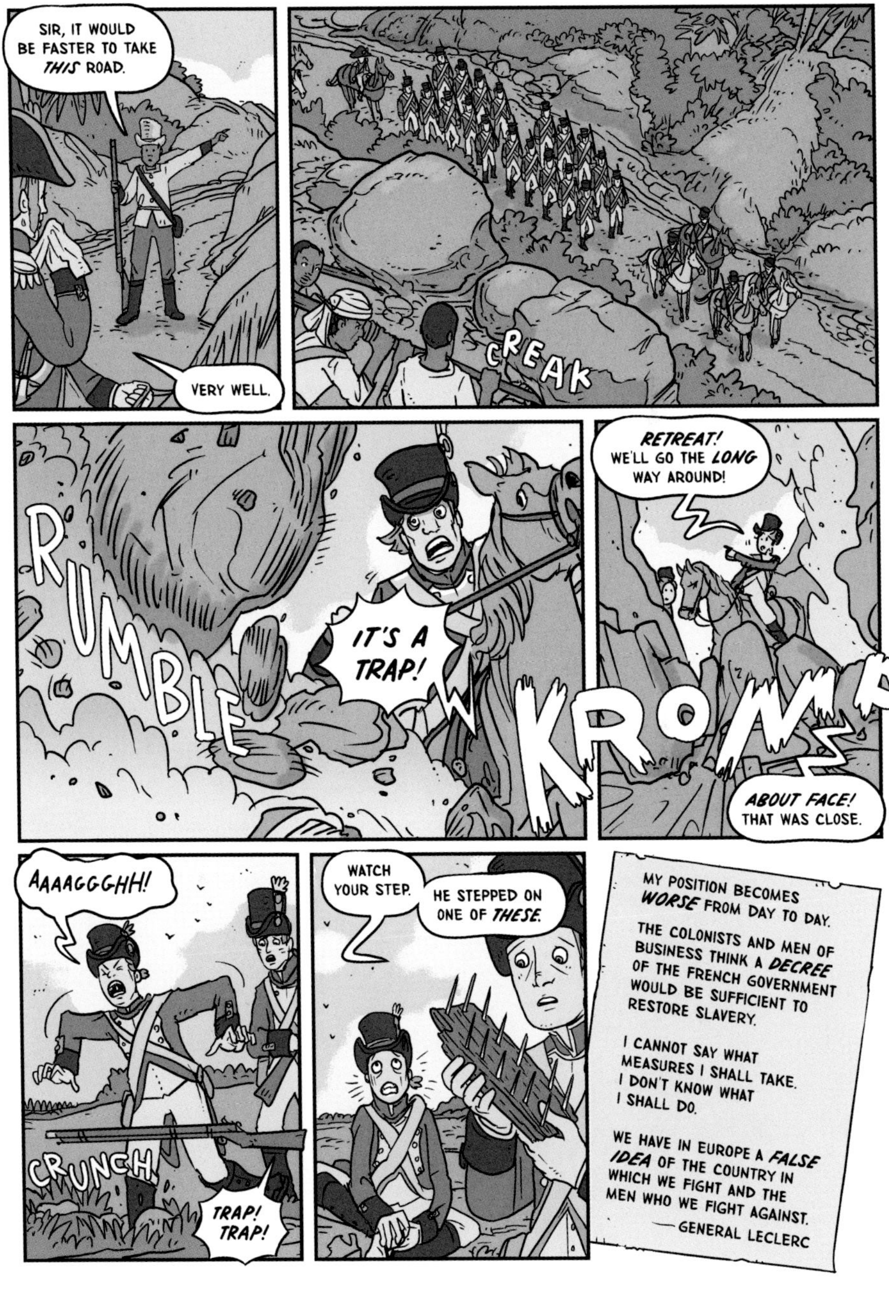
SIR, IT WOULD BE FASTER TO TAKE *THIS* ROAD.
VERY WELL.
CREAK
RUMBLE
IT'S A TRAP!
KROMP
RETREAT! WE'LL GO THE *LONG* WAY AROUND!
ABOUT FACE! THAT WAS CLOSE.
AAAAGGGHH!
CRUNCH
TRAP! TRAP!
WATCH YOUR STEP.
HE STEPPED ON ONE OF *THESE*.
MY POSITION BECOMES *WORSE* FROM DAY TO DAY.
THE COLONISTS AND MEN OF BUSINESS THINK A *DECREE* OF THE FRENCH GOVERNMENT WOULD BE SUFFICIENT TO RESTORE SLAVERY.
I CANNOT SAY WHAT MEASURES I SHALL TAKE. I DON'T KNOW WHAT I SHALL DO.
WE HAVE IN EUROPE A *FALSE IDEA* OF THE COUNTRY IN WHICH WE FIGHT AND THE MEN WHO WE FIGHT AGAINST.
— GENERAL LECLERC

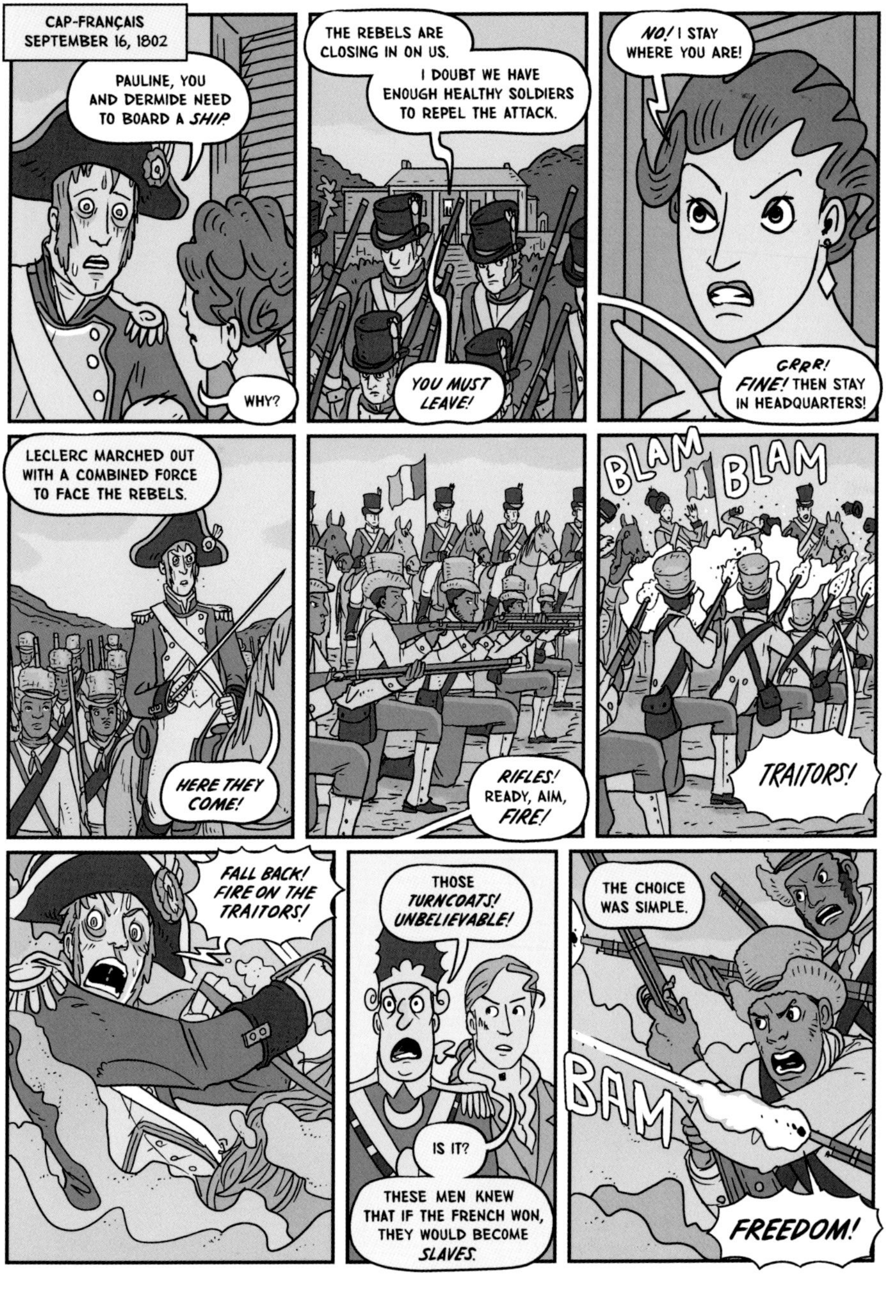
CAP-FRANÇAIS
SEPTEMBER 16, 1802
PAULINE, YOU AND DERMIDE NEED TO BOARD A *SHIP.*
WHY?
THE REBELS ARE CLOSING IN ON US.
I DOUBT WE HAVE ENOUGH HEALTHY SOLDIERS TO REPEL THE ATTACK.
YOU MUST LEAVE!
NO! I STAY WHERE YOU ARE!
GRRR! FINE! THEN STAY IN HEADQUARTERS!
LECLERC MARCHED OUT WITH A COMBINED FORCE TO FACE THE REBELS.
HERE THEY COME!
RIFLES! READY, AIM, *FIRE!*
BLAM BLAM
TRAITORS!
FALL BACK! FIRE ON THE TRAITORS!
THOSE *TURNCOATS! UNBELIEVABLE!*
IS IT?
THESE MEN KNEW THAT IF THE FRENCH WON, THEY WOULD BECOME *SLAVES.*
THE CHOICE WAS SIMPLE.
BAM
FREEDOM!

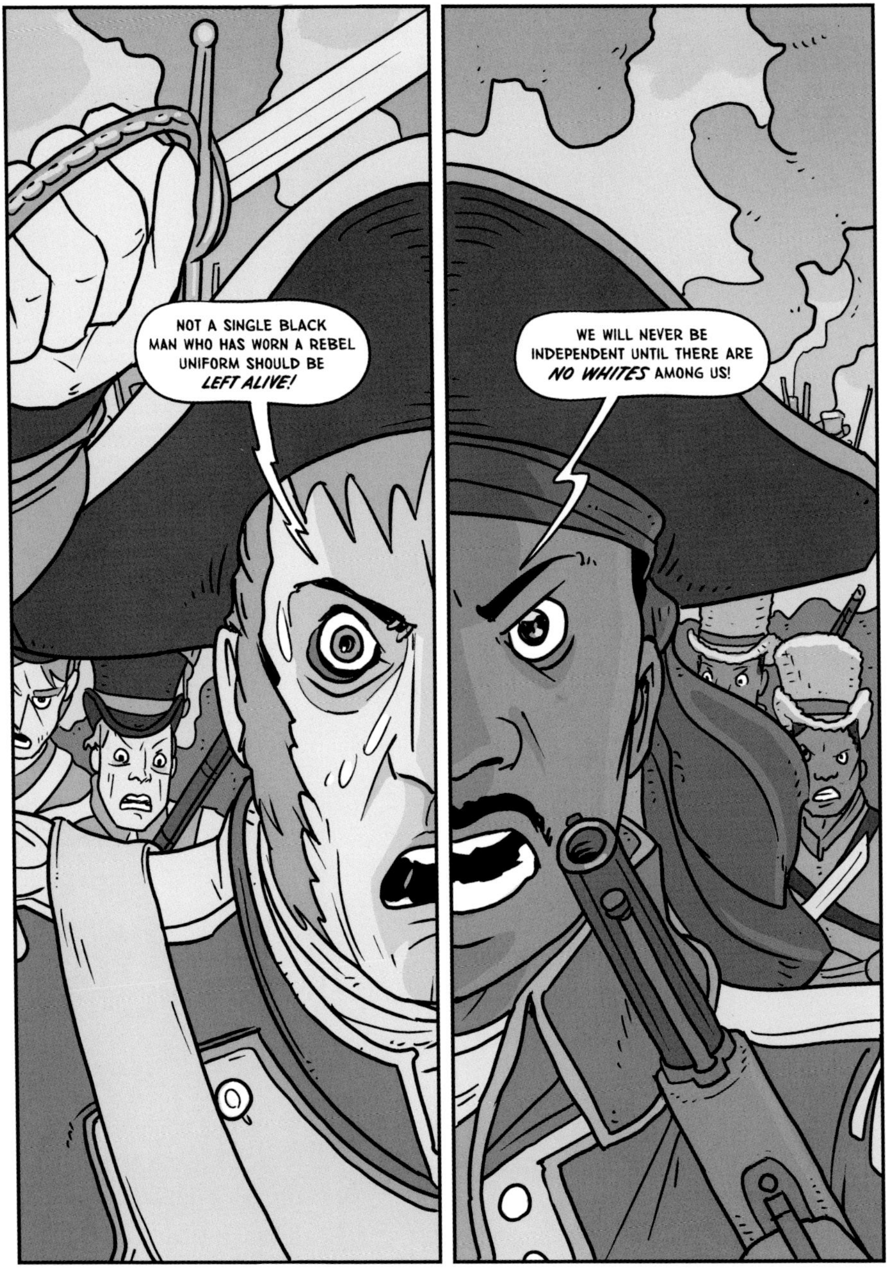
NOT A SINGLE BLACK MAN WHO HAS WORN A REBEL UNIFORM SHOULD BE *LEFT ALIVE!*
WE WILL NEVER BE INDEPENDENT UNTIL THERE ARE *NO WHITES* AMONG US!

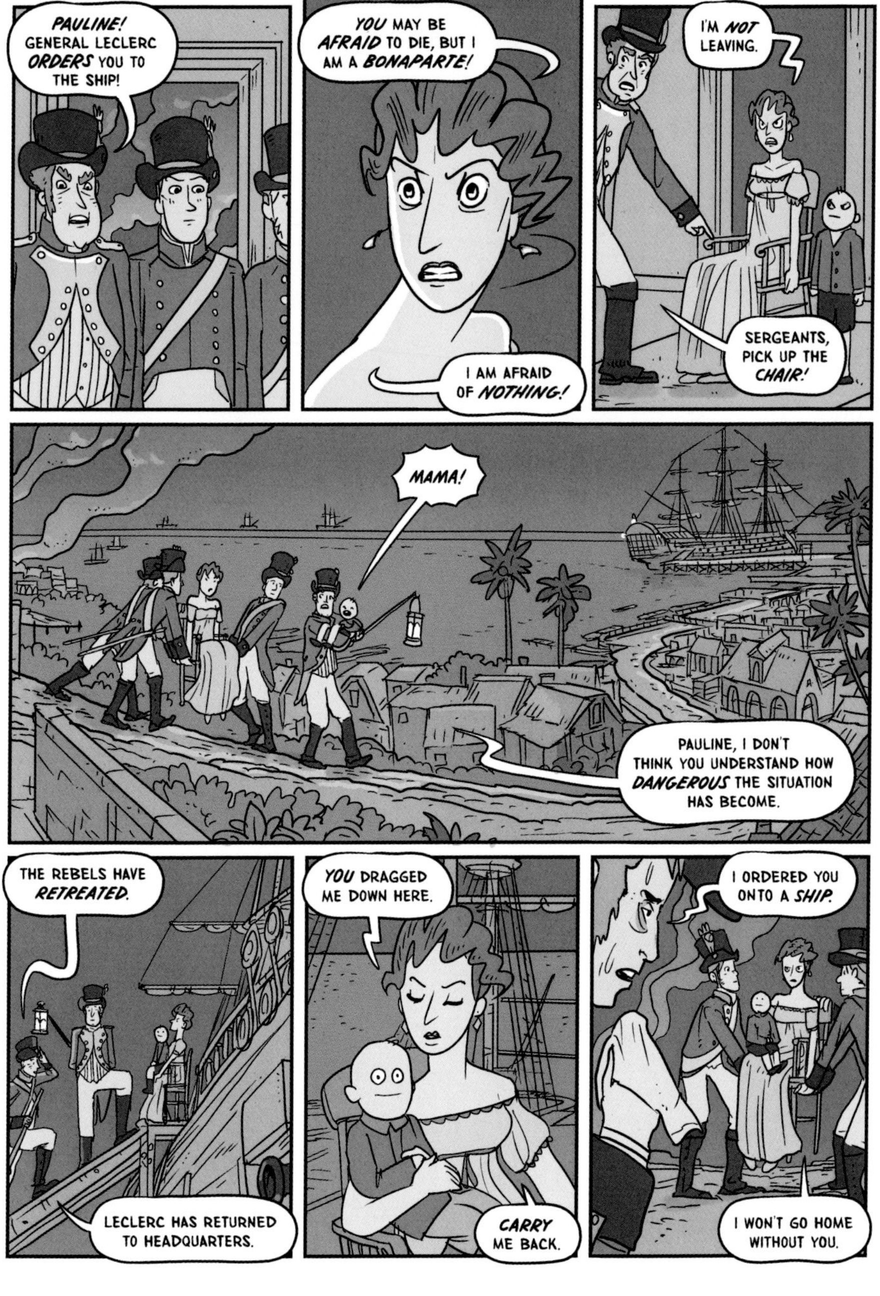
PAULINE! GENERAL LECLERC ORDERS YOU TO THE SHIP!
YOU MAY BE AFRAID TO DIE, BUT I AM A BONAPARTE!
I AM AFRAID OF NOTHING!
I'M NOT LEAVING.
SERGEANTS, PICK UP THE CHAIR!
MAMA!
PAULINE, I DON'T THINK YOU UNDERSTAND HOW DANGEROUS THE SITUATION HAS BECOME.
THE REBELS HAVE RETREATED.
LECLERC HAS RETURNED TO HEADQUARTERS.
YOU DRAGGED ME DOWN HERE.
CARRY ME BACK.
I ORDERED YOU ONTO A SHIP.
I WON'T GO HOME WITHOUT YOU.

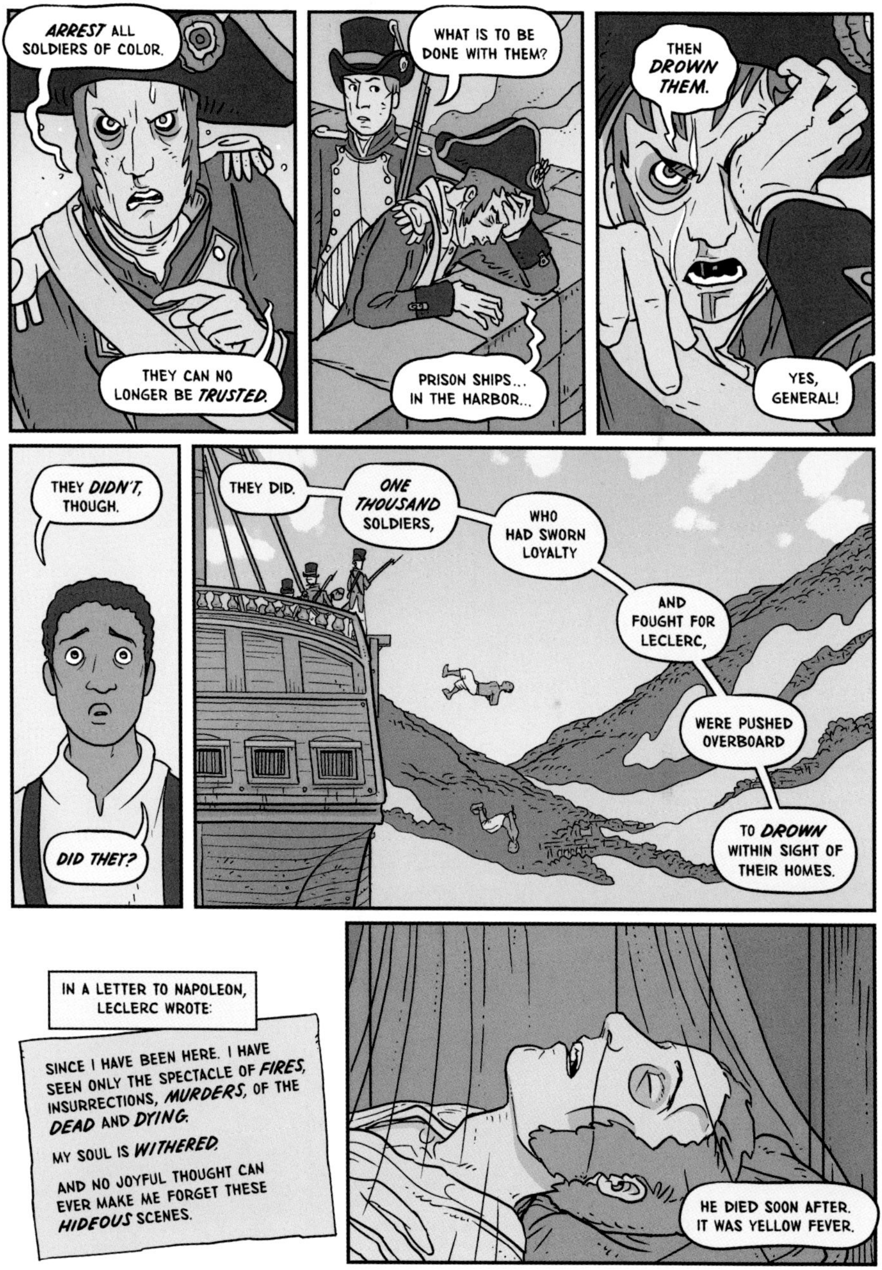
ARREST ALL SOLDIERS OF COLOR.
THEY CAN NO LONGER BE TRUSTED.
WHAT IS TO BE DONE WITH THEM?
PRISON SHIPS... IN THE HARBOR...
THEN DROWN THEM.
YES, GENERAL!
THEY DIDN'T, THOUGH.
DID THEY?
THEY DID.
ONE THOUSAND SOLDIERS,
WHO HAD SWORN LOYALTY
AND FOUGHT FOR LECLERC,
WERE PUSHED OVERBOARD
TO DROWN WITHIN SIGHT OF THEIR HOMES.
IN A LETTER TO NAPOLEON, LECLERC WROTE:
SINCE I HAVE BEEN HERE. I HAVE SEEN ONLY THE SPECTACLE OF FIRES, INSURRECTIONS, MURDERS, OF THE DEAD AND DYING.
MY SOUL IS WITHERED.
AND NO JOYFUL THOUGHT CAN EVER MAKE ME FORGET THESE HIDEOUS SCENES.
HE DIED SOON AFTER. IT WAS YELLOW FEVER.

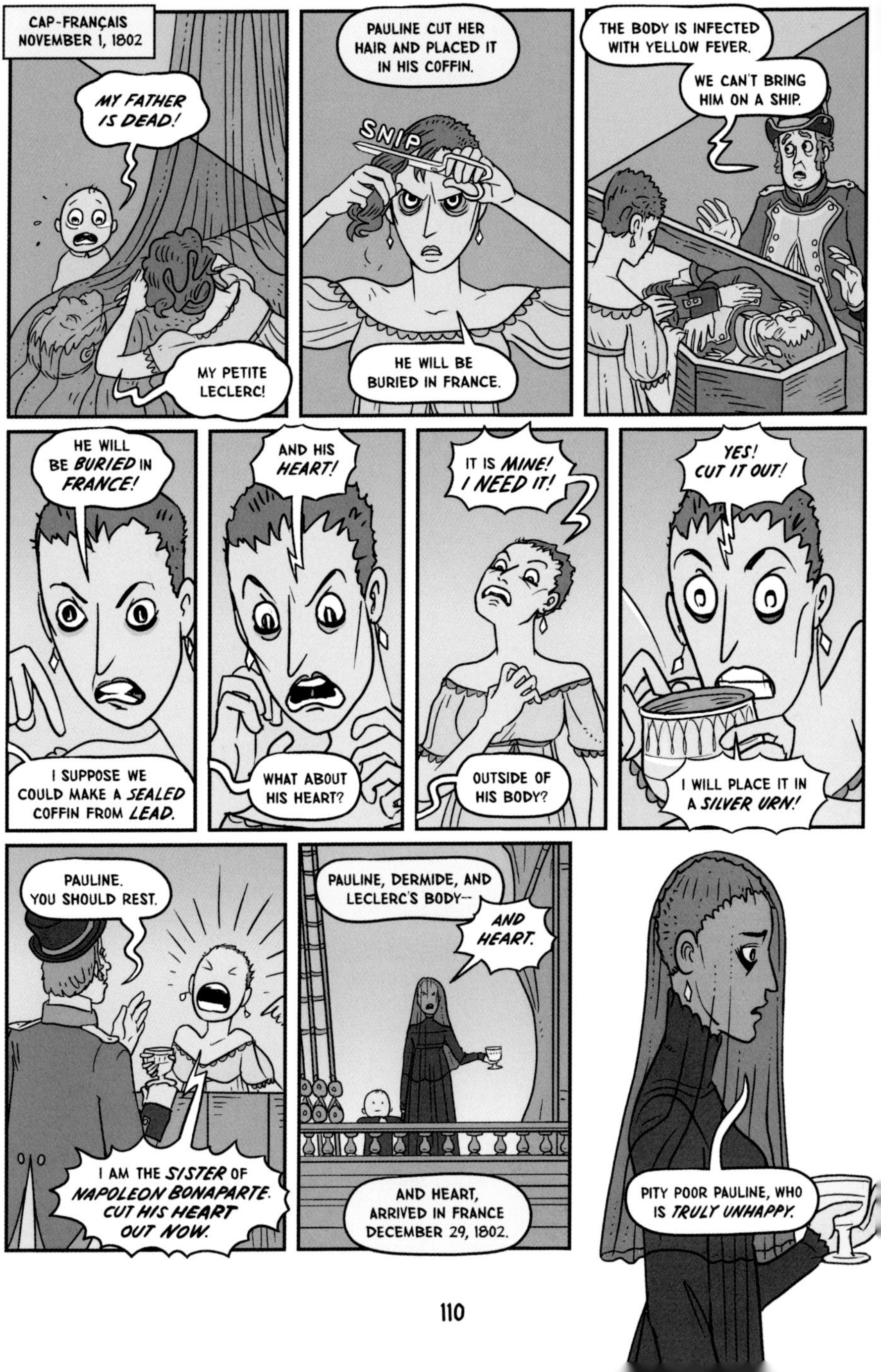
CAP-FRANÇAIS
NOVEMBER 1, 1802
MY FATHER IS DEAD!
MY PETITE LECLERC!
PAULINE CUT HER HAIR AND PLACED IT IN HIS COFFIN.
SNIP
HE WILL BE BURIED IN FRANCE.
THE BODY IS INFECTED WITH YELLOW FEVER.
WE CAN'T BRING HIM ON A SHIP.
HE WILL BE BURIED IN FRANCE!
I SUPPOSE WE COULD MAKE A SEALED COFFIN FROM LEAD.
AND HIS HEART!
WHAT ABOUT HIS HEART?
IT IS MINE! I NEED IT!
OUTSIDE OF HIS BODY?
YES! CUT IT OUT!
I WILL PLACE IT IN A SILVER URN!
PAULINE. YOU SHOULD REST.
I AM THE SISTER OF NAPOLEON BONAPARTE. CUT HIS HEART OUT NOW.
PAULINE, DERMIDE, AND LECLERC'S BODY--
AND HEART.
AND HEART, ARRIVED IN FRANCE DECEMBER 29, 1802.
PITY POOR PAULINE, WHO IS TRULY UNHAPPY.

CHAPTER 9

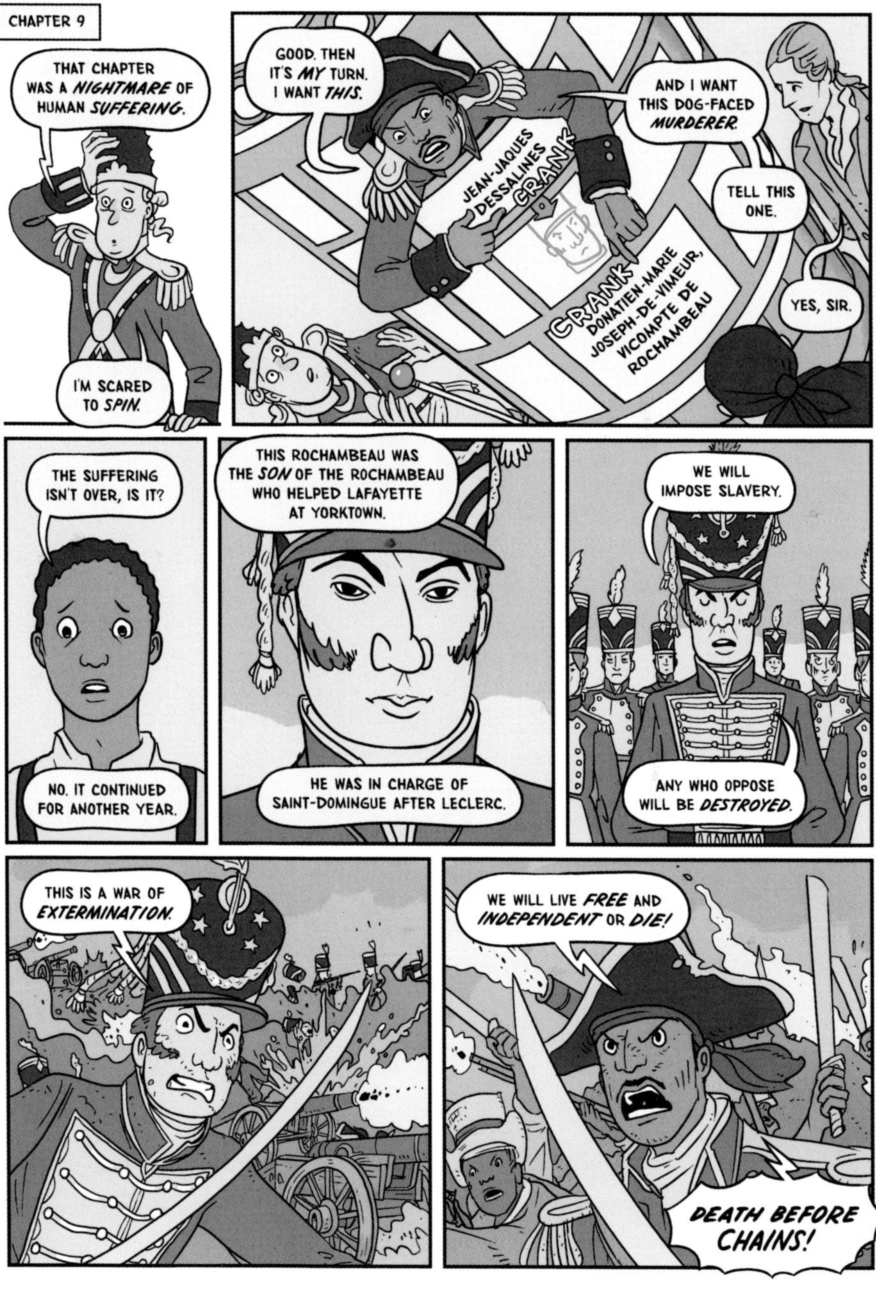
THAT CHAPTER WAS A *NIGHTMARE* OF HUMAN *SUFFERING*.
I'M SCARED TO *SPIN*.
GOOD. THEN IT'S *MY* TURN. I WANT *THIS*.
JEAN-JAQUES DESSALINES
CRANK
CRANK
DONATIEN-MARIE JOSEPH-DE-VIMEUR, VICOMPTE DE ROCHAMBEAU
AND I WANT THIS DOG-FACED *MURDERER*.
TELL THIS ONE.
YES, SIR.
THE SUFFERING ISN'T OVER, IS IT?
NO. IT CONTINUED FOR ANOTHER YEAR.
THIS ROCHAMBEAU WAS THE *SON* OF THE ROCHAMBEAU WHO HELPED LAFAYETTE AT YORKTOWN.
HE WAS IN CHARGE OF SAINT-DOMINGUE AFTER LECLERC.
WE WILL IMPOSE SLAVERY.
ANY WHO OPPOSE WILL BE *DESTROYED*.
THIS IS A WAR OF *EXTERMINATION*.
WE WILL LIVE *FREE* AND *INDEPENDENT* OR *DIE*!
DEATH BEFORE CHAINS!

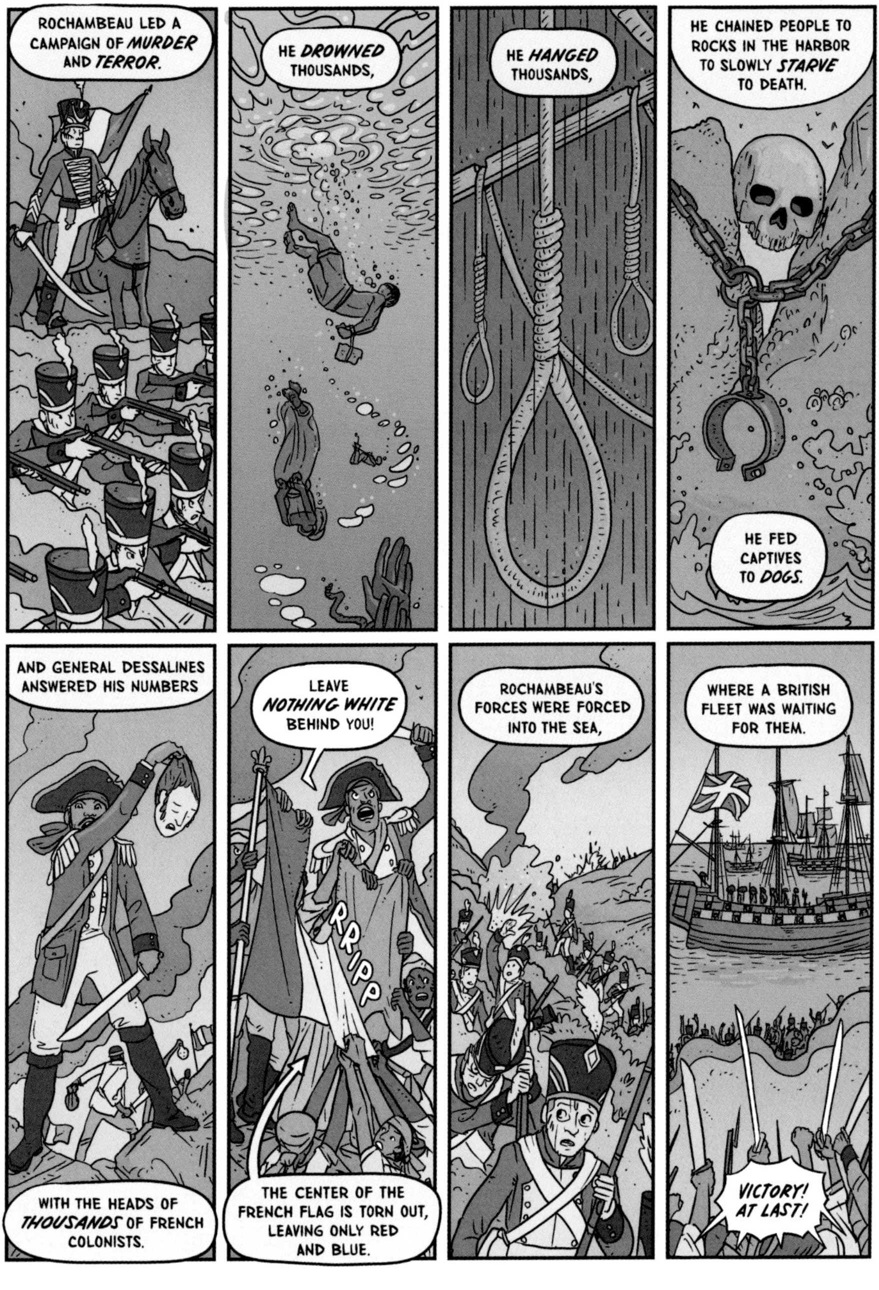
ROCHAMBEAU LED A CAMPAIGN OF *MURDER* AND *TERROR*.
HE *DROWNED* THOUSANDS,
HE *HANGED* THOUSANDS,
HE CHAINED PEOPLE TO ROCKS IN THE HARBOR TO SLOWLY *STARVE* TO DEATH.
HE FED CAPTIVES TO *DOGS*.
AND GENERAL DESSALINES ANSWERED HIS NUMBERS
WITH THE HEADS OF *THOUSANDS* OF FRENCH COLONISTS.
LEAVE *NOTHING WHITE* BEHIND YOU!
RRIPP
THE CENTER OF THE FRENCH FLAG IS TORN OUT, LEAVING ONLY RED AND BLUE.
ROCHAMBEAU'S FORCES WERE FORCED INTO THE SEA,
WHERE A BRITISH FLEET WAS WAITING FOR THEM.
VICTORY! AT LAST!

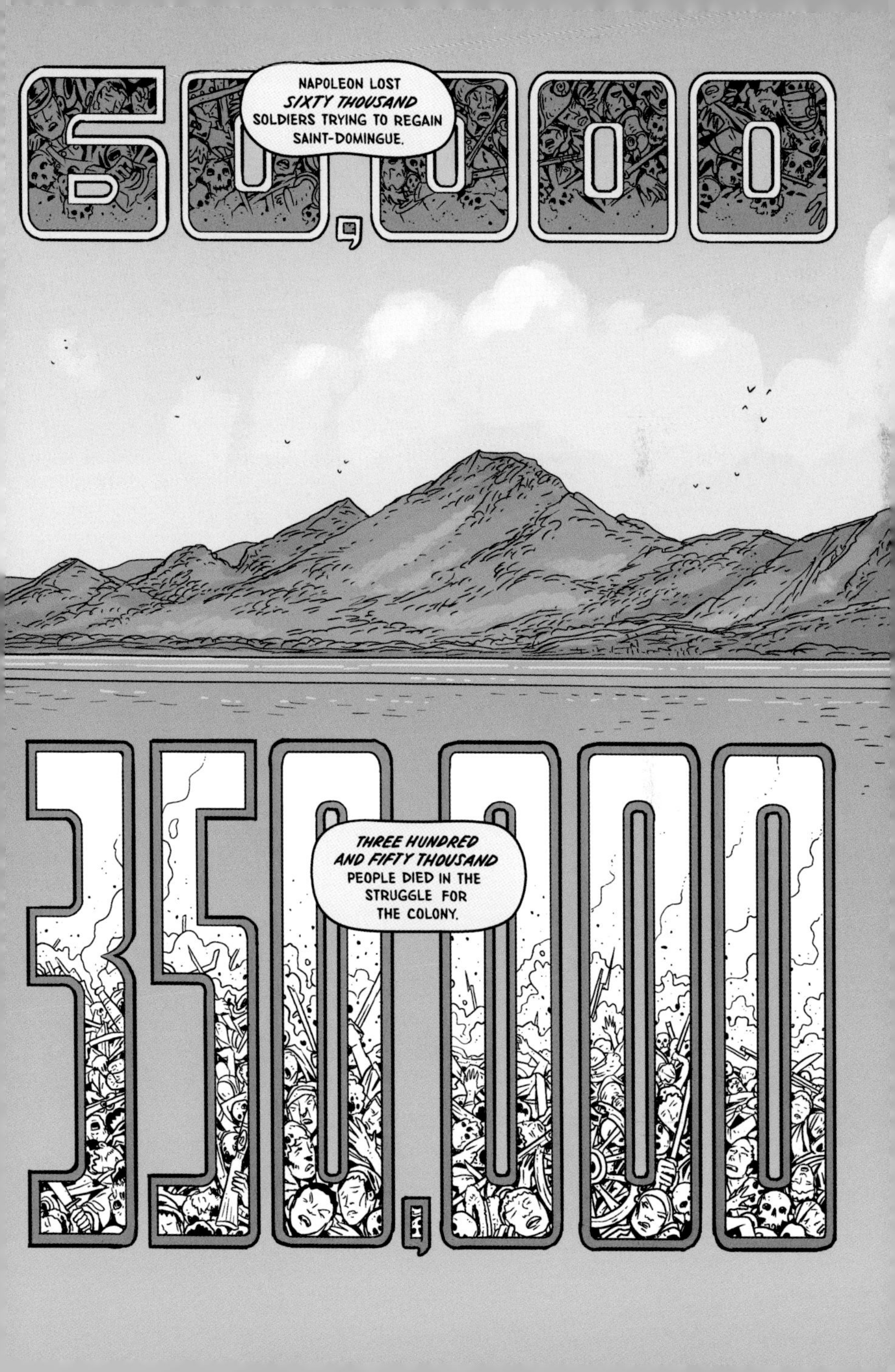
NAPOLEON LOST *SIXTY THOUSAND* SOLDIERS TRYING TO REGAIN SAINT-DOMINGUE.
60,000
THREE HUNDRED AND FIFTY THOUSAND PEOPLE DIED IN THE STRUGGLE FOR THE COLONY.
350,000

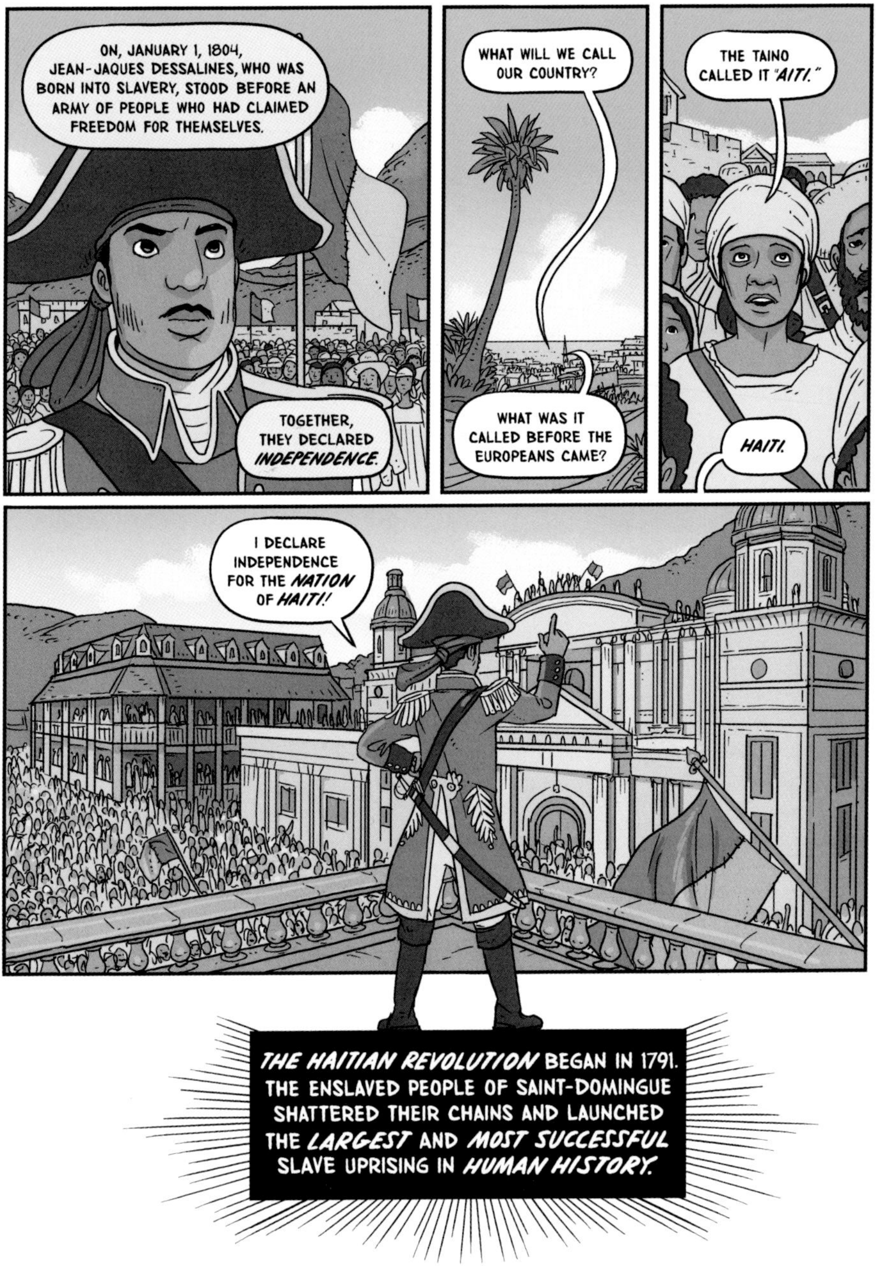
ON, JANUARY 1, 1804, JEAN-JAQUES DESSALINES, WHO WAS BORN INTO SLAVERY, STOOD BEFORE AN ARMY OF PEOPLE WHO HAD CLAIMED FREEDOM FOR THEMSELVES.
TOGETHER, THEY DECLARED *INDEPENDENCE*.
WHAT WILL WE CALL OUR COUNTRY?
WHAT WAS IT CALLED BEFORE THE EUROPEANS CAME?
THE TAINO CALLED IT *"AITI."*
HAITI.
I DECLARE INDEPENDENCE FOR THE *NATION* OF *HAITI!*
THE HAITIAN REVOLUTION BEGAN IN 1791. THE ENSLAVED PEOPLE OF SAINT-DOMINGUE SHATTERED THEIR CHAINS AND LAUNCHED THE *LARGEST* AND *MOST SUCCESSFUL* SLAVE UPRISING IN *HUMAN HISTORY.*

CHAPTER 10

THAT'S THE *END*, RIGHT?

NO, IT ISN'T THE END.

REMEMBER, THIS IS A STORY ABOUT A *LAND PURCHASE*—AND WE HAVEN'T GOTTEN TO IT YET.

NO. END IT *HERE*, WITH THE *SPECTACULAR DESTRUCTION* OF THE *FRENCH!*

NOPE. WE STARTED WITH A *GOAL.* SPIN AGAIN.

SPINNN

VERY WELL. WHO ARE THESE *YAHOOS?*

THOMAS JEFFERSON

LIVINGSTON AND MONROE

REMEMBER THE CHAPTER ABOUT NEW ORLEANS?

YEAH, THE MOST *BORING* CHAPTER.

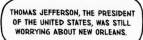

THOMAS JEFFERSON, THE PRESIDENT OF THE UNITED STATES, WAS STILL WORRYING ABOUT NEW ORLEANS.

I *NEEEED* THAT CITY!

ROBERT LIVINGSTON!

EH?

SHOOOP

I WANT YOU TO GO TO *FRANCE.*

BUT I DON'T SPEAK FRENCH.

TELL THEM TO *STAY OUT* OF *NEW ORLEANS.*

IF NAPOLEON CONTROLS THAT PORT, HE CONTROLS TRADE FOR *HALF* OF OUR COUNTRY!

HAVE YOU LOOKED AT EUROPE *LATELY?*

WHEN BONAPARTE GETS A FOOTHOLD HERE, OUR CONTINENT WILL LOOK THE SAME!

WILL THE GOVERNMENT OF FRANCE LISTEN?

FRANCE *LOVES* ME. THEY WILL LISTEN.

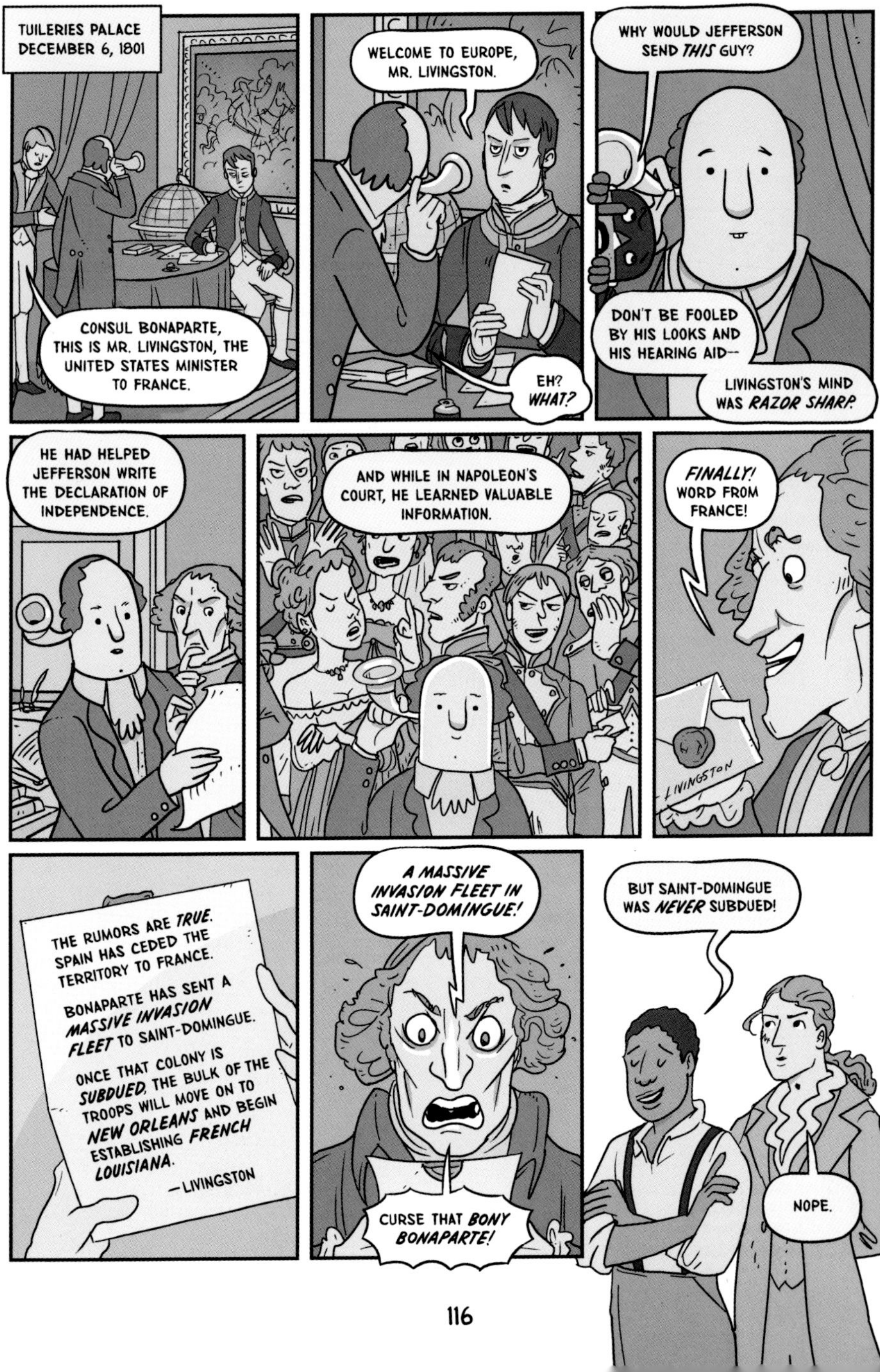
TUILERIES PALACE
DECEMBER 6, 1801
CONSUL BONAPARTE, THIS IS MR. LIVINGSTON, THE UNITED STATES MINISTER TO FRANCE.
WELCOME TO EUROPE, MR. LIVINGSTON.
EH? WHAT?
WHY WOULD JEFFERSON SEND THIS GUY?
DON'T BE FOOLED BY HIS LOOKS AND HIS HEARING AID--
LIVINGSTON'S MIND WAS RAZOR SHARP.
HE HAD HELPED JEFFERSON WRITE THE DECLARATION OF INDEPENDENCE.
AND WHILE IN NAPOLEON'S COURT, HE LEARNED VALUABLE INFORMATION.
FINALLY! WORD FROM FRANCE!
LIVINGSTON
THE RUMORS ARE TRUE. SPAIN HAS CEDED THE TERRITORY TO FRANCE.
BONAPARTE HAS SENT A MASSIVE INVASION FLEET TO SAINT-DOMINGUE.
ONCE THAT COLONY IS SUBDUED, THE BULK OF THE TROOPS WILL MOVE ON TO NEW ORLEANS AND BEGIN ESTABLISHING FRENCH LOUISIANA.
—LIVINGSTON
A MASSIVE INVASION FLEET IN SAINT-DOMINGUE!
CURSE THAT BONY BONAPARTE!
BUT SAINT-DOMINGUE WAS NEVER SUBDUED!
NOPE.

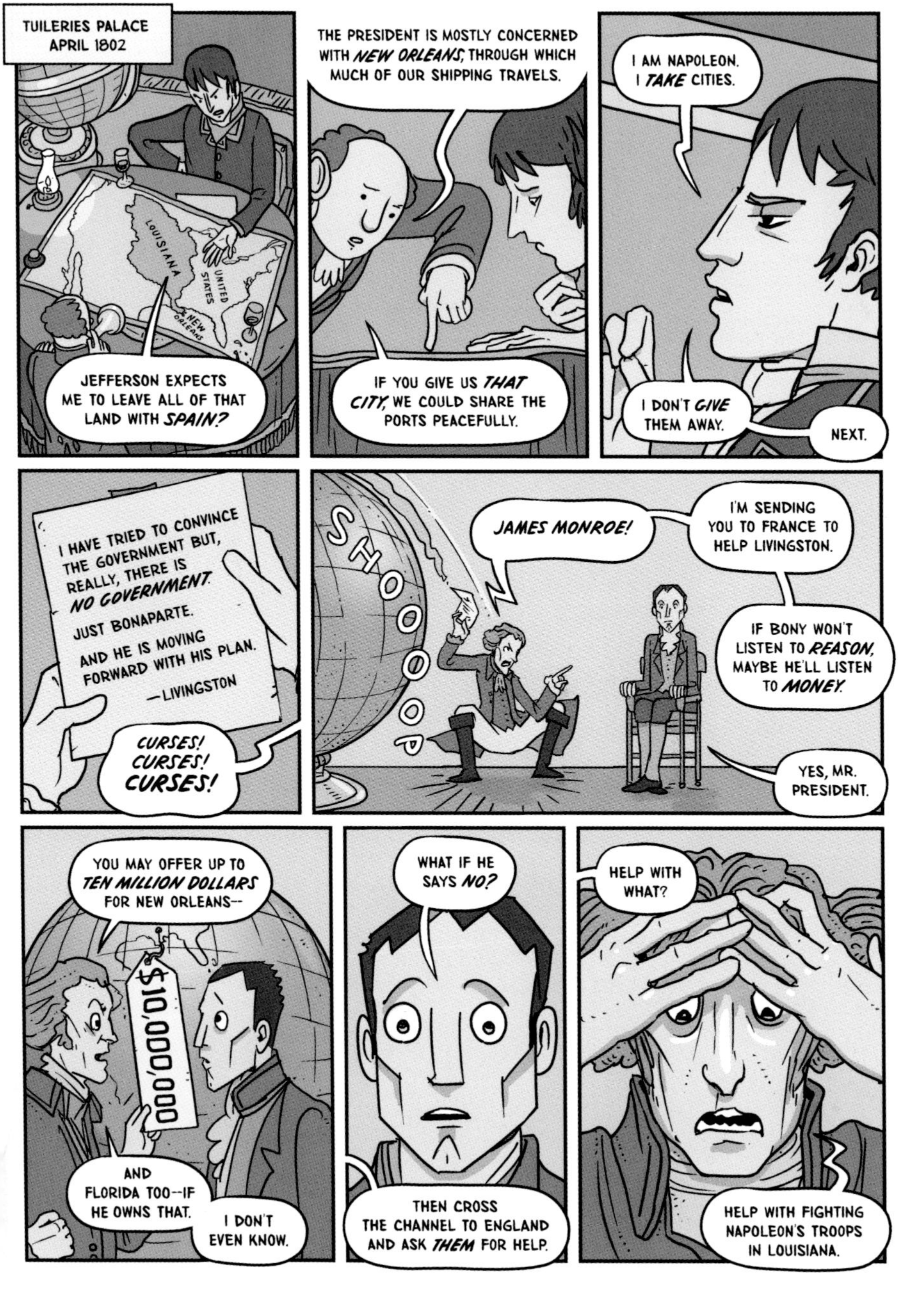
TUILERIES PALACE
APRIL 1802
LOUISIANA
UNITED STATES
NEW ORLEANS
JEFFERSON EXPECTS ME TO LEAVE ALL OF THAT LAND WITH SPAIN?
THE PRESIDENT IS MOSTLY CONCERNED WITH NEW ORLEANS, THROUGH WHICH MUCH OF OUR SHIPPING TRAVELS.
IF YOU GIVE US THAT CITY, WE COULD SHARE THE PORTS PEACEFULLY.
I AM NAPOLEON. I TAKE CITIES.
I DON'T GIVE THEM AWAY.
NEXT.
I HAVE TRIED TO CONVINCE THE GOVERNMENT BUT, REALLY, THERE IS NO GOVERNMENT.
JUST BONAPARTE.
AND HE IS MOVING FORWARD WITH HIS PLAN.
—LIVINGSTON
CURSES! CURSES! CURSES!
SHOOOOP
JAMES MONROE!
I'M SENDING YOU TO FRANCE TO HELP LIVINGSTON.
IF BONY WON'T LISTEN TO REASON, MAYBE HE'LL LISTEN TO MONEY.
YES, MR. PRESIDENT.
YOU MAY OFFER UP TO TEN MILLION DOLLARS FOR NEW ORLEANS--
$10,000,000
AND FLORIDA TOO--IF HE OWNS THAT.
I DON'T EVEN KNOW.
WHAT IF HE SAYS NO?
THEN CROSS THE CHANNEL TO ENGLAND AND ASK THEM FOR HELP.
HELP WITH WHAT?
HELP WITH FIGHTING NAPOLEON'S TROOPS IN LOUISIANA.

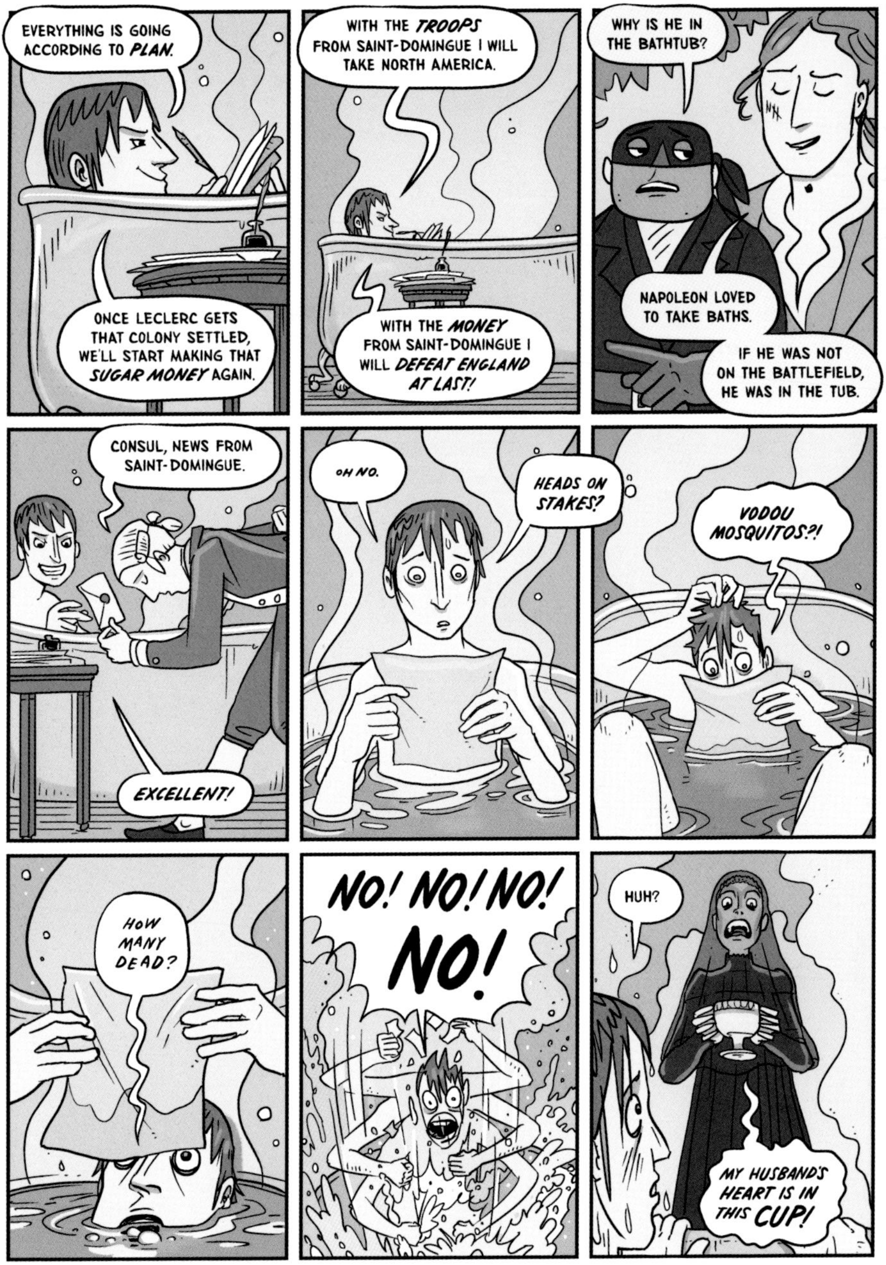
EVERYTHING IS GOING ACCORDING TO *PLAN.*
ONCE LECLERC GETS THAT COLONY SETTLED, WE'LL START MAKING THAT *SUGAR MONEY* AGAIN.
WITH THE *TROOPS* FROM SAINT-DOMINGUE I WILL TAKE NORTH AMERICA.
WITH THE *MONEY* FROM SAINT-DOMINGUE I WILL *DEFEAT ENGLAND AT LAST!*
WHY IS HE IN THE BATHTUB?
NAPOLEON LOVED TO TAKE BATHS.
IF HE WAS NOT ON THE BATTLEFIELD, HE WAS IN THE TUB.
CONSUL, NEWS FROM SAINT-DOMINGUE.
EXCELLENT!
OH NO.
HEADS ON STAKES?
VODOU MOSQUITOS?!
HOW MANY DEAD?
NO! NO! NO!
NO!
HUH?
MY HUSBAND'S HEART IS IN THIS CUP!

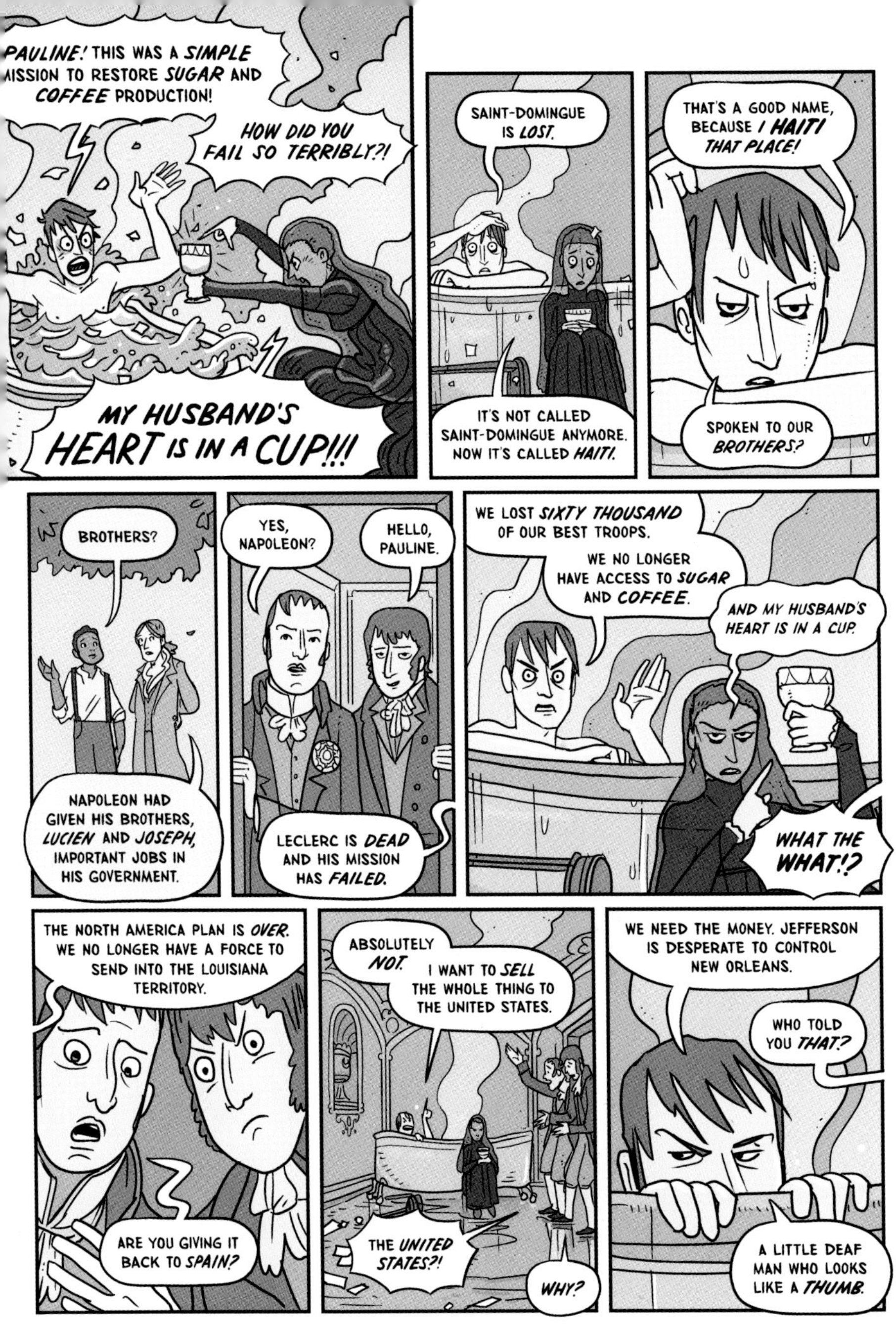
PAULINE! THIS WAS A SIMPLE MISSION TO RESTORE SUGAR AND COFFEE PRODUCTION!
HOW DID YOU FAIL SO TERRIBLY?!
MY HUSBAND'S HEART IS IN A CUP!!!
SAINT-DOMINGUE IS LOST.
IT'S NOT CALLED SAINT-DOMINGUE ANYMORE. NOW IT'S CALLED HAITI.
THAT'S A GOOD NAME, BECAUSE I HAITI THAT PLACE!
SPOKEN TO OUR BROTHERS?
BROTHERS?
NAPOLEON HAD GIVEN HIS BROTHERS, LUCIEN AND JOSEPH, IMPORTANT JOBS IN HIS GOVERNMENT.
YES, NAPOLEON?
HELLO, PAULINE.
LECLERC IS DEAD AND HIS MISSION HAS FAILED.
WE LOST SIXTY THOUSAND OF OUR BEST TROOPS.
WE NO LONGER HAVE ACCESS TO SUGAR AND COFFEE.
AND MY HUSBAND'S HEART IS IN A CUP.
WHAT THE WHAT!?
THE NORTH AMERICA PLAN IS OVER. WE NO LONGER HAVE A FORCE TO SEND INTO THE LOUISIANA TERRITORY.
ARE YOU GIVING IT BACK TO SPAIN?
ABSOLUTELY NOT.
I WANT TO SELL THE WHOLE THING TO THE UNITED STATES.
THE UNITED STATES?!
WHY?
WE NEED THE MONEY. JEFFERSON IS DESPERATE TO CONTROL NEW ORLEANS.
WHO TOLD YOU THAT?
A LITTLE DEAF MAN WHO LOOKS LIKE A THUMB.

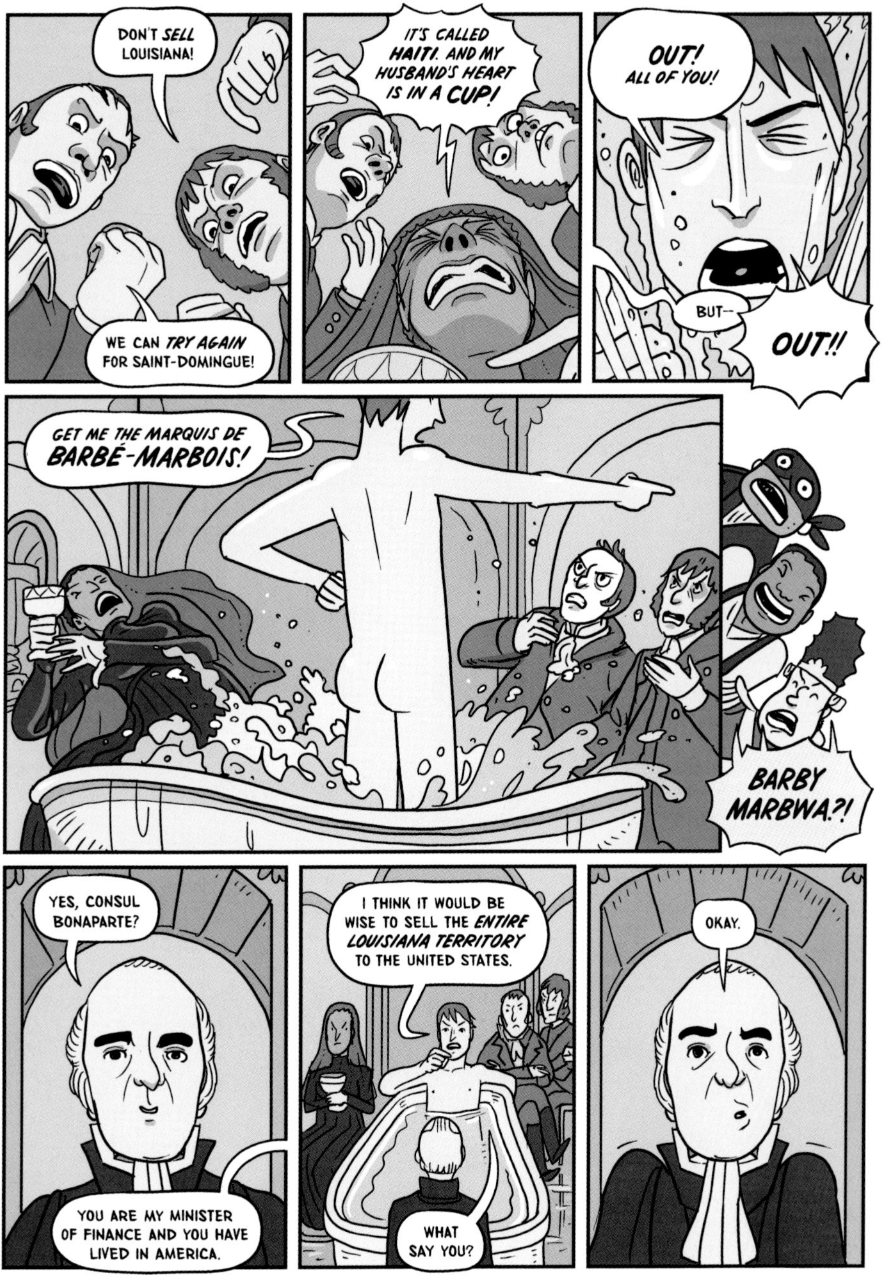
DON'T SELL LOUISIANA!
WE CAN TRY AGAIN FOR SAINT-DOMINGUE!
IT'S CALLED HAITI. AND MY HUSBAND'S HEART IS IN A CUP!
OUT! ALL OF YOU!
BUT--
OUT!!
GET ME THE MARQUIS DE BARBÉ-MARBOIS!
BARBY MARBWA?!
YES, CONSUL BONAPARTE?
YOU ARE MY MINISTER OF FINANCE AND YOU HAVE LIVED IN AMERICA.
WHAT SAY YOU?
I THINK IT WOULD BE WISE TO SELL THE ENTIRE LOUISIANA TERRITORY TO THE UNITED STATES.
OKAY.

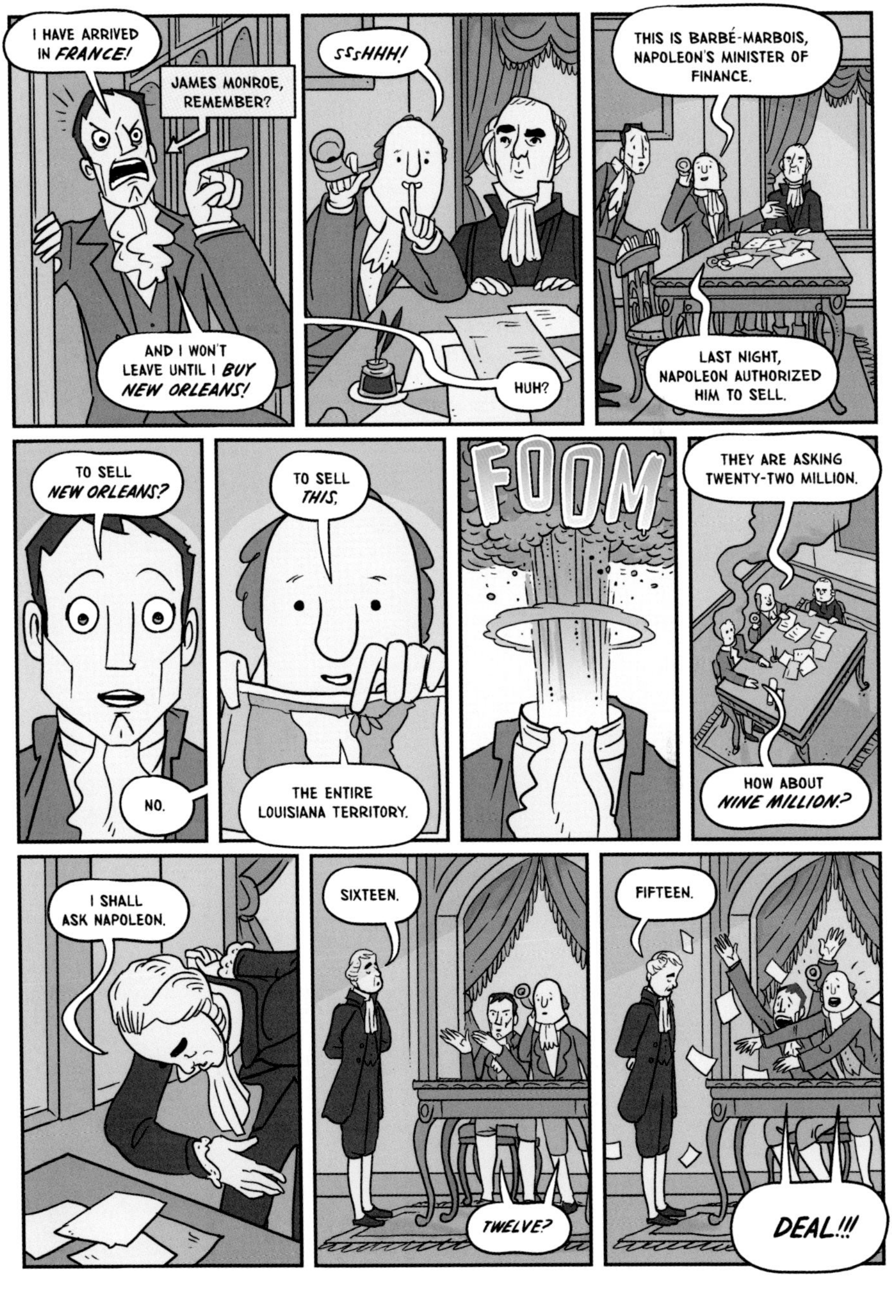
I HAVE ARRIVED IN *FRANCE!*
JAMES MONROE, REMEMBER?
AND I WON'T LEAVE UNTIL I *BUY NEW ORLEANS!*
SSSHHH!
HUH?
THIS IS BARBÉ-MARBOIS, NAPOLEON'S MINISTER OF FINANCE.
LAST NIGHT, NAPOLEON AUTHORIZED HIM TO SELL.
TO SELL *NEW ORLEANS?*
NO.
TO SELL *THIS,*
THE ENTIRE LOUISIANA TERRITORY.
FOOM
THEY ARE ASKING TWENTY-TWO MILLION.
HOW ABOUT *NINE MILLION?*
I SHALL ASK NAPOLEON.
SIXTEEN.
TWELVE?
FIFTEEN.
DEAL!!!

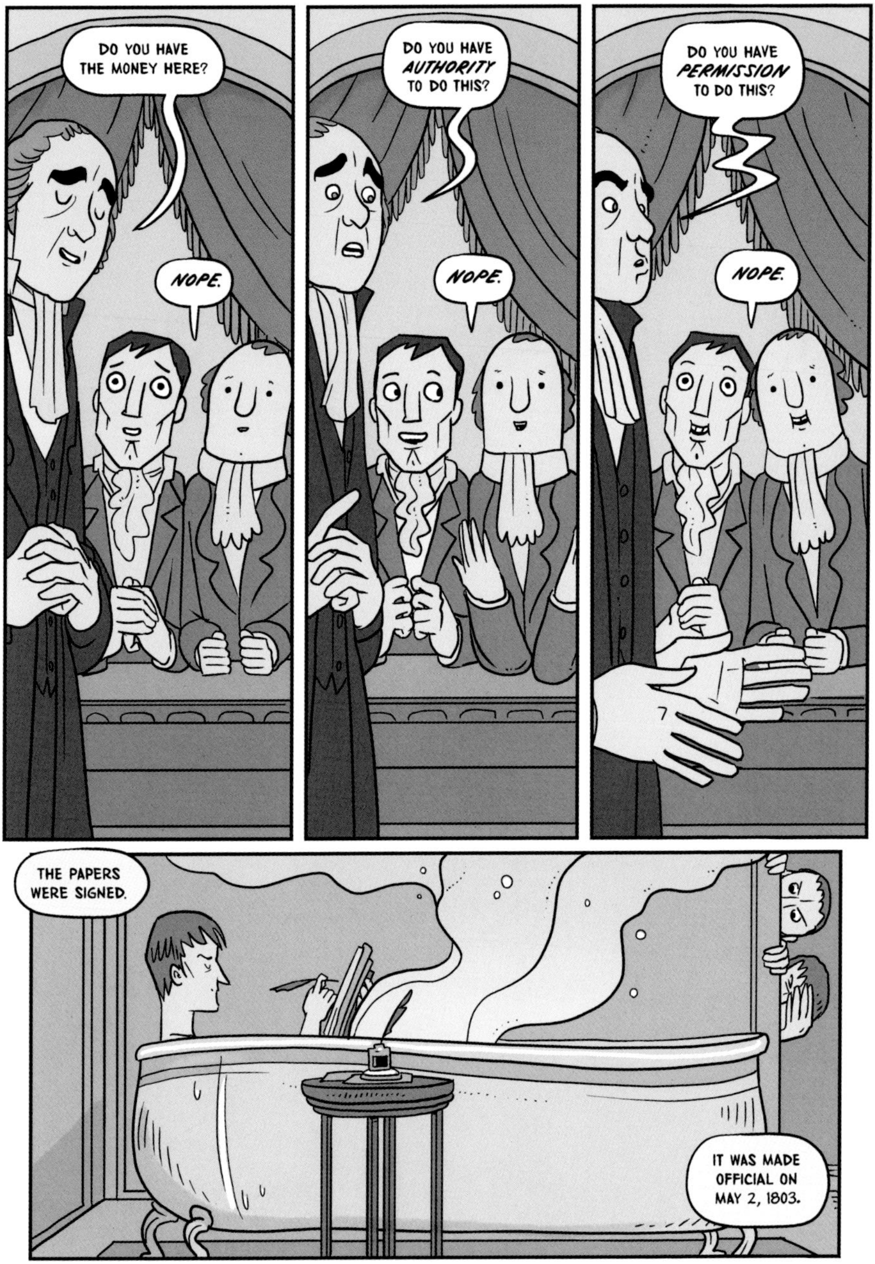
DO YOU HAVE THE MONEY HERE?
NOPE.
DO YOU HAVE *AUTHORITY* TO DO THIS?
NOPE.
DO YOU HAVE *PERMISSION* TO DO THIS?
NOPE.
THE PAPERS WERE SIGNED.
IT WAS MADE OFFICIAL ON MAY 2, 1803.

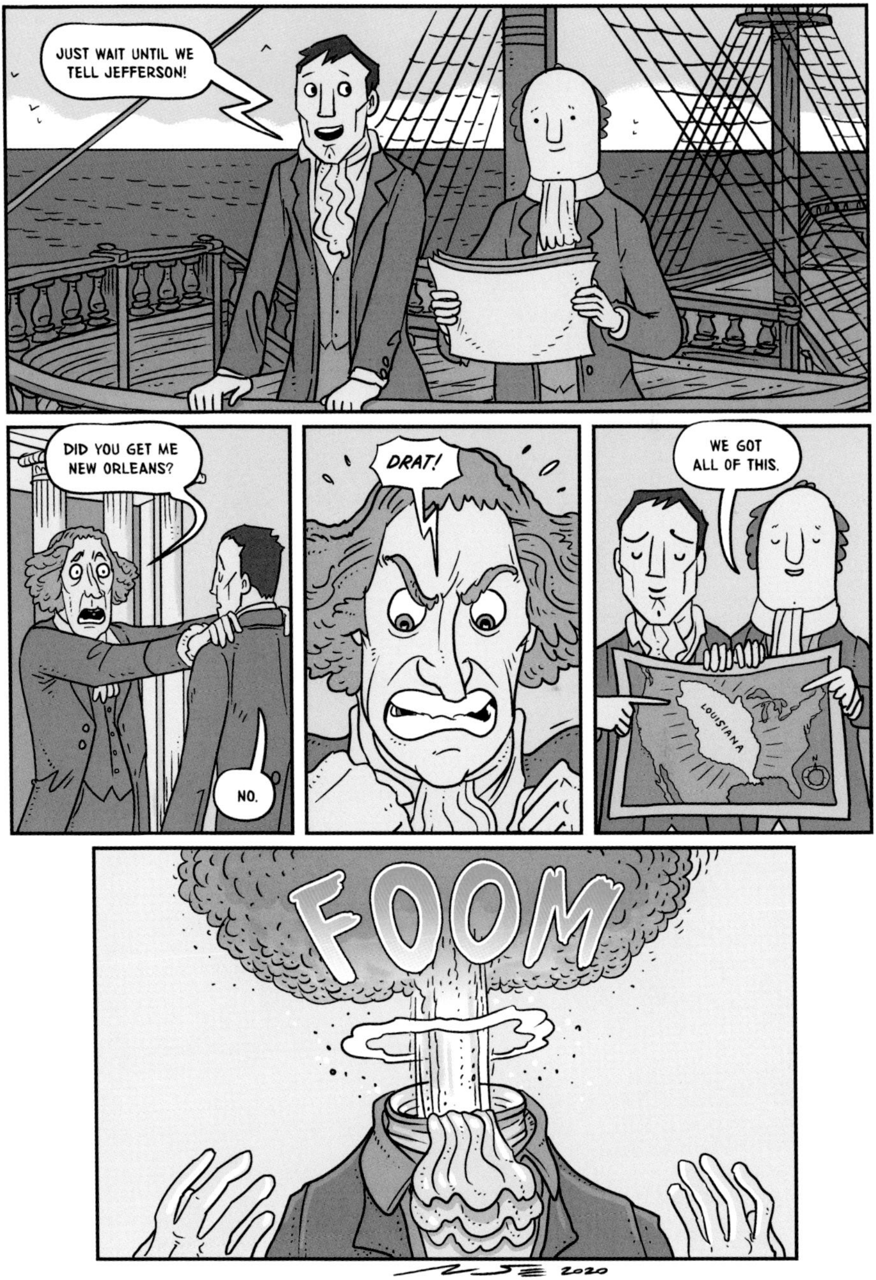
JUST WAIT UNTIL WE TELL JEFFERSON!
DID YOU GET ME NEW ORLEANS?
NO.
DRAT!
WE GOT ALL OF THIS.
LOUISIANA
FOOM
2020

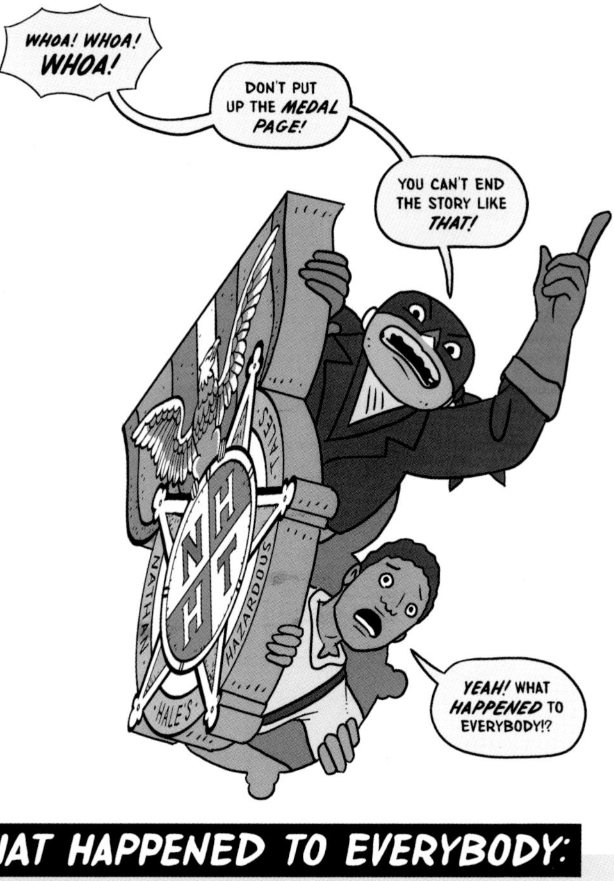
WHOA! WHOA! WHOA!
DON'T PUT UP THE *MEDAL PAGE!*
YOU CAN'T END THE STORY LIKE *THAT!*
NATHAN HALE'S HAZARDOUS TALES
YEAH! WHAT *HAPPENED* TO EVERYBODY!?

WHAT HAPPENED TO EVERYBODY:

RENÉ-ROBERT CAVELIER DE LA SALLE

RETURNED TO THE AMERICAS IN 1684 WITH THREE HUNDRED COLONISTS AND A PLAN TO SETTLE IN THE GULF OF MEXICO.

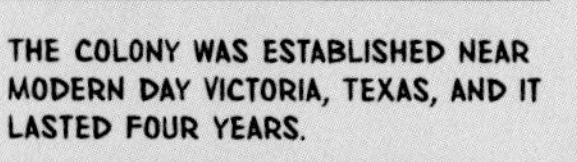

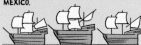

THE COLONY WAS ESTABLISHED NEAR MODERN DAY VICTORIA, TEXAS, AND IT LASTED FOUR YEARS.

DURING THAT TIME SHIPWRECKS, PIRATES, MUTANIES, AND NATIVE AMERICANS WHITTLED THE ORIGINAL THREE HUNDRED DOWN TO ZERO.

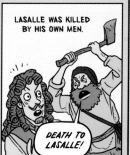

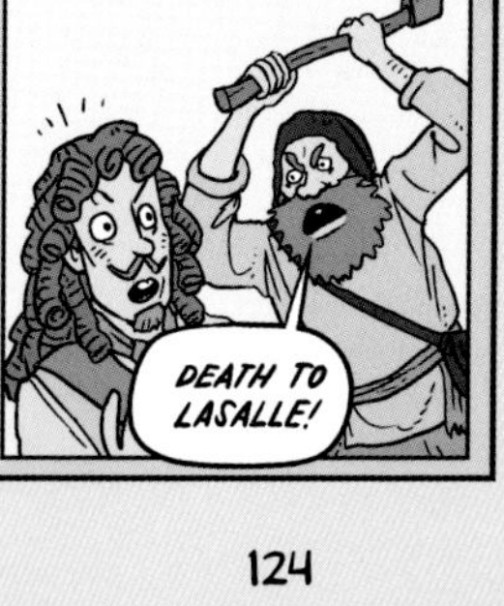
LASALLE WAS KILLED BY HIS OWN MEN.
DEATH TO LASALLE!

AEDES AEGYPTI

ARE ALIVE AND WELL, LIVING IN TROPICAL ZONES AROUND THE WORLD. THEY CARRY YELLOW FEVER, DENGUE FEVER, ZIKA VIRUS, CHIKUNGUNYA, AND MAYARO.

IF YOU ARE GOING ANYWHERE TROPICAL, GET YOUR VACCINE SHOTS AND BRING MOSQUITO REPELLENT!

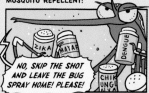

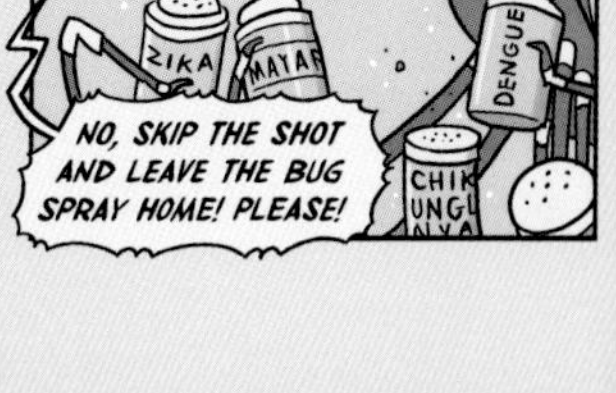
ZIKA
DENGUE
NO, SKIP THE SHOT AND LEAVE THE BUG SPRAY HOME! PLEASE!

LÉGER FÉLICITÉ SONTHONAX

WAS KICKED OUT OF SAINT DOMINGUE IN 1797.

HE RETURNED TO HIS HOME IN OYONNAX, FRANCE.

SONTHONAX FROM OYONNAX.

AWWW! HE'S STILL ADORABLE.

THE REPUBLIC OF HAITI

IS NOW HOME TO OVER ELEVEN MILLION PEOPLE. IT IS THE SECOND MOST POPULOUS COUNTRY IN THE CARIBBEAN, AFTER CUBA.

HAITI REMAINS A FREE AND INDEPENDENT COUNTRY TO THIS DAY.

BLUE
RED

TOUSSAINT L'OUVERTURE

DIED ON APRIL 7TH, 1803, IN A FREEZING FORTRESS IN THE JURA MOUNTAINS OF EASTERN FRANCE. HE WAS 59.

JEAN-JAQUES DESSALINES

CROWNED HIMSELF EMPEROR OF HAITI ON OCTOBER 6TH, 1804. UNDER HIM, SLAVERY IN HAITI WAS COMPLETELY ABOLISHED.

THIS MAKES HAITI THE *FIRST* COUNTRY IN THE AMERICAS TO *END SLAVERY*.

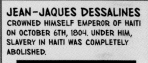

DEATH TO SLAVERY!

HAITI #1

HE ALSO ABOLISHED THE FRENCH IN HAITI, SLAUGHTERING BETWEEN THREE AND FIVE THOUSAND FRENCH PEOPLE IN WHAT WAS CALLED *THE HAITI MASSACRE OF 1804*.

DEATH TO THE FRENCH!

SLAVE OWNERS IN THE AMERICAN SOUTH USED THIS EVENT AS AN ARGUMENT TO MAINTAIN SLAVERY IN THE UNITED STATES.

IF WE FREE OUR SLAVES THEY WILL REENACT THE *HORRORS OF ST. DOMINGO* UPON US!!

DESSALINES WAS ASSASSINATED BY HIS OWN MEN ON OCTOBER 17TH, 1806.

DEATH TO DESSALINES!

ROBERT R. LIVINGSTON MADE FRIENDS WITH

ROBERT FULTON, THE INVENTOR. TOGETHER THEY BUILT THE WORLD'S FIRST STEAMBOAT, THE *CLERMONT*, AND RACED IT DOWN THE HUDSON RIVER.

HELLO TO THE AGE OF STEAM!

JAMES MONROE BECAME THE FIFTH PRESIDENT

OF THE UNITED STATES. IN 1819 HE SIGNED THE ADAMS-ONIS TREATY WITH SPAIN WHICH GAVE FLORIDA TO THE UNITED STATES.

I GOT YOU THE LOUISIANA TERRITORY AND FLORIDA.

YOU'RE WELCOME, AMERICA.

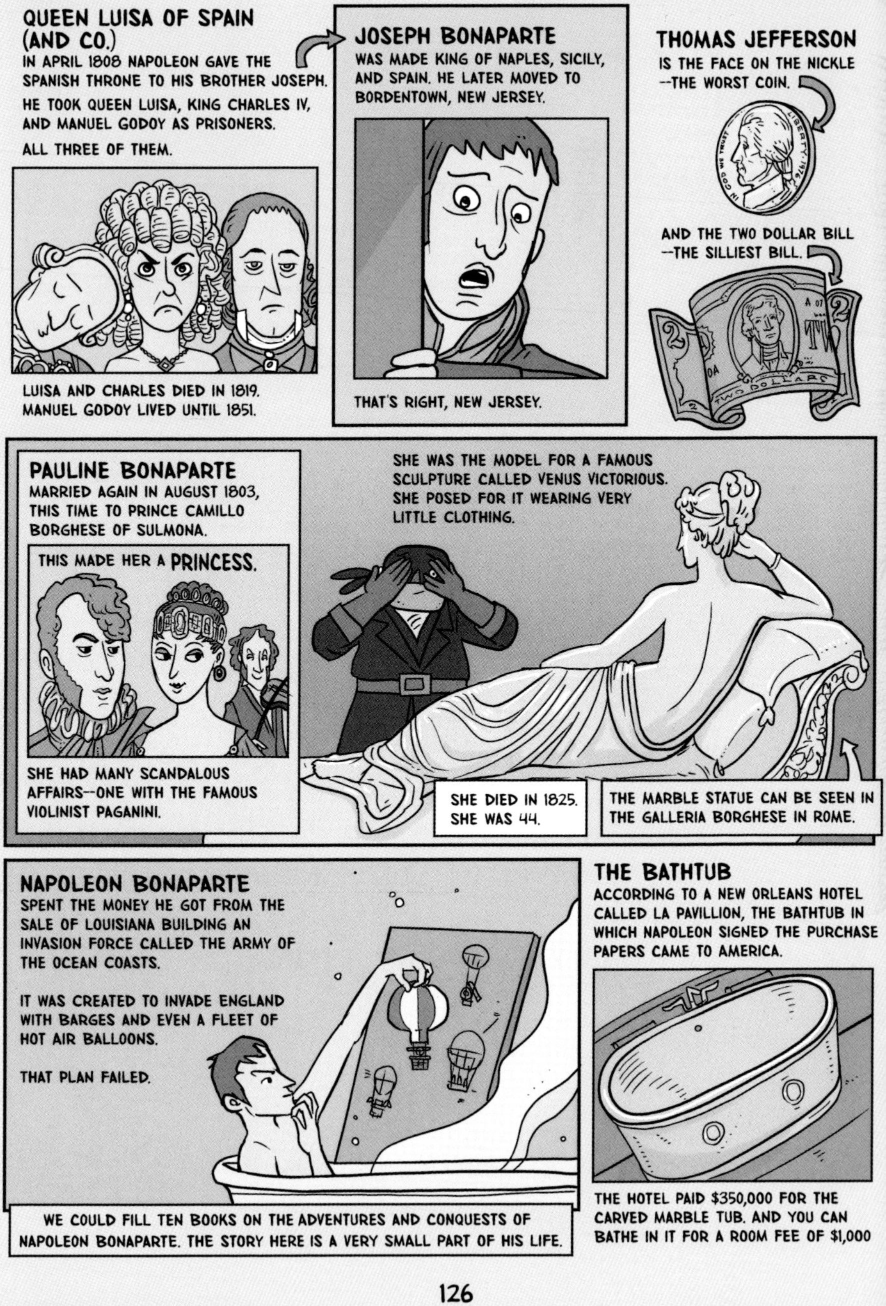
QUEEN LUISA OF SPAIN (AND CO.)
IN APRIL 1808 NAPOLEON GAVE THE SPANISH THRONE TO HIS BROTHER JOSEPH.
HE TOOK QUEEN LUISA, KING CHARLES IV, AND MANUEL GODOY AS PRISONERS.
ALL THREE OF THEM.
LUISA AND CHARLES DIED IN 1819. MANUEL GODOY LIVED UNTIL 1851.
JOSEPH BONAPARTE
WAS MADE KING OF NAPLES, SICILY, AND SPAIN. HE LATER MOVED TO BORDENTOWN, NEW JERSEY.
THAT'S RIGHT, NEW JERSEY.
THOMAS JEFFERSON
IS THE FACE ON THE NICKLE --THE WORST COIN.
AND THE TWO DOLLAR BILL --THE SILLIEST BILL.
PAULINE BONAPARTE
MARRIED AGAIN IN AUGUST 1803, THIS TIME TO PRINCE CAMILLO BORGHESE OF SULMONA.
THIS MADE HER A PRINCESS.
SHE HAD MANY SCANDALOUS AFFAIRS--ONE WITH THE FAMOUS VIOLINIST PAGANINI.
SHE WAS THE MODEL FOR A FAMOUS SCULPTURE CALLED VENUS VICTORIOUS. SHE POSED FOR IT WEARING VERY LITTLE CLOTHING.
SHE DIED IN 1825. SHE WAS 44.
THE MARBLE STATUE CAN BE SEEN IN THE GALLERIA BORGHESE IN ROME.
NAPOLEON BONAPARTE
SPENT THE MONEY HE GOT FROM THE SALE OF LOUISIANA BUILDING AN INVASION FORCE CALLED THE ARMY OF THE OCEAN COASTS.
IT WAS CREATED TO INVADE ENGLAND WITH BARGES AND EVEN A FLEET OF HOT AIR BALLOONS.
THAT PLAN FAILED.
WE COULD FILL TEN BOOKS ON THE ADVENTURES AND CONQUESTS OF NAPOLEON BONAPARTE. THE STORY HERE IS A VERY SMALL PART OF HIS LIFE.
THE BATHTUB
ACCORDING TO A NEW ORLEANS HOTEL CALLED LA PAVILLION, THE BATHTUB IN WHICH NAPOLEON SIGNED THE PURCHASE PAPERS CAME TO AMERICA.
THE HOTEL PAID $350,000 FOR THE CARVED MARBLE TUB. AND YOU CAN BATHE IN IT FOR A ROOM FEE OF $1,000

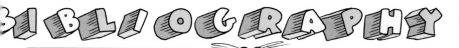

BIBLIOGRAPHY

BLUMBERG, RHODA. WHAT'S THE DEAL? JEFFERSON, NAPOLEON, AND THE LOUISIANA PURCHASE. NEW YORK, NY: SCHOLASTIC, 1999

BROWN, GORDON S. TOUSSAINT'S CLAUSE: THE FOUNDING FATHERS AND THE HAITIAN REVOLUTION. JACKSON, MS. UNIVERSITY PRESS OF MISSISSIPPI, 2005

CERAMI, CHARLES A. JEFFERSON'S GREAT GAMBLE: THE REMARKABLE STORY OF JEFFERSON, NAPOLEON AND THE MEN BEHIND THE LOUISIANA PURCHASE. NAPERVILLE, IL: SOURCEBOOKS, 2003

DAVIS, MARC. MACANDAL: THE INCREDIBLE STORY, HTTPS://MACANDAL.ORG

DUBOIS, LAURENT. AVENGERS OF THE NEW WORLD: THE STORY OF THE HAITIAN REVOLUTION. CAMBRIDGE, MA: HARVARD UNIVERSITY PRESS, 2004

DUBOIS, LAURENT. HAITI: THE AFTERSHOCKS OF HISTORY. NEW YORK, NY: HENRY HOLT, 2012

FICK, CAROLYN E. THE MAKING OF HAITI: THE SAINT DOMINGUE REVOLUTION FROM BELOW. KNOXVILLE, TN: UNIVERSITY OF TENNESSEE PRESS, 1990

FRASER, FLORA. PAULINE BONAPARTE: VENUS OF EMPIRE. NEW YORK, NY: ALFRED A. KNOPF, 2009

JAMES, C.L.R. THE BLACK JACOBINS: TOUSSAINT L'OUVERTURE AND THE SAN DOMINGO REVOLUTION. NEW YORK, NY: RANDOM HOUSE, 1963

KUKLA, JON. A WILDERNESS SO IMMENSE: THE LOUISIANA PURCHASE AND THE DESTINY OF AMERICA. NEW YORK, NY: ALFRED A. KNOPF, 2003

MCNEILL, J.R. MOSQUITO EMPIRES: ECOLOGY AND WAR IN THE GREATER CARIBBEAN 1620-1914. CAMBRIDGE, ENGLAND: CAMBRIDGE UNIVERSITY PRESS, 2010

MUHLSTEIN, ANKA. LA SALLE: EXPLORER OF THE NORTH AMERICAN FRONTIER, TRANSLATED FROM THE FRENCH BY WILLARD WOOD, NEW YORK, NY: ARCADE PUBLISHING, 1994

ORTZEN, LEN. IMPERIAL VENUS: THE STORY OF PAULINE BONAPARTE BORGHESE. SCARBOROUGH HOUSE, 1974

PARKER, MATTHEW. THE SUGAR BARONS: FAMILY, CORRUPTION, EMPIRE, AND WAR IN THE WEST INDIES. NEW YORK, NY: WALKER AND COMPANY, 2011

POOLE, ROBERT M. WHAT BECAME OF THE TAÍNO? SMITHSONIAN MAGAZINE, OCTOBER 2011 WWW.SMITHSONIANMAG.COM

POPKIN, JEREMY D. FACING RACIAL REVOLUTION: EYEWITNESS ACCOUNTS OF THE HAITIAN INSURRECTION. CHICAGO, IL: UNIVERSITY OF CHICAGO PRESS, 2007

RAMSEY, KATE. THE SPIRITS AND THE LAW: VODOU AND POWER IN HAITI. CHICAGO, IL: UNIVERSITY OF CHICAGO PRESS, 2011

ROBERTS, ANDREW. NAPOLEON: A LIFE. NEW YORK, NY: PENGUIN BOOKS, 2014

RODRIGUEZ, JUNIUS P., ED. THE LOUISIANA PURCHASE: A HISTORICAL AND GEOGRAPHICAL ENCYCLOPEDIA. SANTA BARBARA, CA: ABC CLIO, 2002.

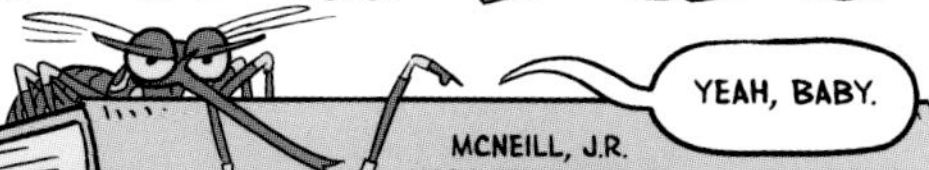

YEAH, BABY.

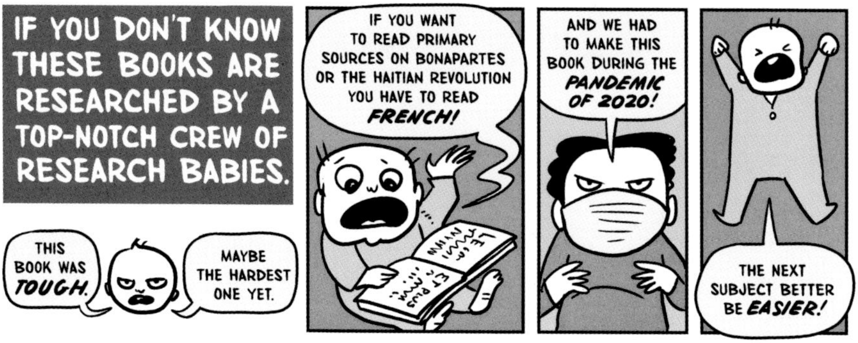

IF YOU DON'T KNOW THESE BOOKS ARE RESEARCHED BY A TOP-NOTCH CREW OF RESEARCH BABIES.
THIS BOOK WAS TOUGH.
MAYBE THE HARDEST ONE YET.
IF YOU WANT TO READ PRIMARY SOURCES ON BONAPARTES OR THE HAITIAN REVOLUTION YOU HAVE TO READ FRENCH!
AND WE HAD TO MAKE THIS BOOK DURING THE PANDEMIC OF 2020!
THE NEXT SUBJECT BETTER BE EASIER!

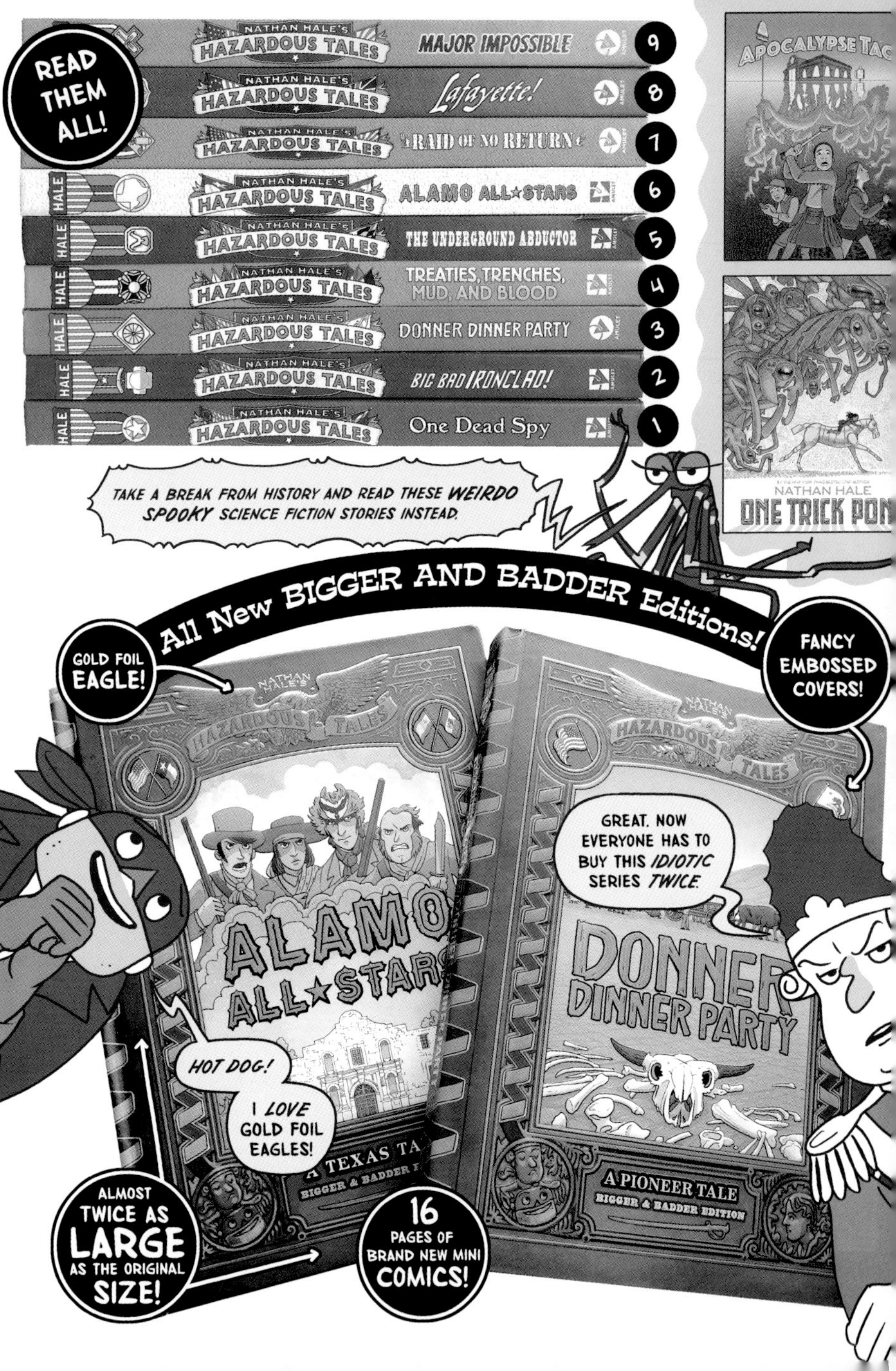
READ THEM ALL!
NATHAN HALE'S HAZARDOUS TALES
MAJOR IMPOSSIBLE 9
Lafayette! 8
RAID OF NO RETURN 7
ALAMO ALL★STARS 6
THE UNDERGROUND ABDUCTOR 5
TREATIES, TRENCHES, MUD, AND BLOOD 4
DONNER DINNER PARTY 3
BIG BAD IRONCLAD! 2
One Dead Spy 1
HALE
APOCALYPSE TAC
NATHAN HALE
ONE TRICK PON
TAKE A BREAK FROM HISTORY AND READ THESE WEIRDO SPOOKY SCIENCE FICTION STORIES INSTEAD.
All New BIGGER AND BADDER Editions!
GOLD FOIL EAGLE!
FANCY EMBOSSED COVERS!
GREAT. NOW EVERYONE HAS TO BUY THIS IDIOTIC SERIES TWICE.
NATHAN HALE'S HAZARDOUS TALES
ALAMO ALL★STARS
HOT DOG!
I LOVE GOLD FOIL EAGLES!
A TEXAS TA
BIGGER & BADDER E
DONNER DINNER PARTY
A PIONEER TALE
BIGGER & BADDER EDITION
ALMOST TWICE AS LARGE AS THE ORIGINAL SIZE!
16 PAGES OF BRAND NEW MINI COMICS!

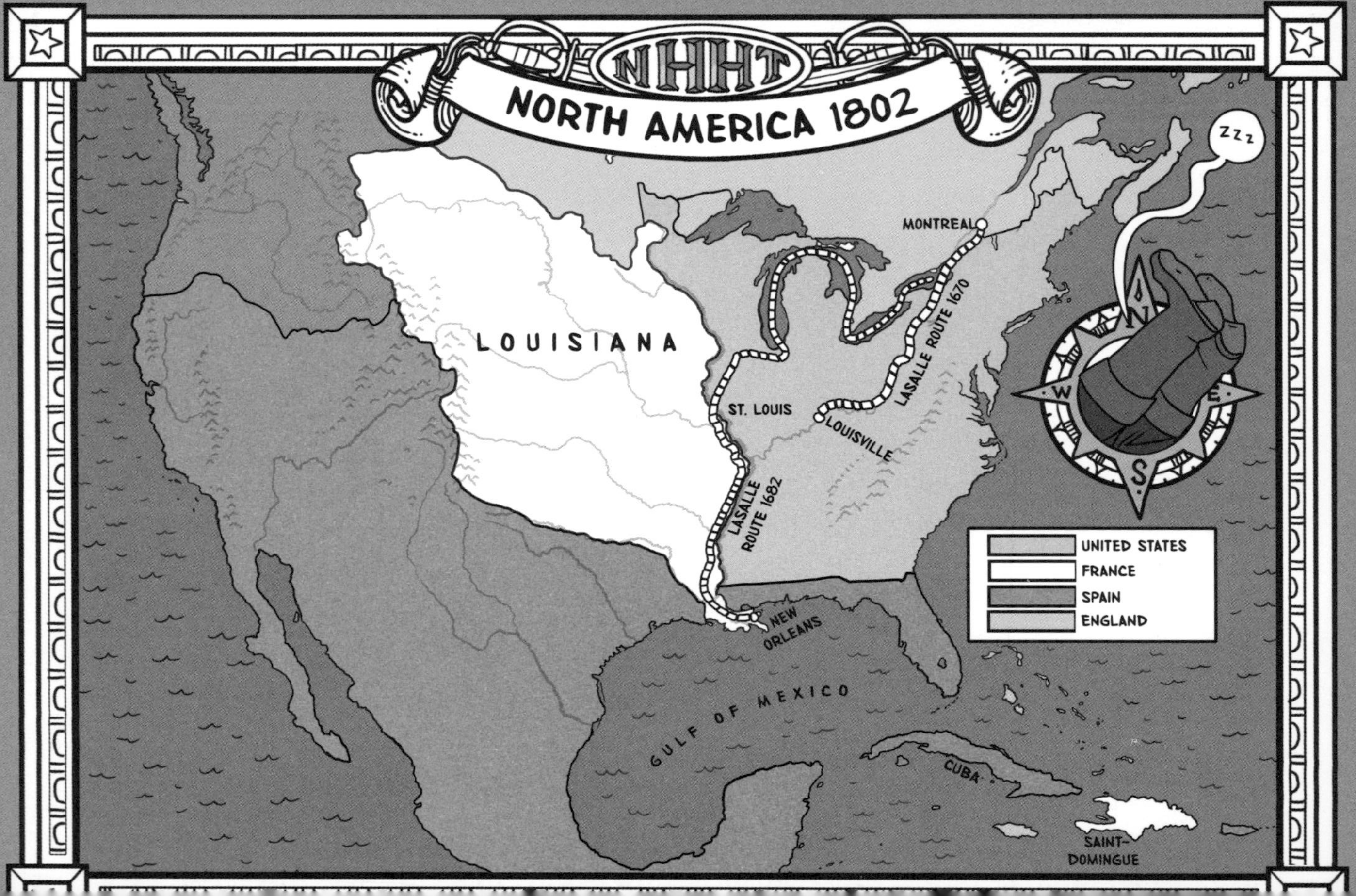
NHHT
NORTH AMERICA 1802
LOUISIANA
MONTREAL
LASALLE ROUTE 1670
ST. LOUIS
LOUISVILLE
LASALLE ROUTE 1682
NEW ORLEANS
GULF OF MEXICO
CUBA
SAINT-DOMINGUE
ZZZ
N
W
E
S
UNITED STATES
FRANCE
SPAIN
ENGLAND